Directgov

Directgov is the place to find all government motoring information and services. From logbooks to licensing, from driving tests to road tax, go to: **direct.gov.uk/motoring**

Theory and practical tests

DSA bookings and enquiries

Online **direct.gov.uk/drivingtest**

Practical & Theory Tests
Enquiries & Bookings **0300 200 1122**
Welsh speakers **0300 200 1133**

Practical Tests
Minicom **0300 200 1144**
Fax **0300 200 1155**

Theory Tests
Minicom **0300 200 1166**
Fax **0300 200 1177**
Customer Enquiry Unit **0300 200 1188**

DVA (Northern Ireland)
Theory test **0845 600 6700**
Practical test **0845 247 2471**

Driving Standards Agency

(Headquarters)

dsa.gov.uk

The Axis Building,
112 Upper Parliament street,
Nottingham NG1 6LP

Tel **0115 936 6666**
Fax **0115 936 6570**

Driver & Vehicle Agency (Testing) in Northern Ireland

dvani.gov.uk

Balmoral Road, Belfast BT12 6QL

Tel **02890 681 831**
Fax **02890 665 520**

Driver & Vehicle Licensing Agency

(GB Licence Enquiries)

dft.gov.uk/dvla

Longview Road, Swansea SA6 7JL

Tel **0300 790 6801**
Fax **0300 123 0798**
Minicom **0300 123 1278**

Driver & Vehicle Agency (Licensing) in Northern Ireland

dvani.gov.uk

County Hall, Castlerock Road,
Coleraine BT51 3TB

Tel **02870 341 469**
24 hour tel **0345 111 222**
Minicom **02870 341 380**

The Driving Standards Agency (DSA) is an executive agency of the Department for Transport. You'll see the DSA logo at theory and practical test centres.

DSA aims to promote road safety through the advancement of driving standards, by

- establishing and developing high standards and best practice in driving and riding on the road; before people start to drive, as they learn, and after they pass their test
- ensuring high standards of instruction for different types of driver and rider
- conducting the statutory theory and practical tests efficiently, fairly and consistently across the country
- providing a centre of excellence for driver training and driving standards
- developing a range of publications and other publicity material designed to promote safe driving for life.

The Driving Standards Agency recognises and values its customers. We will treat all our customers with respect, and deliver our services in an objective, polite and fair way.

dsa.gov.uk

The Driver and Vehicle Agency (DVA) is an executive agency within the Department of the Environment for Northern Ireland.

Its primary aim is to promote and improve road safety through the advancement of driving standards and implementation of the Government's policies for improving the mechanical standards of vehicles.

dvani.gov.uk

CONTENTS

About the theory test

A message from the Chief Driving Examiner 7

Getting started 8

The theory test 12

After the theory test 19

Using the questions and answers section 21

Section one **alertness** 22

Section two **attitude** 42

Section three **safety and your motorcycle** 60

Section four **safety margins** 102

Section five **hazard awareness** 126

Section six **vulnerable road users** 154

Section seven **other types of vehicle** 186

Section eight **motorcycle handling** 200

Section nine **motorway rules** 226

Section ten **rules of the road** 254

Section eleven **road and traffic signs** 280

Section twelve **documents** 346

Section thirteen **incidents, accidents and emergencies** 364

Section fourteen **motorcycle loading** 392

Annexes

1 Case study 408

2 List of theory test centres 411

3 Service standards 413

4 Case study practice - answers 415

introduction
ABOUT THE THEORY TEST

This section covers

- Getting started
- The Theory Test
- After the Theory Test
- Using the questions and answers section

Message from the Chief Driving Examiner

With the ever-increasing volume of traffic on the roads today, it's important to make sure that new riders have a positive attitude and a broad spread of riding knowledge and ability.

The introduction of the separate theory test has been a major step towards improving road safety in Great Britain. In November 2002 the original multiple choice test was extended to include a hazard perception part and in September 2009 we introduced case studies which are aimed at testing your understanding as well as knowledge of riding theory.

All aspects of the theory test are continually monitored, and the bank of questions is regularly updated to take account of changes to legislation and best riding practices. This book contains the whole theory test question bank, set out in an easy-to-read style, with explanations as to why the answers are correct. References to the source material now appear with each question, and at the end of each section there is a short scenario based around topics in that section, with five questions to answer. This gives you an idea of how case study questions test your understanding of the scenario given.

To prepare properly for the test, you should study the source material; this consists of

The Highway Code

Know Your Traffic Signs

The Official DSA Guide to Riding – the essential skills.

To help you practise for the multiple choice questions, *The Official DSA Theory Test for Motorcyclists (CD-Rom)* contains the full question bank and allows you to practise taking multiple choice tests. You can prepare for the hazard perception part of the test by working through *The Official DSA Guide to Hazard Perception (DVD)*.

Using these training aids will give you an extensive knowledge of riding theory, and will help you towards a better understanding of practical riding skills.

You'll never know all the answers. Throughout your driving career there will always be more to learn.

Remember, as a rider you have a responsibility for the safety of your vehicle, any passenger you carry and other road users. By being reliable, efficient and safe you'll be on your way to becoming a better rider.

Trevor Wedge

Trevor Wedge
Chief Driving Examiner and Director for Safer Driving

7

Getting started

Applying for your licence

You must have a valid provisional driving licence before you can ride on the road.

Licences are issued by the Driver and Vehicle Licensing Agency (DVLA). Application forms D1 and D750 can be obtained from any post office. In Northern Ireland the issuing authority is the Driver and Vehicle Agency (Licensing) and the form is a DL1.

Send these forms to the appropriate office, which is shown on the form. You must enclose the required passport-type photographs, as all provisional licences now issued are photocard licences.

When you receive your provisional licence, check that all details are correct before you ride on the road. If you need to contact DVLA, their telephone number is 0300 790 6801 (DVA is 02870 341469).

You will need to show both parts of your provisional licence when you take your theory test.

Residency requirements

You can't take a test or obtain a full licence unless you are normally resident in this country. Normal residence means the place where you reside because of personal or occupational ties. However, if you moved to the United Kingdom (UK) having recently been permanently resident in another state of the EC/EEA (European Economic Area), you must have been normally resident in the UK for 185 days in the 12 months prior to your application for a driving test or full driving licence.

Compulsory Basic Training

Before you take your practical motorcycle test you must attend and successfully complete a Compulsory Basic Training (CBT) course (except in Northern Ireland). CBT courses can be given only by training bodies approved by DSA. Frequent checks are made to ensure a high standard of instruction.

The course will include

- classroom training
- practical skills training.

You can find out about CBT courses from

- DSA (visit **direct.gov.uk/cbt** or call 0115 936 6547)
- your motorcycle dealer
- your local Road Safety Officer (by contacting your local council).

DSA also produces *The Official DSA Guide to Learning to Ride* which will give you details about the course (see page 10 for further details).

About the theory test

The theory test is a screen-based test, and consists of two parts. It has been devised to test your knowledge of riding theory, in particular the rules of the road and best riding practice.

Your knowledge of this information is tested in the first part as a series of multiple choice questions. Some multiple choice questions will be presented in the form of a case study. More information about this part of the test is given on pages 15 and 408. The questions are given in the main part of the book, beginning on page 22.

Each question has an indicator in the coloured bar giving references to the learning material as follows:

> **R-ES 8, HC r162-163, KYTS**

These indicate the section within *Riding – the essential skills* (R-ES), either rule or page in *The Highway Code* (HC r/HC p), and page in *Know Your Traffic Signs* (KYTS). Where no page number is indicated, the reference is to the whole book.

The second part of the theory test is called hazard perception; more information about this is given on page 17.

Can I take the practical test first?

No. You have to pass your theory test before you can book a practical test.

Does everyone have to take the theory test?

Most people in the UK who are learning to ride will have to sit a theory test. However, you won't have to take a motorcycle theory test again to upgrade to a motorcycle licence if you have already passed a motorcycle (A) theory test and then a practical moped test.

Any enquiries about whether you have to take a theory test should be addressed to the Customer Services Unit, DSA, PO Box 280, Newcastle upon Tyne, NE99 1FP. Tel: 0191 201 8161 email: customer.services@dsa.gsi.gov.uk (For Northern Ireland, address enquiries to DVA Theory Test Section, Balmoral Road, Belfast BT12 6QL, tel 02890 681831). Foreign licence holders: If you hold a foreign licence issued outside the EC/EEA, first check with the Driver Vehicle Licensing Agency (telephone 0300 790 6801, for Northern Ireland call 02870 341469), to see whether you can exchange your licence. If you cannot exchange your licence, you will need to apply for a provisional licence and take a theory and practical test.

Preparing for your theory test

Although you have to pass your theory test before you can take your practical test, it's recommended that you start studying for your theory test as soon as possible, but don't actually take it until you have some practical experience of riding.

To prepare for the multiple choice part of the theory test, we strongly recommend that you study the books from which the questions are taken as well as the questions themselves.

It's important that you study, not just to pass the test, but to become a safer rider

The Official Highway Code – this is essential reading for all road users, not just learner drivers and riders. It contains the most up-to-date advice on road safety and the laws which apply to all road users.

Know Your Traffic Signs – this contains the vast majority of signs and road markings that you are likely to encounter.

The Official DSA Guide to Riding – the essential skills – this is the official reference book, giving practical advice and best practice for all riders.

The Official DSA Guide to Learning to Ride – gives full details of basic machine handling for compulsory basic training and the full practical test syllabus.

These books will help you to answer the questions correctly and will also help you when studying for your practical test. The information in them will be relevant throughout your riding life so make sure you always have an up-to-date copy to which you can refer.

Other study aids

The Official DSA Theory Test for Motorcyclists (CD-Rom) – this is an alternative way of preparing for the multiple choice part of the theory test. It contains all the questions and answers and also allows you to take mock tests.

The Official Guide to Hazard Perception (DVD) – We strongly recommend that you use this, preferably with your trainer, to prepare for the hazard perception part of the test.

The DVD is packed with useful tips, quizzes and expert advice. It also includes interactive hazard perception clips, with feedback on your performance.

Better Biking – The Official DSA Training Aid (DVD) – Expert advice on improving your skills – covers all the key skills including negotiating bends, junctions and roundabouts. An ideal solo ride is demonstrated to show the standard of riding to which you can aspire.

Why do the questions keep changing?

To make sure that all candidates are being tested fairly, questions and video clips are under continuous review.

Some questions may be changed as a result of customer feedback. They may also be changed to reflect revised legislation, and DSA publications are updated to reflect such changes.

Can I take a mock test?

You can take mock tests for the multiple choice part of the theory test online at **direct.gov.uk/motoring**

All the official training materials listed are available online at **tsoshop.co.uk/dsa** or by mail order from **0870 241 4523**.

They are also available from bookshops and selected computer software retailers.

The Theory Test

Booking your theory test

The easiest ways to book are online or by phone. You can also book by post.

Booking online or by telephone – by using these methods you'll be given the date and time of your test immediately.

Book online at **direct.gov.uk/booktheorytest** (for Northern Ireland use **dvani.gov.uk**)

To book by telephone, call 0300 200 1122 (0845 600 6700 for Northern Ireland).

If you're deaf and use a minicom machine, call 0300 200 1166 and if you are a Welsh speaker, call 0300 200 1133.

You will need your

- DVLA or DVA driving licence number
- credit or debit card details (the card holder must book the test). We accept Mastercard, Visa, Delta, Switch, Visa Electron and Solo.

You'll be given a booking number and should receive an appointment letter within 10 days.

Where can I take the test?

There are over 150 theory test centres throughout England, Scotland and Wales, and six in Northern Ireland. Most people have a test centre within 20 miles of their home, but this will vary depending on the density of population in your area. You can find a list of test centres on pages 411-412.

What if I don't receive an acknowledgement?

If you don't receive an acknowledgement within the time specified, please visit **direct.gov.uk/changetheorytest** or telephone the booking office to check that an appointment has been made. We can't take responsibility for postal delays. If you miss your test appointment you'll lose your fee.

When are test centres open?

Test centres are usually open on weekdays, some evenings and some Saturdays.

How do I cancel or postpone my test?

You can cancel or postpone your test online by visiting **direct.gov.uk/changetheorytest** or by telephone. You should contact the booking office at least **three clear working days** before your test date, otherwise you'll lose your fee.

Only in exceptional circumstances, such as documented ill-health or family bereavement, can this rule be waived.

Booking by post – If you prefer to book by post, you'll need to fill in an application form. These are available from theory or driving test centres, or your instructor may have one.

You should normally receive an appointment letter within ten days of posting your application form.

If you require a theory test in a language other than English or provision for special needs, please turn to page 14.

Taking your theory test

Arriving at the test centre – You must make sure that when you arrive at the test centre you have all the relevant documents with you, or you won't be able to take your test and you'll lose your fee.

You'll need

- your signed photocard licence and paper counterpart, or
- your signed driving licence and valid passport (your passport doesn't have to be British).

No other form of identification is acceptable.

Other forms of identification may be acceptable in Northern Ireland; please check **dvani.gov.uk** or your appointment letter.

All documents must be original. We can't accept photocopies.

The test centre staff will check your documents and make sure that you take the right category of test.

Remember, if you don't bring your documents your test will be cancelled and you will lose your fee.

Make sure that you arrive in plenty of time so you aren't rushed. If you arrive after the session has started you may not be allowed to take the test.

You'll then be ready to start your test. It's a screen-based test and is made up of a multiple choice part and a hazard perception part.

Languages other than English

In Wales, and at theory test centres on the Welsh borders, you can take your theory test with Welsh text on screen. A voiceover can also be provided in Welsh.

You can listen through a headset to the test being read out in one of 20 other languages as well as English. These are: Albanian, Arabic, Bengali, Cantonese, Dari, Farsi, Gujarati, Hindi, Kashmiri, Kurdish, Mirpuri, Polish, Portuguese, Punjabi, Pushto, Spanish, Tamil, Turkish, Urdu and Welsh.

To take your test in any other language, you may bring a translator with you to certain theory test centres. The translator must be approved by DSA and you must make arrangements when you book your test. You have to arrange and pay for the services of the translator yourself.

Tests with translators can be taken at the following test centres: Aldershot, Birkenhead, Birmingham, Cardiff, Derby, Edinburgh, Glasgow, Ipswich, Leeds, Milton Keynes, Preston, Southgate and all test centres in Northern Ireland.

Provision for special needs

Every effort is made to ensure that the theory test can be taken by all candidates.

It's important that you state your needs when you book your test so that the necessary arrangements can be made.

Reading difficulties – There's an English language voiceover, on a headset, to help you if you have reading difficulties or dyslexia.

You can ask for up to twice the normal time to take the multiple choice part of the test.

You will be asked to provide a letter from a suitable independent person who knows about your reading ability (such as a teacher or employer). Please check with the Special Needs section (on the normal booking number, see page 12), if you're unsure who to ask.

We can't guarantee to return any original documents, so please send copies only.

Hearing difficulties – If you're deaf or have other hearing difficulties, the multiple choice part and the introduction to the hazard perception part of the test can be delivered in British Sign Language (BSL) by an on-screen signer.

A BSL interpreter, signer or lip speaker can be provided if requested at the time of booking. If you have any other requirements please call the Special Needs section on the normal booking number (see page 12).

Physical disabilities – If you have a physical disability which would make it difficult for you to use a mouse button in the theory test, we may be able to make special arrangements for you to use a different method if you let us know when you book your test.

Multiple choice questions

The first part of the theory test consists of 50 multiple choice questions. Some of these multiple choice questions will be presented to you on test in the form of a case study. You select your answers for this part of the test by simply touching the screen or using the mouse.

Before you start you'll be given the chance to work through a practice session for up to 15 minutes to get used to the system. Staff at the test centre will be available to help you if you have any difficulties.

The questions will cover a variety of topics relating to road safety, the environment and documentation. Only one question will appear on the screen at a time.

Most questions will ask you to mark one correct answer from four possible answers given. Some questions may ask for two or more correct answers from a selection, but this is shown clearly on the screen. If you try to move on without marking the correct number of answers you'll be reminded that more answers are needed.

To answer, you need to mark the box alongside the answer or answers you think are correct. If you change your mind and don't want that answer to be selected, mark it again. You can then choose another answer.

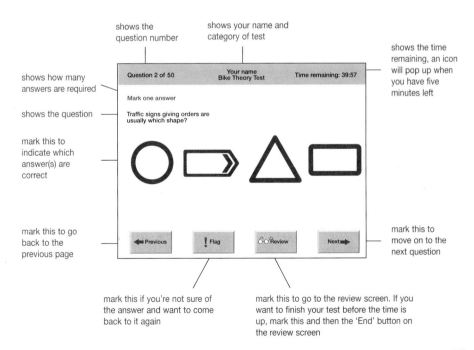

shows the question number

shows your name and category of test

shows the time remaining, an icon will pop up when you have five minutes left

shows how many answers are required

shows the question

mark this to indicate which answer(s) are correct

mark this to go back to the previous page

Question 2 of 50

Your name
Bike Theory Test

Time remaining: 39:57

Mark one answer

Traffic signs giving orders are usually which shape?

Previous   ! Flag   Review   Next

mark this to move on to the next question

mark this if you're not sure of the answer and want to come back to it again

mark this to go to the review screen. If you want to finish your test before the time is up, mark this and then the 'End' button on the review screen

Case studies

Some of the multiple choice questions will be presented as part of a case study. Case studies are designed to test

- knowledge (basic recall of facts)
- comprehension (basic understanding)
- application (practical use of knowledge and understanding).

This is done by creating a scenario or a set of circumstances that you may encounter in a real-life situation. You will then be asked a number of questions, relating to the scenario, which will require you to consider how you would react/behave in each case. For an example of a case study, see page 408.

Take your time and read the questions carefully. You're given 57 minutes for this part of the test, so relax and don't rush.

Some questions will take longer to answer than others, but there are no trick questions. The time remaining is displayed on screen. Extra time can be provided if you have special needs and you let us know when you book your test.

You'll be able to move backwards and forwards through the questions and you can also 'flag' questions that you'd like to look at again. It's easy to change your answer if you want to. Try to answer all the questions. If you're well prepared you shouldn't find them difficult.

Before you finish this part of the test, if you have time, you can use the 'review' feature to check your answers. If you want to finish your test before the full time, mark the 'review' button and then the 'end' button on the review screen. When you mark the review button you will see the following screen.

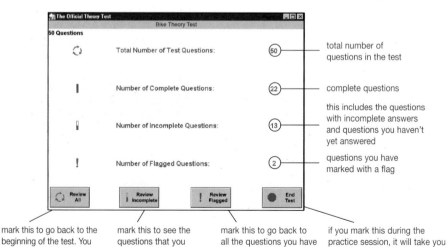

mark this to go back to the beginning of the test. You can look at all questions again and change your answers if you want

mark this to see the questions that you haven't answered or have marked with the wrong number of answers

mark this to go back to all the questions you have marked with a flag. You can then work through all the flagged questions

if you mark this during the practice session, it will take you to the start of the test. **During the actual test this button will end the test session**

Further practice for case studies

The case studies at the end of each section set out scenarios and then ask you relevant questions. This is to help you test your knowledge in a format similar to the case studies in the theory test. However, note that they are not shown in the same layout used in the theory test screens. The answers for these are on pages 415-416.

Hazard perception

After you've finished the multiple choice part, there is a break of up to three minutes before you start the hazard perception part of the test. You cannot leave your seat during this break. This part of the test will consist of a series of film clips, shown from a rider's point of view.

Before you start this part of the test you'll be shown a short tutorial video that explains how the test works and gives you a chance to see a sample film clip. This will help you to understand what you need to do. You can run this video again if you wish.

During the hazard perception part of the test you'll be shown 14 film clips. Each clip contains one or more developing hazards. You should respond by pressing the mouse button **as soon as you see** a hazard developing that may result in you, the rider, having to take some action, such as changing speed or direction.

The earlier you notice a developing hazard and make a response, the higher your score. There are 15 scoreable hazards in total.

Your response will not cause the scene in the video to change in any way. However, a red flag will appear on the bottom of the screen to show that your response has been noted.

Before each clip starts, there will be a 10-second pause to allow you to see the new road situation.

The hazard perception part of the test lasts about 20 minutes. For this part of the test there is no extra time available, and you can't repeat any of the clips – you don't get a second chance to see a hazard when you're riding on the road.

Trial questions

We're constantly checking the questions and clips to help us decide whether to use them in future tests. After the hazard perception part of the test you may be asked to try a few trial questions and clips. You don't have to do these if you don't want to, and if you answer them they won't count towards your final score.

Customer satisfaction survey

We want to ensure our customers are completely satisfied with the service they receive. At the end of your test you'll be shown some questions designed to give us information about you and how happy you are with the service you received from us.

Your answers will be treated in the strictest confidence. They are not part of the test and they won't be used in determining your final score or for marketing purposes. You'll be asked if you want to complete the survey, but there's no obligation to do so.

The result

You should receive your result at the test centre within 10 minutes of completing the test.

You'll be given a score for each part of the test (the multiple choice part and the hazard perception part). You'll need to pass both parts to pass the theory test. If you fail one of the parts you'll have to take the whole test again.

Why do I have to retake both parts of the test if I only fail one?

It's really only one test. The theory test has always included questions relating to hazard awareness – the second part simply tests the same skills in a more effective way. The two parts are only presented separately in the theory test because different scoring methods are used.

What's the pass mark?

To pass the multiple choice part of the theory test you must answer at least 43 questions correctly. For learner car drivers and bike riders the pass mark for the hazard perception part is 44 out of 75.

If I don't pass, when can I take the test again?

If you fail your test, you've shown that you're not fully prepared. You'll have to wait at least three clear working days before you take the theory test again.

Good preparation will save you both time and money.

After the theory test

When you pass your theory test you'll be given a certificate. Keep this safe, as you'll need it when you go for your practical test.

This certificate has a life of two years from the date of your test. This means that you have to take and pass the practical test within this two-year period. If you don't, you'll have to take and pass the theory test again before you can book your practical test.

Your practical test

Your next step is to prepare for and take a practical test. To help you prepare for this, *The Official DSA Guide to Learning to Ride* has details of the practical test. As well as giving the full test syllabus, it explains the skills you should show and faults you should avoid when taking your test.

Please refer to the back of this book for information about other publications which will help you prepare for your practical test.

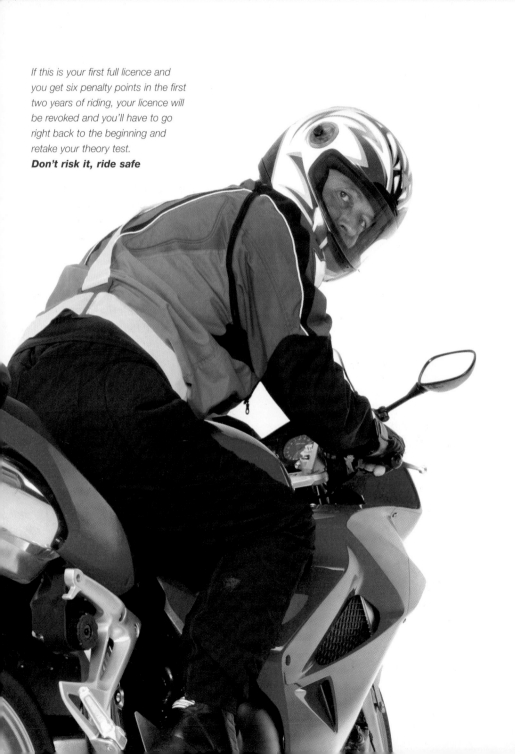

If this is your first full licence and you get six penalty points in the first two years of riding, your licence will be revoked and you'll have to go right back to the beginning and retake your theory test.

Don't risk it, ride safe

Using the questions and answers section

The following part of the book contains all the questions that could be used in the multiple choice part of the theory test.

For easy reference, and to help you to study, the questions have been divided into topics and put into sections. Although this isn't how you'll find them in your test, it's helpful if you want to refer to particular subjects.

The questions are in the left-hand column with a choice of answers beneath. On the right-hand side of the page you'll find the correct answers and a brief explanation of why they are correct. There will also be some advice on correct riding procedures and some brief references to the relevant source materials to help you further. At the start of each topic, before the questions, a few pages of useful information is provided to help you learn more about each topic.

Don't just learn the answers. It's important that you know why the answers are correct. To help you do this, there is a brief scenario at the end of each question section, with five associated questions to answer. This will give you an idea of how the case study part of the theory test will assess your understanding of the subject covered. This knowledge will help you with your practical skills and prepare you to become a safe and confident rider.

Taking exams or tests is rarely a pleasant experience, but you can make your test less stressful by being confident that you have the knowledge to answer the questions correctly.

Make studying more enjoyable by involving friends and relations. Take part in a question and answer game. Test those 'experienced' riders who've had their licence a while: they might learn something too!

Best wishes for your test. Once you're on the road, don't forget everything you've learnt

Some of the questions in this book will not be used in Northern Ireland theory tests. These questions are marked as follows: *NI EXEMPT*

section **one**
ALERTNESS

This section covers
- Observation
- Anticipation
- Concentration
- Awareness
- Distraction
- Boredom

Alertness

Observation

Riding safely takes a lot of concentration. Look around constantly and assess the changing situations as you ride. Be aware of traffic all around you. Before you carry out any manoeuvre, such as moving off, stopping, turning or changing lanes, you should

- use your mirrors to assess how your actions will affect traffic behind you
- look all around, including checking the 'blind areas' not covered by your mirrors
- signal if necessary
- take a final rearward glance (the 'lifesaver' look) as an extra check, before making any manoeuvre.

R-ES 8, HC r159-161

If your elbows obstruct your view in the mirrors, you should extend the mirror arms until your view is unobstructed. Having mirrors fitted to both sides of your motorcycle will give you the best view of the road behind.

Looking over your shoulder before manoeuvring will also warn other drivers that you may be about to change lane, direction or speed.

If you can't see when emerging from a junction because your view is obstructed by parked cars, move forward slowly and carefully until you can get a proper view.

Be particularly careful before you overtake. Ensure that

- the manoeuvre is necessary, safe and legal
- you have a clear view of the road ahead – there shouldn't be any bends or dips
- you have enough time to complete the manoeuvre safely.

R-ES 8, HC r162-163

It's also important for other road users to know you're there.

Where you can't be seen, such as at a hump-back bridge, consider using your horn.

HC r113-115

When following a large vehicle, stay well back. This will help the driver to see you in their mirrors. If you can't see their mirrors, they can't see you. Staying back will also help you see the road ahead much more clearly.

HC r164

Anticipation and awareness

Look at the road signs and markings; these give you information about any hazards. You should

- follow their advice
- react accordingly.

Watch other road users. Try to anticipate their actions so you're ready if you need to slow down or change direction.

R-ES 7, KYTS 10 & 62

When turning right onto a dual carriageway, first check that the central reservation is wide enough for your vehicle.

Be aware of other, more vulnerable road users. Watch out for

- pedestrians, especially where they may be hidden or approaching a crossing
- cyclists – always pass slowly and leave plenty of room
- horses, which may be startled by the noise of your vehicle – again, pass them slowly and leave plenty of room.

R-ES 10, HC r204-218

If you're approaching traffic lights that have been green for some time, be prepared to stop because they may change.

However well prepared you are, you may still have to stop quickly in an emergency. Keep both hands on the handlebars as you brake to keep control of your vehicle.

R-ES 6, 7 & 10, HC r204-218

Concentration

Always plan your journey so you

- know what route you need to take
- have regular rest stops.

You'll not be able to concentrate properly if you're tired. It's particularly easy to feel sleepy on a motorway, so

- don't ride continuously for more than two hours
- if you feel tired, leave at the next exit. Find a safe place to stop and take a break.

Have two cups of coffee or other caffeinated drink, if appropriate. However, this is only a short-term countermeasure and should not be considered as a substitute for proper rest.

R-ES 1, HC r91 & r262

It's just as easy to lose concentration if you are cold. Although it's not cheap, proper motorcycle clothing will keep you warm and also offers safety benefits in the event of a road traffic incident too.

Distraction and boredom

Remember, you can be distracted by using such things as hands-free phones, intercom systems or iPlayers, as your concentration is split between your attention on the road ahead and whatever you are hearing at the time. Lapses in concentration, or just taking your eyes off the road for a second, could be disastrous. In that second, at 60 mph, your vehicle will travel 27 metres.

R-ES 1, HC r149-150

You can also be distracted by an incident scene which may have occurred, for example, on the other side of a motorway. Don't slow down or try to see what is happening – continue on with your journey and keep your concentration.

Be safe, and don't be distracted in any way. Don't listen to music via an earpiece while riding; switch off any phones or hands-free kits and use the mail retrieval service. Wait until you're parked in a safe and proper place before you

- retrieve any messages
- make any calls
- send or receive texts.

If you are riding on a motorway you should leave the motorway and stop in a safe place before using your phone or adjusting a navigation system.

R-ES 1, 16 & 18

FAQs

What should I do if I'm dazzled by the main beam of an oncoming vehicle?

Slow down or stop until your eyes have adjusted. When using your main beam at night, also remember to dip your lights to avoid dazzling oncoming vehicles, or as soon as another vehicle overtakes you.

R-ES 13, HC r115

I've noticed curved white arrows in the centre of the road, pointing to the left. What do they mean?

These markings advise road users to move back into the left after overtaking. There will be some sort of hazard or change of road layout ahead, such as a junction, or perhaps there are two lanes merging into one single lane.

R-ES 7, KYTS p63

I've seen yellow lines painted at intervals across the road. What do they mean?

These encourage drivers and riders to reduce their speed. Some may also be red. You often see them on approach to a

- *hazard (such as a roundabout or dangerous junction)*
- *reduced speed limit.*

R-ES 7, KYTS p68 & p75

I have heard the term 'blind spot'. What does this mean?

Blind spots are areas that can't be seen either when using normal forward vision or when using the mirrors.

Remember that a driver of a large vehicle can't see you in the mirrors if you're close behind. Keep well back so you're visible.

R-ES 5, HC r159

I'm getting a new motorcycle – before riding it for the first time, is there anything I should know?

Yes – make sure you are familiar with the layout of all the switches and controls. Control layouts are usually similar, but you should be aware of any differences before you start riding, to ensure you stay safe and confident in your ability to control the motorcycle.

R-ES 5

1.1   *Mark **one** answer*   **R-ES 8, HC r179-181**

You are about to turn right. What should you do just before you turn?

- ⊙ Give the correct signal
- ⊙ Take a 'lifesaver' glance over your shoulder
- ⊙ Select the correct gear
- ⊙ Get in position ready for the turn

⊙ **Take a 'lifesaver' glance over your shoulder**

When you are turning right, plan your approach to the junction. Signal and select the correct gear in good time. Just before you turn, take a 'lifesaver' glance for a final check behind and to the side of you.

1.2   *Mark **one** answer*   **R-ES 8, HC r180**

What is the 'lifesaver' when riding a motorcycle?

- ⊙ A certificate every motorcyclist must have
- ⊙ A final, rearward glance before changing direction
- ⊙ A part of the motorcycle tool kit
- ⊙ A mirror fitted to check blind spots

⊙ **A final, rearward glance before changing direction**

This action makes you aware of what's happening behind and alongside you. The 'lifesaver' glance should be timed so that you still have time to react if it isn't safe to perform the manoeuvre.

1.3   *Mark **one** answer*   **R-ES 7 & 9**

You see road signs showing a sharp bend ahead. What should you do?

- ⊙ Continue at the same speed
- ⊙ Slow down as you go around the bend
- ⊙ Slow down as you come out of the bend
- ⊙ Slow down before the bend

⊙ **Slow down before the bend**

Always look for any advance warning of hazards, such as road signs and hazard warning lines. Use this information to plan ahead and to help you avoid the need for late, harsh braking. Your motorcycle should be upright and moving in a straight line when you brake. This will help you to keep maximum control when dealing with the hazard.

*Mark **one** answer*

You are riding at night and are dazzled by the headlights of an oncoming car. You should

⊙ slow down or stop

⊙ close your eyes

⊙ flash your headlight

⊙ turn your head away

⊙ **slow down or stop**

If you are dazzled by lights when riding, slow down or stop until your eyes have adjusted. Taking a hand off the handlebars to adjust your visor while riding could lead to loss of control. A dirty or scratched visor could cause dazzle and impair vision further.

*Mark **one** answer*

When riding, your shoulders obstruct the view in your mirrors. To overcome this you should

⊙ indicate earlier than normal

⊙ fit smaller mirrors

⊙ extend the mirror arms

⊙ brake earlier than normal

⊙ **extend the mirror arms**

It's essential that you have a clear view all around. Adjust your mirrors to give you the best view of the road behind. If your elbows obscure the view try fitting mirrors with longer stems.

*Mark **one** answer*

On a motorcycle you should only use a mobile telephone when you

⊙ have a pillion passenger to help

⊙ have parked in a safe place

⊙ have a motorcycle with automatic gears

⊙ are travelling on a quiet road

⊙ **have parked in a safe place**

It's important that you're in full control at all times. Even using a hands-free kit can distract your attention from the road. Don't take the risk. If you need to use a mobile phone stop at a safe and convenient place.

1.7 *Mark **one** answer* **R-ES 13, HC r114-115**

You are riding at night. You have your headlight on main beam. Another vehicle is overtaking you. When should you dip your headlight?

⊙ When the other vehicle signals to overtake

⊙ As soon as the other vehicle moves out to overtake

⊙ As soon as the other vehicle passes you

⊙ After the other vehicle pulls in front of you

⊙ **As soon as the other vehicle passes you**

At night you should dip your headlight to avoid dazzling oncoming drivers or those ahead of you. If you're being overtaken, dip your headlight as the other vehicle comes past. When you switch to dipped beam your view of the road ahead will be reduced, so look ahead for hazards on your side of the road before you do so.

1.8 *Mark **one** answer* **R-ES 6 & 8, HC r159**

To move off safely from a parked position you should

⊙ signal if other drivers will need to slow down

⊙ leave your motorcycle on its stand until the road is clear

⊙ give an arm signal as well as using your indicators

⊙ look over your shoulder for a final check

⊙ **look over your shoulder for a final check**

Before you move off from the side of the road on a motorcycle you must take a final look around over your shoulder. There may be another road user who is not visible in your mirrors.

1.9 *Mark **one** answer* **R-ES 1, 4 & 12**

Riding a motorcycle when you are cold could cause you to

⊙ be more alert

⊙ be more relaxed

⊙ react more quickly

⊙ lose concentration

⊙ **lose concentration**

It can be difficult to keep warm when riding a motorcycle. Although it isn't cheap, proper motorcycle clothing will help to keep you warm and is essential. It also helps to protect you if you fall off or are involved in a crash.

1.10

R-ES 13, HC r114-115

You are riding at night and are dazzled by the lights of an approaching vehicle. What should you do?

⊙ Switch off your headlight

⊙ Switch to main beam

⊙ Slow down and stop

⊙ Flash your headlight

⊙ **Slow down and stop**

If your view of the road ahead is restricted because you are being dazzled by approaching headlights, slow down and if you need to, pull over and stop.

1.11

R-ES 6, HC r159

You should always check the 'blind areas' before

⊙ moving off

⊙ slowing down

⊙ changing gear

⊙ giving a signal

⊙ **moving off**

These are the areas behind and to either side of you which are not covered by your mirrors. You should always check these areas before moving off or changing direction.

1.12

R-ES 6 & 8, HC r159-160 & r179-190

The 'blind area' should be checked before

⊙ giving a signal

⊙ applying the brakes

⊙ changing direction

⊙ giving an arm signal

⊙ **changing direction**

The areas not covered by your mirrors are called blind spots. They should always be checked before changing direction. This check is so important that it is called the 'lifesaver'.

1.13   *Mark **one** answer*   **R-ES 6 & 8, HC r264 & r167-268**

It is vital to check the 'blind area' before

⊙ changing gear

⊙ giving signals

⊙ slowing down

⊙ changing lanes

⊙ **changing lanes**

Other vehicles may be hidden in the blind spots that are not covered by your mirrors. Always make sure it is safe before changing lanes by taking a 'lifesaver' check.

1.14   *Mark **one** answer*   **R-ES 8**

Why can it be helpful to have mirrors fitted on each side of your motorcycle ?

⊙ To judge the gap when filtering in traffic

⊙ To give protection when riding in poor weather

⊙ To make your motorcycle appear larger to other drivers

⊙ To give you the best view of the road behind

⊙ **To give you the best view of the road behind**

When riding on the road you need to know as much about following traffic as you can. A mirror fitted on each side of your motorcycle will help give you the best view of the road behind.

1.15   *Mark **one** answer*   **R-ES 6 & 8**

In motorcycling, the term 'lifesaver' refers to

⊙ a final rearward glance

⊙ an approved safety helmet

⊙ a reflective jacket

⊙ the two-second rule

⊙ **a final rearward glance**

Mirrors on motorcycles don't always give a clear view behind. There will be times when you need to look round to see the full picture.

31

*Mark **one** answer*

You are about to emerge from a junction. Your pillion passenger tells you it's clear. When should you rely on their judgement?

- ⊙ Never, you should always look for yourself
- ⊙ When the roads are very busy
- ⊙ When the roads are very quiet
- ⊙ Only when they are a qualified rider

⊙ **Never, you should always look for yourself**

Your passenger may be inexperienced in judging traffic situations, have a poor view and not have seen a potential hazard. You are responsible for your own safety and your passenger. Always make your own checks to be sure it is safe to pull out.

---

*Mark **one** answer*

You are about to emerge from a junction. Your pillion passenger tells you it's safe to go. What should you do?

- ⊙ Go, if you are sure they can see clearly
- ⊙ Check for yourself before pulling out
- ⊙ Take their advice and ride on
- ⊙ Ask them to check again before you go

⊙ **Check for yourself before pulling out**

You must rely on your own judgement when making decisions. Only you know your own capabilities and the performance of your machine.

---

*Mark **one** answer*

What must you do before stopping normally?

- ⊙ Put both feet down
- ⊙ Select first gear
- ⊙ Use your mirrors
- ⊙ Move into neutral

⊙ **Use your mirrors**

Check your mirrors before slowing down or stopping as there could be vehicles close behind you. If necessary, look behind before stopping.

1.19 — Mark **two** answers — R-ES 6 & 8

You want to change lanes in busy, moving traffic. Why could looking over your shoulder help?

- Mirrors may not cover blind spots
- To avoid having to give a signal
- So traffic ahead will make room for you
- So your balance will not be affected
- Drivers behind you would be warned

⊙ **Mirrors may not cover blind spots**

⊙ **Drivers behind you would be warned**

Before changing lanes make sure there's a safe gap to move into. Looking over your shoulder allows you to check the area not covered by your mirrors, where a vehicle could be hidden from view. It also warns following drivers that you want to change lanes.

1.20 — Mark **one** answer — R-ES 6 & 8

You have been waiting for some time to make a right turn into a side road. What should you do just before you make the turn?

- Move close to the kerb
- Select a higher gear
- Make a 'lifesaver' check
- Wave to the oncoming traffic

⊙ **Make a 'lifesaver' check**

Remember your 'lifesaver' glance before you start to turn. If you've been waiting for some time and a queue has built up behind you, a vehicle further back may try to overtake. It is especially important to look out for other motorcycles in this situation which may be approaching at speed.

1.21 — Mark **one** answer — R-ES 9, HC r173

You are turning right onto a dual carriageway. What should you do before emerging?

- Stop, and then select a very low gear
- Position in the left gutter of the side road
- Check that the central reservation is wide enough
- Check there is enough room for vehicles behind you

⊙ **Check that the central reservation is wide enough**

Before emerging right onto a dual carriageway make sure that the central reservation is wide enough to protect your vehicle. If it's not, you should treat it as one road and check that it's clear in both directions before pulling out. Otherwise, you could obstruct part of the carriageway and cause a hazard, both for yourself and other road users.

*Mark **one** answer*

When riding a different motorcycle you should

- ask someone to ride with you for the first time
- ride as soon as possible as all controls and switches are the same
- leave your gloves behind so switches can be operated more easily
- be sure you know where all controls and switches are

⊙ **be sure you know where all controls and switches are**

Before you ride any motorcycle make sure you're familiar with the layout of all the controls and switches. While control layouts are generally similar, there may be differences in their feel and method of operation.

---

*Mark **one** answer*

You are turning right at a large roundabout. Before you leave the roundabout you should

- take a 'lifesaver' glance over your left shoulder
- give way to all traffic from the right
- put on your right indicator
- cancel the left indicator

⊙ **take a 'lifesaver' glance over your left shoulder**

You need to be aware of what's happening behind and alongside you. Looking left, just before you move across gives you time to react if it isn't safe to make the manoeuvre.

---

*Mark **one** answer*

You are turning right at a large roundabout. Before you cross a lane to reach your exit you should

- take a 'lifesaver' glance over your right shoulder
- put on your right indicator
- take a 'lifesaver' glance over your left shoulder
- cancel the left indicator

⊙ **take a 'lifesaver' glance over your left shoulder**

On busy roundabouts traffic may be moving very quickly and changing lanes suddenly. You need to be aware of what's happening all around you. Before crossing lanes to the left make sure you take a 'lifesaver' glance to the left. This gives you time to react if it's not safe to make the manoeuvre.

1.25   *Mark **one** answer*   R-ES 6 & 8, HC r184-190

You are positioned to turn right on a multi-lane roundabout. What should you do before moving to a lane on your left?

- ⊙ Take a 'lifesaver' glance over your right shoulder
- ⊙ Cancel the left signal
- ⊙ Signal to the right
- ⊙ Take a 'lifesaver' glance over your left shoulder

⊙ **Take a 'lifesaver' glance over your left shoulder**

Beware of traffic changing lanes quickly and at the last moment on these roundabouts. Be aware of all signs and road markings so that you can position correctly in good time. Your life could depend on you knowing where other vehicles are.

1.26   *Mark **one** answer*   R-ES 6 & 8, HC r184-190

You are turning right on a multi-lane roundabout. When should you take a 'lifesaver' glance over your left shoulder?

- ⊙ After moving into the left lane
- ⊙ After leaving the roundabout
- ⊙ Before signalling to the right
- ⊙ Before moving into the left lane

⊙ **Before moving into the left lane**

The 'lifesaver' is essential to motorcyclists and is exactly what it says. It could save your life. It's purpose is to check the blind spot that is not covered by your mirrors. Understand and learn how and when you should use it.

1.27   *Mark **one** answer*   R-ES 11 & 16, HC r282

You are on a motorway. You see an incident on the other side of the road. Your lane is clear. You should

- ⊙ assist the emergency services
- ⊙ stop, and cross the road to help
- ⊙ concentrate on what is happening ahead
- ⊙ place a warning triangle in the road

⊙ **concentrate on what is happening ahead**

Always concentrate on the road ahead. Try not to be distracted by an incident on the other side of the road. Many motorway collisions occur due to traffic slowing down. This is because drivers are looking at something on the other side of the road.

1.28
*Mark **one** answer* R-ES 8, HC r159-161

Before you make a U-turn in the road, you should

- ⊙ give an arm signal as well as using your indicators
- ⊙ signal so that other drivers can slow down for you
- ⊙ look over your shoulder for a final check
- ⊙ select a higher gear than normal

- ⊙ **look over your shoulder for a final check**

If you want to make a U-turn, slow down and ensure that the road is clear in both directions. Make sure that the road is wide enough to carry out the manoeuvre safely.

1.29
*Mark **three** answers* HC r113-115

As you approach this bridge you should

- ⊙ move into the middle of the road to get a better view
- ⊙ slow down
- ⊙ get over the bridge as quickly as possible
- ⊙ consider using your horn
- ⊙ find another route
- ⊙ beware of pedestrians

- ⊙ **slow down**
- ⊙ **consider using your horn**
- ⊙ **beware of pedestrians**

This sign gives you a warning. The brow of the hill prevents you seeing oncoming traffic so you must be cautious. The bridge is narrow and there may not be enough room for you to pass an oncoming vehicle at this point. There is no footpath, so pedestrians may be walking in the road. Consider the hidden hazards and be ready to react if necessary.

1.30
*Mark **one** answer* R-ES 8, HC r163

In which of these situations should you avoid overtaking?

- ⊙ Just after a bend
- ⊙ In a one-way street
- ⊙ On a 30 mph road
- ⊙ Approaching a dip in the road

- ⊙ **Approaching a dip in the road**

As you begin to think about overtaking, ask yourself if it's really necessary. If you can't see well ahead stay back and wait for a safer place to pull out.

1.31   *Mark **one** answer*   **HC r162-167, KYTS p10 & 63**

This road marking warns

⊙ drivers to use the hard shoulder

⊙ overtaking drivers there is a bend to the left

⊙ overtaking drivers to move back to the left

⊙ drivers that it is safe to overtake

⊙ **overtaking drivers to move back to the left**

You should plan your overtaking to take into account any hazards ahead. In this picture the marking indicates that you are approaching a junction. You will not have time to overtake and move back into the left safely.

1.32   *Mark **one** answer*   **HC r149-150**

Your mobile phone rings while you are travelling. You should

⊙ stop immediately

⊙ answer it immediately

⊙ pull up in a suitable place

⊙ pull up at the nearest kerb

⊙ **pull up in a suitable place**

The safest option is to switch off your mobile phone before you set off, and use a message service. Even hands-free systems are likely to distract your attention. Don't endanger other road users. If you need to make a call, pull up in a safe place when you can, you may need to go some distance before you can find one. It's illegal to use a hand-held mobile or similar device when driving or riding, except in a genuine emergency.

Why are these yellow lines painted across the road?

⊙ To help you choose the correct lane

⊙ To help you keep the correct separation distance

⊙ To make you aware of your speed

⊙ To tell you the distance to the roundabout

⊙ **To make you aware of your speed**

These lines are often found on the approach to a roundabout or a dangerous junction. They give you extra warning to adjust your speed. Look well ahead and do this in good time.

You are approaching traffic lights that have been on green for some time. You should

⊙ accelerate hard

⊙ maintain your speed

⊙ be ready to stop

⊙ brake hard

⊙ **be ready to stop**

The longer traffic lights have been on green, the greater the chance of them changing. Always allow for this on approach and be prepared to stop.

Which of the following should you do before stopping?

⊙ Sound the horn

⊙ Use the mirrors

⊙ Select a higher gear

⊙ Flash your headlights

⊙ **Use the mirrors**

Before pulling up check the mirrors to see what is happening behind you. Also assess what is ahead and make sure you give the correct signal· if it helps other road users.

1.36   Mark **one** answer   R-ES 7, HC r221

When following a large vehicle you should keep well back because this

⊙ allows you to corner more quickly

⊙ helps the large vehicle to stop more easily

⊙ allows the driver to see you in the mirrors

⊙ helps you to keep out of the wind

⊙ **allows the driver to see you in the mirrors**

If you're following a large vehicle but are so close to it that you can't see the exterior mirrors, the driver can't see you.

Keeping well back will also allow you to see the road ahead by looking past either side of the large vehicle.

1.37   Mark **one** answer   R-ES 8, HC r159-161

When you see a hazard ahead you should use the mirrors. Why is this?

⊙ Because you will need to accelerate out of danger

⊙ To assess how your actions will affect following traffic

⊙ Because you will need to brake sharply to a stop

⊙ To check what is happening on the road ahead

⊙ **To assess how your actions will affect following traffic**

You should be constantly scanning the road for clues about what is going to happen next. Check your mirrors regularly, particularly as soon as you spot a hazard. What is happening behind may affect your response to hazards ahead.

1.38   Mark **one** answer   R-ES 8 & 10

You are waiting to turn right at the end of a road. Your view is obstructed by parked vehicles. What should you do?

⊙ Stop and then move forward slowly and carefully for a proper view

⊙ Move quickly to where you can see so you only block traffic from one direction

⊙ Wait for a pedestrian to let you know when it is safe for you to emerge

⊙ Turn your vehicle around immediately and find another junction to use

⊙ **Stop and then move forward slowly and carefully for a proper view**

At junctions your view is often restricted by buildings, trees or parked cars. You need to be able to see in order to judge a safe gap. Edge forward slowly and keep looking all the time. Don't cause other road users to change speed or direction as you emerge.

Case study practice 1 – Alertness

The morning is clear and fine but very cold. Joan is riding her motorcycle and is using dipped headlights. Further on, there is an unmarked junction. Joan looks over her right shoulder before turning right. Ahead, there is a dip in the road. Later, she reaches a school crossing patrol area. The officer is signalling traffic to stop while children are crossing.

1.1 Why would Joan be using dipped headlights?

*Mark **one** answer*

- ⊙ To help her see the road ahead.
- ⊙ To help her be seen by others.
- ⊙ To help her see other road users.
- ⊙ To help others see the road ahead.

R-ES 4, HC r86

1.2 How should Joan behave at this junction?

*Mark **one** answer*

- ⊙ Check quickly and cross as fast as possible.
- ⊙ Move slowly while flashing her headlights.
- ⊙ Check carefully and proceed with great care.
- ⊙ Wait for someone else to wave her onwards.

R-ES 9, HC r176

1.3 What is the name of the final look that Joan gives before turning right?

*Mark **one** answer*

- ⊙ Lifecycle.
- ⊙ Lifepreserver.
- ⊙ Lifeblood.
- ⊙ Lifesaver.

R-ES 8

1.4 How could the dip affect Joan?

*Mark **one** answer*

- ⊙ Obstruct her view of the road.
- ⊙ Increase her fuel consumption.
- ⊙ Improve her brake function.
- ⊙ Cause more wear on her tyres.

R-ES 8

1.5 How **MUST** Joan react to the school crossing patrol warden's signal?

*Mark **one** answer*

- ⊙ Stop her vehicle and wait patiently.
- ⊙ Rev up and inch her vehicle forward.
- ⊙ Stop and wave the children across.
- ⊙ Move forward slowly with headlights on.

R-ES 8, HC r105 & p105

section **two**
ATTITUDE

This section covers
- Consideration
- Close following
- Courtesy
- Priority

Attitude

Safe riding is all about developing the correct attitude and approach together with a sound knowledge of riding techniques. However good, fast or expensive your motorcycle, it's you, the rider, who determines how safe it is.

Consideration

Be considerate to other road users. Other types of vehicle, cyclists and horse riders have just as much right to use the road as you. Don't ride in a competitive way – people who do this can create an increased risk for everyone on the road.

Horses become frightened easily and the rider could lose control. When passing them, keep your speed right down and give them plenty of room. Also take care if there are animals, such as sheep, on the road. Stop and switch off your engine if necessary or if you're asked to do so.

R-ES 10, HC r214-215

Help other road users know your intention by signalling correctly and taking up the correct position at junctions in good time. For instance, if you want to turn right, get into the right-hand lane. A badly positioned vehicle could prevent following vehicles proceeding.

R-ES 8 & 9, HC r143

If you are riding a slow-moving moped, consider the other road users behind you. If there's a queue, pull over as soon as you can do so safely and let the traffic pass.

R-ES 10, HC r169

Following safely

Keep a safe distance from the vehicle in front.

- In good, dry conditions leave a two-second gap.
- In wet weather leave a four-second gap.

R-ES 8, 10 & 11, HC r156

Tailgating – riding too close to the vehicle in front – is

- very dangerous
- intimidating for the road user in front.

Travelling too close to another vehicle means your view of the road ahead is reduced, so keep well back, especially from a large vehicle. By being able to see further down the road, you can be prepared for any hazards. Keeping well back also allows

- the road user in front to see you in their mirrors
- traffic emerging from junctions ahead to see you more easily.

R-ES 8 & 10

If the road user behind is following too closely, gradually increase the gap between you and the vehicle in front. This will give you a greater safety margin.

HC r168

If another road user cuts in front of you, drop back to maintain your correct separation distance.

Courtesy

Be patient with other road users. Be aware that not everyone obeys the rules. Try to be calm and tolerant, however difficult it seems. For instance, if a vehicle pulls out in front of you at a junction, slow down and don't get annoyed with them. Only sound your horn if there's danger and you need to let others know you're there. Don't sound it through impatience.

R-ES 5, 6 & 10, HC r147

At night, don't dazzle other road users. Dip your lights when you're following, or meeting, another vehicle.

R-ES 8 & 10, HC r112

Priority

Give priority to emergency vehicles. It's important for them to proceed quickly through traffic. Someone's life might depend on it. Pull over to let them through as soon as you can do so safely. As well as the normal fire, police and ambulance services the following may also use a blue flashing light:

- coastguard
- bomb disposal
- mountain rescue
- blood transfusion.

Doctors may use green flashing lights when answering an emergency call.

R-ES 8, HC r219

Give priority to buses pulling out from bus stops, as long as you can do so safely. In some areas, bus lanes allow buses to proceed quickly through traffic. Be aware of road signs and markings so you don't use bus lanes while they're in operation unless permitted to do so.

At unmarked crossroads no one has priority. Slow down and look both ways before pulling out.

R-ES 7, 8 & 10, HC r223

Watch out for pedestrians at or approaching a zebra crossing:

- be prepared to slow down and stop
- be patient if they're a bit slow
- don't encourage them to cross by waving or flashing your headlights – there may be another vehicle coming.

R-ES 8, HC r195

If you're approaching a pelican crossing and the amber light is flashing

- give way to pedestrians on the crossing
- don't move off until the crossing is clear.

R-ES 8, HC r196-198

Puffin crossings are electronically controlled. Sensors mean the red light stays on until the person has reached a safe position. There's no flashing amber phase – the sequence follows that of normal traffic lights, eg with a steady amber light.

R-ES 8, HC r196-198

Toucan crossings allow cyclists to cross at the same time as pedestrians.

FAQs

I've seen this sign – what does it mean?

This sign applies to trams only. Even if there aren't any trams where you live, you still need to know how to deal with them in case you ever visit a town which has them.

Give cyclists extra room where there are tram rails. The slippery rails may be difficult for them to negotiate. This also applies to motorcyclists so take extra care yourself when crossing tram rails.

R-ES 8, HC r300-306, KYTS p31

Why do large vehicles 'hog' the road?

Larger vehicles need more room to manoeuvre. This will affect their position when approaching junctions, especially when turning left. Keep well back and don't try to pass them on the left as the rear of the vehicle will cut in.

R-ES 10, HC r221

A large vehicle is trying to overtake me, but is taking a long time, what should I do?

Slow down and let them pass. They will need more time than a car to pass you.

R-ES 8, HC r168

What do I do if I'm travelling at the speed limit and a driver comes up behind flashing their headlights or trying to overtake?

Keep a steady course and allow them to overtake. Don't try to stop them, they could become more frustrated.

R-ES 8 & 11, HC r168

I'm never too sure when I should flash my headlights.

Only flash your headlights to show other road users you're there. It's not a signal to show priority or impatience, nor to greet others.

R-ES 6 & 10, HC r110-111

2.1

Mark **one** answer

R-ES 1 & 8, HC r195

You are riding towards a zebra crossing. Pedestrians are waiting to cross. You should

⊙ give way to the elderly and infirm only

⊙ slow down and prepare to stop

⊙ use your headlight to indicate they can cross

⊙ wave at them to cross the road

⊙ **slow down and prepare to stop**

Look for people waiting to cross and be ready to slow down or stop. Some pedestrians may be hesitant. Children can be unpredictable and may hesitate or run out unexpectedly.

2.2

Mark **one** answer

R-ES 1 & 8, HC r221

You are riding a motorcycle and following a large vehicle at 40 mph. You should position yourself

⊙ close behind to make it easier to overtake the vehicle

⊙ to the left of the road to make it easier to be seen

⊙ close behind the vehicle to keep out of the wind

⊙ well back so that you can see past the vehicle

⊙ **well back so that you can see past the vehicle**

You need to be able to see well down the road and be ready for any hazards. Staying too close to the vehicle will reduce your view of the road ahead and the driver of the vehicle in front may not be able to see you either. Without a safe separation gap you do not have the time and space necessary to react to any hazards.

2.3

Mark **one** answer

R-ES 1 & 10, HC r214-215

You are riding on a country road. Two horses with riders are in the distance. You should

⊙ continue at your normal speed

⊙ change down the gears quickly

⊙ slow down and be ready to stop

⊙ flash your headlight to warn them

⊙ **slow down and be ready to stop**

Animals are easily frightened by moving motor vehicles. If you're approaching horses keep your speed down and watch to see if the rider has any difficulty keeping control. Always be ready to stop if necessary.

You are approaching a red light at a puffin crossing. Pedestrians are on the crossing. The red light will stay on until

⊙ you start to edge forward on to the crossing

⊙ the pedestrians have reached a safe position

⊙ the pedestrians are clear of the front of your motorcycle

⊙ a driver from the opposite direction reaches the crossing

⊙ **the pedestrians have reached a safe position**

The electronic device will automatically detect when the pedestrians have reached a safe position. Don't proceed until the green light shows it is safe to do so.

You are riding a slow-moving scooter on a narrow winding road. You should

⊙ keep well out to stop vehicles overtaking dangerously

⊙ wave vehicles behind you to pass, if you think they can overtake quickly

⊙ pull in safely when you can, to let vehicles behind you overtake

⊙ give a left signal when it is safe for vehicles to overtake you

⊙ **pull in safely when you can, to let vehicles behind you overtake**

Try not to hold up a queue of traffic. This might lead to other road users becoming impatient and attempting dangerous manoeuvres.

If you're riding a slow-moving scooter or small motorcycle on a narrow road and a queue of traffic has built up behind you, look out for a safe place to pull in.

When riding a motorcycle your normal road position should allow

⊙ other vehicles to overtake on your left

⊙ the driver ahead to see you in their mirrors

⊙ you to prevent vehicles behind from overtaking

⊙ you to be seen by traffic that is emerging from junctions ahead

⊙ you to ride within half a metre (1 foot 8 ins) of the kerb

⊙ **the driver ahead to see you in their mirrors**

⊙ **you to be seen by traffic that is emerging from junctions ahead**

Aim to ride in the middle of your lane. Avoid riding in the gutter or in the centre of the road, where you might obstruct overtaking traffic or put yourself in danger from oncoming traffic. Riding in this position could also encourage other traffic to overtake you on the left.

2.7 — Mark *one* answer — R-ES 1

Young, inexperienced and newly qualified motorcyclists can often be involved in crashes. This is due to

- being too cautious at junctions
- riding in the middle of their lane
- showing off and being competitive
- wearing full weather protection

⊙ **showing off and being competitive**

Over-confidence, lack of experience and poor judgement can lead to disaster. No matter what anyone says, don't do anything that could endanger lives. It's not worth the risk.

2.8 — Mark *one* answer — R-ES 8, HC r195

At a pelican crossing the flashing amber light means you MUST

- stop and wait for the green light
- stop and wait for the red light
- give way to pedestrians waiting to cross
- give way to pedestrians already on the crossing

⊙ **give way to pedestrians already on the crossing**

Pelican crossings are signal-controlled crossings operated by pedestrians. Push-button controls change the signals. Pelican crossings have no red-and-amber stage before green. Instead, they have a flashing amber light, which means you MUST give way to pedestrians already on the crossing, but if it is clear, you may continue.

2.9 — Mark *one* answer — R-ES 8, HC r195

You should never wave people across at pedestrian crossings because

- there may be another vehicle coming
- they may not be looking
- it is safer for you to carry on
- they may not be ready to cross

⊙ **there may be another vehicle coming**

If people are waiting to use a pedestrian crossing, slow down and be prepared to stop. Don't wave them across the road since another driver may not have seen them, not have seen your signal and may not be able to stop safely.

*Mark **one** answer* **R-ES 8, 10, 11, HC r126**

'Tailgating' means

- using the rear door of a hatchback car
- reversing into a parking space
- following another vehicle too closely
- driving with rear fog lights on

⊙ **following another vehicle too closely**

'Tailgating' is used to describe this dangerous practice, often seen in fast-moving traffic and on motorways. Following the vehicle in front too closely is dangerous because it

- restricts your view of the road ahead
- leaves you no safety margin if the vehicle in front slows down or stops suddenly.

*Mark **one** answer* **R-ES 8 & 10**

Following this vehicle too closely is unwise because

- your brakes will overheat
- your view ahead is increased
- your engine will overheat
- your view ahead is reduced

⊙ **your view ahead is reduced**

Staying back will increase your view of the road ahead. This will help you to see any hazards that might occur and allow you more time to react.

*Mark **one** answer* **R-ES 8, 10, 11, HC r126**

You are following a vehicle on a wet road. You should leave a time gap of at least

- one second
- two seconds
- three seconds
- four seconds

⊙ **four seconds**

Wet roads will reduce your tyres' grip on the road. The safe separation gap of at least two seconds in dry conditions should be doubled in wet weather.

2.13 — Mark *one* answer — R-ES 8, HC r168

A long, heavily-laden lorry is taking a long time to overtake you. What should you do?

- ⊙ Speed up
- ⊙ Slow down
- ⊙ Hold your speed
- ⊙ Change direction

⊙ **Slow down**

A long lorry with a heavy load will need more time to pass you than a car, especially on an uphill stretch of road. Slow down and allow the lorry to pass.

2.14 — Mark *three* answers — R-ES 8, HC r219

Which of the following vehicles will use blue flashing beacons?

- ⊙ Motorway maintenance
- ⊙ Bomb disposal
- ⊙ Blood transfusion
- ⊙ Police patrol
- ⊙ Breakdown recovery

⊙ **Bomb disposal**

⊙ **Blood transfusion**

⊙ **Police patrol**

When you see emergency vehicles with blue flashing beacons, move out of the way as soon as it is safe to do so.

2.15 — Mark *three* answers — R-ES 8, HC r219

Which THREE of these emergency services might have blue flashing beacons?

- ⊙ Coastguard
- ⊙ Bomb disposal
- ⊙ Gritting lorries
- ⊙ Animal ambulances
- ⊙ Mountain rescue
- ⊙ Doctors' cars

⊙ **Coastguard**

⊙ **Bomb disposal**

⊙ **Mountain rescue**

When attending an emergency these vehicles will be travelling at speed. You should help their progress by pulling over and allowing them to pass. Do so safely. Don't stop suddenly or in a dangerous position.

*Mark **one** answer* **R-ES 8, HC r219**

When being followed by an ambulance showing a flashing blue beacon you should

- ⊙ pull over as soon as safely possible to let it pass
- ⊙ accelerate hard to get away from it
- ⊙ maintain your speed and course
- ⊙ brake harshly and immediately stop in the road

⊙ **pull over as soon as safely possible to let it pass**

Pull over in a place where the ambulance can pass safely. Check that there are no bollards or obstructions in the road that will prevent it from doing so.

2.17 *Mark **one** answer* **R-ES 7, 8, 10, HC r223**

What type of emergency vehicle is fitted with a green flashing beacon?

- ⊙ Fire engine
- ⊙ Road gritter
- ⊙ Ambulance
- ⊙ Doctor's car

⊙ **Doctor's car**

A green flashing beacon on a vehicle means the driver or passenger is a doctor on an emergency call. Give way to them if it's safe to do so. Be aware that the vehicle may be travelling quickly or may stop in a hurry.

2.18 *Mark **one** answer* **R-ES 7, 8, 10, HC r223**

A flashing green beacon on a vehicle means

- ⊙ police on non-urgent duties
- ⊙ doctor on an emergency call
- ⊙ road safety patrol operating
- ⊙ gritting in progress

⊙ **doctor on an emergency call**

If you see a vehicle with a flashing green beacon approaching, allow it to pass when you can do so safely. Be aware that someone's life could depend on the driver making good progress through traffic.

2.19 *Mark **one** answer* **R-ES 8, HC r300-306, KYTS p31**

Diamond-shaped signs give instructions to

- ⊙ tram drivers
- ⊙ bus drivers
- ⊙ lorry drivers
- ⊙ taxi drivers

⊙ **tram drivers**

These signs only apply to trams. They are directed at tram drivers but you should know their meaning so that you're aware of the priorities and are able to anticipate the actions of the driver.

2.20 *Mark **one** answer* **R-ES 8, HC r306, KYTS p31**

On a road where trams operate, which of these vehicles will be most at risk from the tram rails?

- ⊙ Cars
- ⊙ Cycles
- ⊙ Buses
- ⊙ Lorries

⊙ **Cycles**

The narrow wheels of a bicycle can become stuck in the tram rails, causing the cyclist to stop suddenly, wobble or even lose balance altogether. The tram lines are also slippery which could cause a cyclist to slide or fall off.

2.21 *Mark **one** answer* **R-ES 5, 6, 10, HC r112**

What should you use your horn for?

- ⊙ To alert others to your presence
- ⊙ To allow you right of way
- ⊙ To greet other road users
- ⊙ To signal your annoyance

⊙ **To alert others to your presence**

Your horn must not be used between 11.30 pm and 7 am in a built-up area or when you are stationary, unless a moving vehicle poses a danger. Its function is to alert other road users to your presence.

You are in a one-way street and want to turn right. You should position yourself

- in the right-hand lane
- in the left-hand lane
- in either lane, depending on the traffic
- just left of the centre line

⊙ **in the right-hand lane**

If you're travelling in a one-way street and wish to turn right you should take up a position in the right-hand lane. This will enable other road users not wishing to turn to proceed on the left. Indicate your intention and take up your position in good time.

You wish to turn right ahead. Why should you take up the correct position in good time?

- To allow other drivers to pull out in front of you
- To give a better view into the road that you're joining
- To help other road users know what you intend to do
- To allow drivers to pass you on the right

⊙ **To help other road users know what you intend to do**

If you wish to turn right into a side road take up your position in good time. Move to the centre of the road when it's safe to do so. This will allow vehicles to pass you on the left. Early planning will show other traffic what you intend to do.

At which type of crossing are cyclists allowed to ride across with pedestrians?

- Toucan
- Puffin
- Pelican
- Zebra

⊙ **Toucan**

A toucan crossing is designed to allow pedestrians and cyclists to cross at the same time. Look out for cyclists approaching the crossing at speed.

2.25
*Mark **one** answer*

R-ES 8 & 11, HC r168

You are travelling at the legal speed limit. A vehicle comes up quickly behind, flashing its headlights. You should

⊙ accelerate to make a gap behind you

⊙ touch the brakes sharply to show your brake lights

⊙ maintain your speed to prevent the vehicle from overtaking

⊙ allow the vehicle to overtake

⊙ **allow the vehicle to overtake**

Don't enforce the speed limit by blocking another vehicle's progress. This will only lead to the other driver becoming more frustrated. Allow the other vehicle to pass when you can do so safely.

2.26
*Mark **one** answer*

R-ES 6 & 10, HC r110-111

You should ONLY flash your headlights to other road users

⊙ to show that you are giving way

⊙ to show that you are about to turn

⊙ to tell them that you have right of way

⊙ to let them know that you are there

⊙ **to let them know that you are there**

You should only flash your headlights to warn others of your presence. Don't use them to greet others, show impatience or give priority to other road users. They could misunderstand your signal.

2.27
*Mark **one** answer*

R-ES 8, HC r176

You are approaching unmarked crossroads. How should you deal with this type of junction?

⊙ Accelerate and keep to the middle

⊙ Slow down and keep to the right

⊙ Accelerate looking to the left

⊙ Slow down and look both ways

⊙ **Slow down and look both ways**

Be extra-cautious, especially when your view is restricted by hedges, bushes, walls and large vehicles etc. In the summer months these junctions can become more difficult to deal with when growing foliage may obscure your view.

You are approaching a pelican crossing. The amber light is flashing. You must

- ⊙ give way to pedestrians who are crossing
- ⊙ encourage pedestrians to cross
- ⊙ not move until the green light appears
- ⊙ stop even if the crossing is clear

⊙ **give way to pedestrians who are crossing**

While the pedestrians are crossing don't encourage them to cross by waving or flashing your headlights: other road users may misunderstand your signal. Don't harass them by creeping forward or revving your engine.

The conditions are good and dry. You could use the 'two-second rule'

- ⊙ before restarting the engine after it has stalled
- ⊙ to keep a safe gap from the vehicle in front
- ⊙ before using the 'Mirror-Signal-Manoeuvre' routine
- ⊙ when emerging on wet roads

⊙ **to keep a safe gap from the vehicle in front**

To measure this, choose a fixed reference point such as a bridge, sign or tree. When the vehicle ahead passes the object, say to yourself 'Only a fool breaks the two-second rule.' If you reach the object before you finish saying this, you're TOO CLOSE.

A vehicle has a flashing green beacon. What does this mean?

- ⊙ A doctor is answering an emergency call
- ⊙ The vehicle is slow-moving
- ⊙ It is a motorway police patrol vehicle
- ⊙ The vehicle is carrying hazardous chemicals

⊙ **A doctor is answering an emergency call**

A doctor attending an emergency may show a green flashing beacon on their vehicle. Give way to them when you can do so safely as they will need to reach their destination quickly. Be aware that they might pull over suddenly.

2.31 *Mark **one** answer* **R-ES 8, 10, 11, HC r126**

You are in a line of traffic. The driver behind you is following very closely. What action should you take?

⊙ Ignore the following driver and continue to travel within the speed limit

⊙ Slow down, gradually increasing the gap between you and the vehicle in front

⊙ Signal left and wave the following driver past

⊙ Move over to a position just left of the centre line of the road

⊙ **Slow down, gradually increasing the gap between you and the vehicle in front**

It can be worrying to see that the car behind is following you too closely. Give yourself a greater safety margin by easing back from the vehicle in front.

2.32 *Mark **one** answer* **R-ES 8, HC r199**

At a puffin crossing, which colour follows the green signal?

⊙ Steady red
⊙ Flashing amber
⊙ Steady amber
⊙ Flashing green

⊙ **Steady amber**

Puffin crossings have infra-red sensors which detect when pedestrians are crossing and hold the red traffic signal until the crossing is clear. The use of a sensor means there is no flashing amber phase as there is with a pelican crossing.

2.33 *Mark **one** answer* **R-ES 7, 8, 10, HC r223**

A bus has stopped at a bus stop ahead of you. Its right-hand indicator is flashing. You should

⊙ flash your headlights and slow down
⊙ slow down and give way if it is safe to do so
⊙ sound your horn and keep going
⊙ slow down and then sound your horn

⊙ **slow down and give way if it is safe to do so**

Give way to buses whenever you can do so safely, especially when they signal to pull away from bus stops. Look out for people leaving the bus and crossing the road.

Case study practice 2 – Attitude

David rides his motorcycle to a motorcycle show. The single-carriageway road surface is damp from overnight rain. David comes up behind two horse riders on the single-carriageway road. He passes them in an appropriate manner. Near the showground, the traffic volume increases. There's a large vehicle in front, so David drops back. He sees a green flashing light in his mirrors so he makes room for the vehicle to pass.

2.1 What is the national speed limit for motorcycles on this road?

*Mark **one** answer*

⊙ 40 mph.
⊙ 50 mph.
⊙ 60 mph.
⊙ 70 mph.

HC r124 & p40

2.2 How should David ride on this road surface?

*Mark **one** answer*

⊙ Carefully, while increasing the distance from the vehicle in front.
⊙ Faster, as this will help warm the tyres and dry the road surface.
⊙ Very slowly, to help prevent surface water spraying over others.
⊙ As close as possible to the vehicle in front, for added protection.

R-ES 8, HC r126

2.3 What is the recommended safest way to pass horse riders?

*Mark **one** answer*

- ⊙ Quickly, while flashing headlights.
- ⊙ Slowly, while sounding the horn.
- ⊙ Quickly, leaving a large gap.
- ⊙ Slowly, leaving plenty of room.

R-ES 10, HC r214-215

2.4 Why did David drop back?

*Mark **one** answer*

- ⊙ To avoid any buffeting from the wind.
- ⊙ To allow space for other road users to pull in.
- ⊙ To avoid any mud splashing up from the tyres.
- ⊙ To allow the driver to see him in the mirrors.

R-ES 10, HC r164

2.5 Which vehicle would show a green flashing light?

*Mark **one** answer*

- ⊙ Fire fighter driving to the fire station.
- ⊙ Doctor attending emergency call.
- ⊙ Police officer driving home after duty.
- ⊙ Council worker driving snow plough.

HC r219

section **three**
SAFETY AND YOUR MOTORCYCLE

This section covers
- Fault detection
- Defects
- Safety equipment
- Emissions
- Noise

Safety and your motorcycle

Basic maintenance

Regular care and maintenance should ensure that your motorcycle is safe and roadworthy. It will also help fuel economy as well as keeping exhaust emissions to a minimum. Check the following items on a regular basis

- **Engine** – fuel, oil (engine, gearbox and final drive), coolant (liquid cooled engines), brake fluid, air filter

- **Suspension and steering** – suspension, steering head bearings, wheels, tyres (eg splits, tread depth, worn spots, debris in the tread)

- **Controls** – brakes, throttle, clutch (if cable-operated, keep cable oiled)

- **Electrical systems** – battery, lights, horn, indicators.

Lights and number plates should be kept clean at all times.

R-ES 6 & 15, HC p128

There are other items which can develop problems or produce adverse effects if not checked regularly, such as

- **the drive chain** – this can lock the rear wheel if loose or worn. When adjusting, check wheel alignment too as this can increase tyre wear and instability when cornering

R-ES 15

- **tyre pressures** – check when cold, increase pressure when carrying passengers or loads or if riding at high speeds. Under-inflation can affect braking and steering, and increase fuel consumption. Check owner's manual for correct pressures

- **tread** – depth must be more than 1mm to be legal. When replacing tyres, replace tubes as well if necessary. Check wheel alignment after refitting rear wheel. Ride carefully on new tyres till the shiny surface wears off.

R-ES 15, HC p129

Defects and fault detection

If you've a basic understanding of how your motorcycle works it'll help you recognise the signs of a defect. It's important that your vehicle is checked regularly by a qualified mechanic, especially the brakes.

Warning lights on the instrument panel monitor the performance of the engine and give you warning of any defects.

- Check your vehicle handbook for their meaning.
- Don't ignore the warning – it could affect your safety.

R-ES 5 & 15, HC p128

Motorcycles fitted with anti-lock brake systems (ABS) will have a warning light on the instrument panel which should go out at a speed of 5-10 mph. If it doesn't, have it checked by a qualified mechanic.

Remember to check oil seals for leakage – leaks of damping oil from shock absorbers or front forks can

- make the motorcycle difficult to control
- increase your stopping distance
- find its way onto the wheel, tyre and brake disc or drum, causing skidding or brake problems.

Don't overfill your motorcycle with oil as this could cause oil leaks and damage to engine seals.

Consult a garage as soon as possible if

- the steering vibrates – the wheels may need balancing
- the motorcycle becomes difficult to control – the steering head bearings may be worn or need adjustment
- indicators flash too fast – they should flash between one and two times a second
- you notice uneven tyre wear – this can indicate faults with the brakes, suspension or wheel alignment.

R-ES 6 & 15

If, while riding

- the oil light comes on – stop as quickly as possible and investigate
- a tyre bursts – slow gently to a stop,

holding the handlebars firmly

- you forget to switch the choke off – do so as soon as you realise. Leaving it on can cause pollution, engine wear and waste fuel.

Other points to remember are

- to regularly check brake fluid levels – low levels can affect braking efficiency
- to check oil and water levels before a long journey, as well as tyre pressures
- to check battery fluid levels if necessary – top up with distilled water to just above the cell plates.

R-ES 6 & 15, HC p128

Carrying passengers or loads

Once you have passed your practical test you can carry a passenger if your motorcycle is designed to do so. You are responsible for ensuring that any passenger you carry is sitting properly, facing forward, on a proper seat with appropriate footrests, and wearing appropriate headgear which is correctly fastened.

Make sure you properly secure any load or luggage to ensure it does not fall off or affect your control of the motorcycle.

R-ES 14, HC r83 & r85

Safety issues

Before riding, adjust the mirrors to maximise your field of vision. Convex mirrors give a wider view but can make vehicles look further away than they are.

Use dipped headlights. It's important for other road users to see you. If there's thick fog, use your fog lights. You can maximise your visibility in other ways as well, by wearing a white helmet, brightly coloured clothing and a high-visibility or reflective jacket or vest. Reflective clothing is especially important at night.

There is no substitute for wearing proper protective clothing and footwear at all times – they can protect you in all types of weather and in the event of an incident. Having touring fairings fitted to your motorcycle will protect your hands, legs and feet from bad weather and cold winds.

R-ES 4, HC r83-88

Helmet visors and goggles should be

- kept clean – wash or clean them in soapy water (but also check manufacturer's guidelines for advice)
- undamaged – if they become scratched, replace them as soon as possible.

If visors or goggles become fogged up during a ride, stop as soon as possible and wipe them.

R-ES 4, HC r83-88

When leaving your vehicle on a two-way road at night, park in the direction of the traffic. If the speed limit is over 30 mph (46 km/h), switch on your parking lights. If hazard warning lights are fitted, you can warn drivers of a hazard ahead, such as

- when you've broken down
- queuing traffic on a dual carriageway or motorway.

Don't use them as an excuse to park illegally, even for a short time.

R-ES 11, HC r116, r274, r277-8

Security

Make it as difficult as you can for a thief to either damage your motorcycle or steal it:

- engage the steering lock
- secure it to an immovable object or another motorcycle
- use an additional locking device, ie high-tension steel cable or chain with high-quality padlock, a U-lock or disc lock
- at night, park in a well-lit area.

To make it more difficult for the opportunist thief you can

- fit an anti-theft alarm or immobiliser
- have the vehicle security marked, which involves having the Vehicle Identification Number (VIN) put on the motorcycle.

Consider joining a vehicle watch scheme if there's one in your area.

R-ES 8

63

Considering other road users

Avoid parking your vehicle where it would cause an obstruction to other road users, such as

- in front of a property entrance
- at or near a bus stop
- near the brow of a hill
- at a dropped kerb.

Never stop or park on or near a level crossing, or on the zigzag lines at a pedestrian crossing. This would block the view of pedestrians and other road users, as well as endangering people trying to use the crossing.

R-ES 8, HC r239-250 & r291

If you do have to park on an incline, leave your motorcycle in a low gear and block a wheel or wedge it against the kerb, which will stop it rolling away.

Environment

Motor vehicles can harm the environment, resulting in air pollution, damage to buildings and the using up of natural resources.

Road transport accounts for 20% of all emissions. Help the environment by riding in an eco-safe manner – you will improve road safety, reduce exhaust emissions and improve your fuel consumption. You should

- reduce your speed – vehicles travelling at 70 mph (112 km/h) use more fuel than those travelling at 50 mph (80 km/h)
- plan well ahead so that you can ride

smoothly – avoiding rapid acceleration and heavy braking can cut your fuel bill by up to 15%

- use selective gear changing – missing out some gears can help reduce the amount of time you are accelerating, which is when your vehicle uses most fuel
- have your vehicle serviced and tuned properly
- make sure your tyres are correctly inflated.

Don't

- carry unnecessary weight
- over-rev in lower gears
- leave the engine running unnecessarily – if your vehicle is stationary and likely to remain so for some time, switch off the engine.

Never leave your vehicle unattended with the engine running. Always switch off the engine and secure the vehicle before leaving it. Use the steering lock and, if possible, chain the motorcycle to an immovable object for extra security.

Try not to use your vehicle to make a lot of short journeys – think about walking or cycling instead. Using public transport or sharing a vehicle can reduce the volume of traffic and the emissions it creates. Modern trams use electric power. They can help reduce traffic and noise pollution.

Make sure your filler cap is securely fastened. If it's loose, it could spill fuel which wastes energy and money. Spilt diesel fuel makes the road slippery for other road users. Check out any strong smell of petrol in the interests of safety. Use the engine cut-out switch in an emergency.

Having your motorcycle serviced regularly will give better fuel economy and your exhaust emissions will be cleaner. If your vehicle is over three years old (over four years old in Northern Ireland), it will have to pass an emissions test as part of the MOT test. If you service your own vehicle, dispose of old engine oil and batteries responsibly. Take them to a local authority site or a garage. Don't pour oil down the drain.

Also bear in mind noise pollution. In built-up areas don't use your horn between 11.30 pm and 7.00 am, unless another vehicle poses a danger.

R-ES 8 &17, HC r123

Avoiding congestion

You will have an easier and more pleasant journey if you plan your route before starting out. Try to avoid busy times, if possible. Also, you should allow plenty of time for your journey, especially if you have an appointment to keep or a connection to make. Plan your route by

- looking at a map
- using satellite navigation equipment
- checking with a motoring organisation
- using a route planner on the internet.

If you are travelling on a new or unfamiliar route, it is a good idea to print out or write down the route, and also to plan an alternative in case your original route is blocked. If you can avoid travelling at busy times, you will be less likely to be delayed. This will also help to ease congestion for those who have to travel at these times.

In some areas those using congested road space have to pay a congestion charge. In London, those exempt from paying include

- disabled people who hold a Blue Badge
- riders of two-wheeled vehicles
- people living within the area.

R-ES 18

FAQs

What is a catalytic converter?

A catalytic converter is fitted to the exhaust and reduces emissions. It acts like a filter, removing some of the toxic exhaust gas waste.

R-ES 15

I've been offered a second-hand helmet – is this a good idea?

No. Even if the helmet has no obvious damage, it could have damage which is not visible to the naked eye. This means it could be unreliable in a road traffic incident, so it's best not to take the risk.

R-ES 4

Road humps have been installed in our area. What other types of traffic-calming measures are there?

As well as road humps, road narrowing and chicanes may be used as traffic-calming measures. These are used to slow the traffic down, so keep your speed down throughout the area.

A reduced speed limit of 20 mph (32 km/h) is being introduced into many narrow residential streets. Look out for the signs, and remember the measures are there for a good reason; they could save lives.

R-ES 7, HC r153

On a trip to London I saw red lines on the side of the road. What are they for?

These indicate 'red routes'. They help the traffic flow by restricting stopping on these routes, and can now also be found in other cities.

R-ES 18, HC r240, r247 & p115

3.1 *Mark one answer* R-ES 15 & 17

A loose drive chain on a motorcycle could cause

- the front wheel to wobble
- the ignition to cut out
- the brakes to fail
- the rear wheel to lock

⊙ **the rear wheel to lock**

Drive chains are subject to wear and require frequent adjustment to maintain the correct tension. Allowing the drive chain to run dry will greatly increase the rate of wear, so it is important to keep it lubricated. If the chain becomes worn or slack it can jump off the sprocket and lock the rear wheel.

3.2 *Mark one answer* R-ES 15 & 17

What is the most important reason why you should keep your motorcycle regularly maintained?

- To accelerate faster than other traffic
- So the motorcycle can carry panniers
- To keep the machine roadworthy
- So the motorcycle can carry a passenger

⊙ **To keep the machine roadworthy**

Whenever you use any motorcycle on the road it must be in a roadworthy condition. Regular maintenance should identify any faults at an early stage and help prevent more serious problems.

3.3 *Mark one answer* R-ES 15

How should you ride a motorcycle when NEW tyres have just been fitted?

- Carefully, until the shiny surface is worn off
- By braking hard especially into bends
- Through normal riding with higher air pressures
- By riding at faster than normal speeds

⊙ **Carefully, until the shiny surface is worn off**

New tyres have a shiny finish which needs to wear off before the tyre will give the best grip. Take extra care if the road surface is wet or slippery.

3.4

R-ES 4, HC r87

When riding and wearing brightly coloured clothing you will

- ⊙ dazzle other motorists on the road
- ⊙ be seen more easily by other motorists
- ⊙ create a hazard by distracting other drivers
- ⊙ be able to ride on unlit roads at night with sidelights

⊙ **be seen more easily by other motorists**

For your own safety you need other road users to see you easily. Wearing brightly coloured or fluorescent clothing will help you to achieve this during daylight. At night, wearing clothing that includes reflective material is the best way of helping others to see you.

3.5

R-ES 4

You are riding a motorcycle in very hot weather. You should

- ⊙ ride with your visor fully open
- ⊙ continue to wear protective clothing
- ⊙ wear trainers instead of boots
- ⊙ slacken your helmet strap

⊙ **continue to wear protective clothing**

Always wear your protective clothing, whatever the weather.

In very hot weather it's tempting to ride in light summer clothes. Don't take the risk. If you fall from your motorcycle you'll have no protection from the hard road surface.

3.6

R-ES 4, HC r86

Why should you wear fluorescent clothing when riding in daylight?

- ⊙ It reduces wind resistance
- ⊙ It prevents injury if you come off the machine
- ⊙ It helps other road users to see you
- ⊙ It keeps you cool in hot weather

⊙ **It helps other road users to see you**

Motorcycles are smaller and therefore harder to see than most other vehicles on the road. You need to make yourself as visible as possible to other road users. Fluorescent and reflective clothing will help achieve this. You must be visible from all sides.

3.7   *Mark **one** answer*   R-ES 4, HC r87

Why should riders wear reflective clothing?

- To protect them from the cold
- To protect them from direct sunlight
- To be seen better in daylight
- To be seen better at night

⊙ **To be seen better at night**

Fluorescent clothing will help others to see you during the day. At night, however, you should wear clothing that reflects the light. This allows other road users to see you more easily in their headlights. Ask your local motorcycle dealer about fluorescent and reflective clothing.

3.8   *Mark **one** answer*   R-ES 4

Which of the following fairings would give you the best weather protection?

- Handlebar
- Sports
- Touring
- Windscreen

⊙ **Touring**

Fairings give protection to the hands, legs and feet. They also make riding more comfortable by keeping you out of the wind.

3.9   *Mark **one** answer*   R-ES 4, HC r84

Your visor becomes badly scratched. You should

- polish it with a fine abrasive
- replace it
- wash it in soapy water
- clean it with petrol

⊙ **replace it**

Your visor protects your eyes from wind, rain, insects and road dirt. It's therefore important to keep it clean and in good repair. A badly scratched visor can, obscure your view and cause dazzle from lights of oncoming vehicles.

3.10
Mark one answer

R-ES 15, HC p129

The legal minimum depth of tread for motorcycle tyres is

- ⊙ 1 mm
- ⊙ 1.6 mm
- ⊙ 2.5 mm
- ⊙ 4 mm

⊙ **1 mm**

The entire original tread should be continuous. Don't ride a motorcycle with worn tyres. Your tyres are your only contact with the road so it's very important that you ensure they are in good condition.

3.11
Mark three answers

R-ES 4, HC r84-85

Which of the following makes it easier for motorcyclists to be seen?

- ⊙ Using a dipped headlight
- ⊙ Wearing a fluorescent jacket
- ⊙ Wearing a white helmet
- ⊙ Wearing a grey helmet
- ⊙ Wearing black leathers
- ⊙ Using a tinted visor

⊙ **Using a dipped headlight**

⊙ **Wearing a fluorescent jacket**

⊙ **Wearing a white helmet**

Many incidents and collisions involving motorcyclists occur because another road user didn't see them. Do what you can to make yourself more visible to others. Be aware that you are vulnerable and ride defensively.

3.12
Mark one answer

R-ES 15 & 17

Your oil light comes on as you are riding. You should

- ⊙ go to a dealer for an oil change
- ⊙ go to the nearest garage for their advice
- ⊙ ride slowly for a few miles to see if the light goes out
- ⊙ stop as quickly as possible and try to find the cause

⊙ **stop as quickly as possible and try to find the cause**

If the oil pressure warning light comes on when the engine is running you may have a serious problem. Pull over as soon as you can, stop the engine and investigate the cause.

3.13   *Mark **two** answers*   R-ES 15

Motorcycle tyres MUST

- ⊙ have the same tread pattern
- ⊙ be correctly inflated
- ⊙ be the same size, front and rear
- ⊙ both be the same make
- ⊙ have sufficient tread depth

⊙ **be correctly inflated**

⊙ **have sufficient tread depth**

Your safety and that of others may depend on the condition of your tyres. Before you ride you must check they are correctly inflated and have sufficient tread depth. Make sure these checks become part of a routine.

3.14   *Mark **one** answer*   R-ES 15 & 17

Riding your motorcycle with a slack or worn drive chain may cause

- ⊙ an engine misfire
- ⊙ early tyre wear
- ⊙ increased emissions
- ⊙ a locked wheel

⊙ **a locked wheel**

Check your drive chain regularly; adjust and lubricate it if necessary. It needs to be adjusted until the free play is as specified in the vehicle handbook.

3.15   *Mark **one** answer*   R-ES 5

You forget to switch the choke off after the engine warms up. This could

- ⊙ flatten the battery
- ⊙ reduce braking distances
- ⊙ use less fuel
- ⊙ cause much more engine wear

⊙ **cause much more engine wear**

Leaving the choke on for too long will cause unnecessary engine wear and waste fuel.

3.16
*Mark **one** answer*

R-ES 15

When riding your motorcycle a tyre bursts. What should you do?

⊙ Slow gently to a stop

⊙ Brake firmly to a stop

⊙ Change to a high gear

⊙ Lower the side stand

⊙ **Slow gently to a stop**

If a tyre bursts, close the throttle smoothly and slow gently to a stop, holding the handlebars firmly to help you keep a straight course.

3.17
*Mark **one** answer*

R-ES 15 & 17

A motorcycle engine that is properly maintained will

⊙ use much more fuel

⊙ have lower exhaust emissions

⊙ increase your insurance premiums

⊙ not need to have an MOT

⊙ **have lower exhaust emissions**

A badly maintained engine can emit more exhaust fumes than one that is correctly serviced. This can be damaging to the environment and also cost you more in fuel.

3.18
*Mark **one** answer*

R-ES 4

What should you clean visors and goggles with?

⊙ Petrol

⊙ White spirit

⊙ Antifreeze

⊙ Soapy water

⊙ **Soapy water**

It is very important to keep your visor or goggles clean. Clean them using warm soapy water. Do not use solvents or petrol.

3.19 *Mark **one** answer* R-ES 4

You are riding on a quiet road. Your visor fogs up. What should you do?

- Continue at a reduced speed
- Stop as soon as possible and wipe it
- Build up speed to increase air flow
- Close the helmet air vents

- **Stop as soon as possible and wipe it**

In cold and wet weather your visor may fog up. If this happens when you are riding choose somewhere safe to stop, and wipe it clean with a damp cloth. Special anti-fog products are available at motorcycle dealers.

3.20 *Mark **one** answer* R-ES 4

You are riding in hot weather. What is the safest type of footwear?

- Sandals
- Trainers
- Shoes
- Boots

- **Boots**

It is important to wear good boots when you ride a motorcycle. Boots protect your feet and shins from knocks, and give some protection in a crash. They also help keep you warm and dry in cold or wet weather.

3.21 *Mark **one** answer* R-ES 4, HC r83

Which of the following should not be used to fasten your safety helmet?

- Double D ring fastening
- Velcro tab
- Quick release fastening
- Bar and buckle

- **Velcro tab**

Some helmet straps have a velcro tab in addition to the main fastening, which is intended to secure the strap so that it does not flap in the wind. It should NOT be used on its own to fasten the helmet.

After warming up the engine you leave the choke ON. What will this do?

⊙ Discharge the battery

⊙ Use more fuel

⊙ Improve handling

⊙ Use less fuel

⊙ **Use more fuel**

Leaving the choke on for too long could waste fuel and cause unnecessary pollution.

You want to ride your motorcycle in the dark. What could you wear to be seen more easily ?

⊙ A black leather jacket

⊙ Reflective clothing

⊙ A white helmet

⊙ A red helmet

⊙ **Reflective clothing**

⊙ **A white helmet**

When riding in the dark you will be easier to see if you wear reflective clothing and a white helmet. A light-coloured helmet contrasts starkly with the surrounding darkness, while reflective clothing reflects the light from other vehicles and makes the rider much more visible.

Your motorcycle has a catalytic converter. Its purpose is to reduce

⊙ exhaust noise

⊙ fuel consumption

⊙ exhaust emissions

⊙ engine noise

⊙ **exhaust emissions**

Catalytic converters reduce the toxic and polluting gases given out by the engine. Never use leaded or lead replacement petrol in a vehicle with a catalytic converter, as even one tankful can permanently damage the system.

3.25   *Mark **one** answer*   R-ES 15 & 17

Refitting which of the following will disturb your wheel alignment?

⊙ front wheel
⊙ front brakes
⊙ rear brakes
⊙ rear wheel

⊙ **rear wheel**

When refitting the rear wheel or adjusting the drive chain it is possible to disturb the wheel alignment. Incorrect alignment can cause instability, especially when cornering, and increased tyre wear.

3.26   *Mark **one** answer*   R-ES 15 & 17

After refitting your rear wheel what should you check?

⊙ Your steering damper
⊙ Your side stand
⊙ Your wheel alignment
⊙ Your suspension preload

⊙ **Your wheel alignment**

After refitting the rear wheel or adjusting the drive chain you should check your wheel alignment. Incorrect alignment will result in excessive tyre wear and poor road holding.

3.27   *Mark **one** answer*   R-ES 15 & 17

You are checking your direction indicators. How often per second must they flash?

⊙ Between 1 and 2 times
⊙ Between 3 and 4 times
⊙ Between 5 and 6 times
⊙ Between 7 and 8 times

⊙ **Between 1 and 2 times**

You should check that all your lights work properly before every journey. Make sure that any signals you give can be clearly seen.

If you're not sure whether your signals can be seen you can use arm signals as well to make your intentions clear. Only do this if you're going slowly.

75

After adjusting the final drive chain what should you check?

- ⊙ The rear wheel alignment
- ⊙ The suspension adjustment
- ⊙ The rear shock absorber
- ⊙ The front suspension forks

⊙ **The rear wheel alignment**

Always check the rear wheel alignment after adjusting the chain tension. Marks on the chain adjuster may be provided to make this easy. Incorrect alignment can cause instability and increased tyre wear.

Your steering feels wobbly. Which of these is a likely cause?

- ⊙ Tyre pressure is too high
- ⊙ Incorrectly adjusted brakes
- ⊙ Worn steering head bearings
- ⊙ A broken clutch cable

⊙ **Worn steering head bearings**

Worn bearings in the steering head can make your motorcycle very difficult to control. They should be checked for wear and correct adjustment.

You see oil on your front forks. Should you be concerned about this?

- ⊙ No, unless the amount of oil increases
- ⊙ No, lubrication here is perfectly normal
- ⊙ Yes, it is illegal to ride with an oil leak
- ⊙ Yes, oil could drip onto your tyre

⊙ **Yes, oil could drip onto your tyre**

Oil leaking from your forks could get on to your tyre or brake disc. This could result in your tyre losing grip, or your brakes being less effective. A loss of front fork oil will also affect handling and stability.

3.31 *Mark one answer* R-ES 15 & 17

You have a faulty oil seal on a shock absorber. Why is this a serious problem?

⊙ It will cause excessive chain wear

⊙ Dripping oil could reduce the grip of your tyre

⊙ Your motorcycle will be harder to ride uphill

⊙ Your motorcycle will not accelerate so quickly

⊙ **Dripping oil could reduce the grip of your tyre**

Leaking oil could affect the grip of your tyres and also the effectiveness of your brakes. This could result in a loss of control, putting you and other road users in danger.

3.32 *Mark one answer* R-ES 15 & 17

Oil is leaking from your forks. Why should you NOT ride a motorcycle in this condition?

⊙ Your brakes could be affected by dripping oil

⊙ Your steering is likely to seize up

⊙ The forks will quickly begin to rust

⊙ The motorcycle will become too noisy

⊙ **Your brakes could be affected by dripping oil**

Oil dripping from forks and shock absorbers is dangerous if it gets onto brakes and tyres. Replace faulty oil seals immediately.

3.33 *Mark one answer* R-ES 15 & 17

You have adjusted your drive chain. If this is not done properly, what problem could it cause?

⊙ Inaccurate speedometer reading

⊙ Loss of braking power

⊙ Incorrect rear wheel alignment

⊙ Excessive fuel consumption

⊙ **Incorrect rear wheel alignment**

After carrying out drive chain adjustment, you should always check the rear wheel alignment. Many motorcycles have alignment guides stamped onto the frame to help you do this correctly.

Mark one answer

You have adjusted your drive chain. Why is it also important to check rear wheel alignment?

- ⊙ Your tyre may be more likely to puncture
- ⊙ Fuel consumption could be greatly increased
- ⊙ You may not be able to reach top speed
- ⊙ Your motorcycle could be unstable on bends

⊙ **Your motorcycle could be unstable on bends**

Rear wheel alignment can be disturbed by adjustments to the drive chain. It's very important to make sure that the wheel is still properly aligned after doing this.

Mark one answer

There is a cut in the sidewall of one of your tyres. What should you do about this?

- ⊙ Replace the tyre before riding the motorcycle
- ⊙ Check regularly to see if it gets any worse
- ⊙ Repair the puncture before riding the motorcycle
- ⊙ Reduce pressure in the tyre before you ride

⊙ **Replace the tyre before riding the motorcycle**

A cut in the sidewall can be very dangerous. The tyre is in danger of blowing out if you ride the motorcycle in this condition.

Mark one answer

You need to put air into your tyres. How would you find out the correct pressure to use?

- ⊙ It will be shown on the tyre wall
- ⊙ It will be stamped on the wheel
- ⊙ By checking the vehicle owner's manual
- ⊙ By checking the registration document

⊙ **By checking the vehicle owner's manual**

Tyre pressures should be checked regularly. Use your vehicle manual to find advice on the correct pressures to use.

3.37   *Mark one answer*   R-ES 15 & 17

You can prevent a cable operated clutch from becoming stiff by keeping the cable

⊙ tight

⊙ dry

⊙ slack

⊙ oiled

⊙ **oiled**

Keeping the cable oiled will help it to move smoothly through its outer casing. This will extend the life of the cable and assist your control of the motorcycle.

3.38   *Mark one answer*   R-ES 15 & 17

When adjusting your chain it is important for the wheels to be aligned accurately. Incorrect wheel alignment can cause

⊙ a serious loss of power

⊙ reduced braking performance

⊙ increased tyre wear

⊙ reduced ground clearance

⊙ **increased tyre wear**

If a motorcycle's wheels are incorrectly aligned tyres may wear unevenly and the motorcycle can become unstable, especially when cornering.

3.39   *Mark one answer*   R-ES 15 & 17

What problem can incorrectly aligned wheels cause?

⊙ Faulty headlight adjustment

⊙ Reduced braking performance

⊙ Better ground clearance

⊙ Instability when cornering

⊙ **Instability when cornering**

Wheels should be aligned accurately after refitting your rear wheel. Incorrect wheel alignment can cause uneven tyre wear and poor handling. Most motorcycles have wheel alignment guides stamped onto the swinging arm.

3.40
*Mark **one** answer*

R-ES 15 & 17

What is most likely to be affected by incorrect wheel alignment?

- ⊙ Braking performance
- ⊙ Stability
- ⊙ Acceleration
- ⊙ Suspension preload

⊙ **Stability**

It is important that your wheels are aligned accurately. It will be necessary to do this after removing your rear wheel or adjusting the chain. Incorrect alignment can cause instability, especially when cornering. It can also increase tyre wear.

3.41
*Mark **one** answer*

R-ES 4

Why should you wear specialist motorcycle clothing when riding?

- ⊙ Because the law requires you to do so
- ⊙ Because it looks better than ordinary clothing
- ⊙ Because it gives best protection from the weather
- ⊙ Because it will reduce your insurance

⊙ **Because it gives best protection from the weather**

If you become cold and wet when riding, this can have a serious effect on your concentration and control of your motorcycle.

Proper riding gear can help shield you from the weather, as well as giving protection in the event of a crash.

3.42
*Mark **one** answer*

R-ES 8

When leaving your motorcycle parked, you should always

- ⊙ remove the battery lead
- ⊙ pull it onto the kerb
- ⊙ use the steering lock
- ⊙ leave the parking light on.

⊙ **use the steering lock**

When leaving your motorcycle you should always use the steering lock. You should also consider using additional locking devices such as a U-lock, disc lock or chain. If possible fasten it to an immovable post or another motorcycle.

3.43   *Mark one answer*   R-ES 8

You are parking your motorcycle. Chaining it to an immovable object will

⊙ be against the law
⊙ give extra security
⊙ be likely to cause damage
⊙ leave the motorcycle unstable

⊙ **give extra security**

Theft of motorcycles is a very common crime. If you can, secure your vehicle to a lamp post or other such object, to help reduce the chances of it being stolen.

3.44   *Mark one answer*   R-ES 8

You are parking your motorcycle and sidecar on a hill. What is the best way to stop it rolling away?

⊙ Leave it in neutral
⊙ Put the rear wheel on the pavement
⊙ Leave it in a low gear
⊙ Park very close to another vehicle

⊙ **Leave it in a low gear**

To make sure a sidecar outfit doesn't roll away when parking you should leave it in a low gear, and wedge it against the kerb or place a block behind the wheel.

3.45   *Mark one answer*   R-ES 5

An engine cut-out switch should be used to

⊙ reduce speed in an emergency
⊙ prevent the motorcycle being stolen
⊙ stop the engine normally
⊙ stop the engine in an emergency

⊙ **stop the engine in an emergency**

If you are involved in a collision or crash, using the engine cut-out switch will help to reduce any fire hazard. When stopping the engine normally, use the ignition switch.

*Mark **one** answer*

You enter a road where there are road humps. What should you do?

- ◉ Maintain a reduced speed throughout
- ◉ Accelerate quickly between each one
- ◉ Always keep to the maximum legal speed
- ◉ Ride slowly at school times only

◉ **Maintain a reduced speed throughout**

The humps are there for a reason; to reduce the speed of the traffic. Don't accelerate harshly between them, as this means you will only have to brake sharply to negotiate the next hump.

Harsh braking and acceleration uses more fuel as well as causing wear and tear to your vehicle.

---

*Mark **one** answer*

When should you especially check the engine oil level?

- ◉ Before a long journey
- ◉ When the engine is hot
- ◉ Early in the morning
- ◉ Every 6000 miles

◉ **Before a long journey**

As well as the oil you will also need to check other items. These include, fuel, water and tyres.

---

*Mark **one** answer*

You service your own motorcycle. How should you get rid of the old engine oil?

- ◉ Take it to a local authority site
- ◉ Pour it down a drain
- ◉ Tip it into a hole in the ground
- ◉ Put it into your dustbin

◉ **Take it to a local authority site**

Never pour the oil down any drain. The oil is highly pollutant and could harm wildlife. Confine it in a container and dispose of it properly at an authorised site.

3.49 — Mark *one* answer — R-ES 17

What safeguard could you take against fire risk to your motorcycle?

- Keep water levels above maximum
- Check out any strong smell of petrol
- Avoid riding with a full tank of petrol
- Use unleaded petrol

⊙ **Check out any strong smell of petrol**

The fuel in your motorcycle can be a dangerous fire hazard. DON'T use a naked flame if you can smell fuel, or smoke when refuelling.

3.50 — Mark *one* answer — R-ES 4, HC r86

Which of the following would NOT make you more visible in daylight?

- Wearing a black helmet
- Wearing a white helmet
- Switching on your dipped headlight
- Wearing a fluorescent jacket

⊙ **Wearing a black helmet**

Wearing bright or fluorescent clothes will help other road users to see you. Wearing a white or brightly coloured helmet can also make you more visible.

3.51 — Mark *one* answer — R-ES 4

It would be illegal to ride with a helmet on when

- the helmet is not fastened correctly
- the helmet is more than four years old
- you have borrowed someone else's helmet
- the helmet does not have chin protection

⊙ **the helmet is not fastened correctly**

A helmet that is incorrectly fastened or not fastened at all is likely to come off in a crash. It will provide little or no protection. By law, you must wear a helmet when riding on the road and it must be correctly fastened (members of the Sikh religion who wear a turban are exempt).

83

When may you have to increase the tyre pressures on your motorcycle?

⊙ When carrying a passenger
⊙ After a long journey
⊙ When carrying a load
⊙ When riding at high speeds
⊙ When riding in hot weather

⊙ **When carrying a passenger**

⊙ **When carrying a load**

⊙ **When riding at high speeds**

Read the manufacturer's handbook to see if they recommend increasing tyre pressures under certain conditions.

Which TWO of these items on a motorcycle MUST be kept clean?

⊙ Number plate
⊙ Wheels
⊙ Engine
⊙ Fairing
⊙ Headlight

⊙ **Number plate**

⊙ **Headlight**

Maintenance is a vital part of road safety. Lights, indicators, reflectors and number plates MUST be kept clean and clear.

You should use the engine cut-out switch on your motorcycle to

⊙ save wear and tear on the battery
⊙ stop the engine for a short time
⊙ stop the engine in an emergency
⊙ save wear and tear on the ignition

⊙ **stop the engine in an emergency**

Only use the engine cut-out switch in an emergency. When stopping the engine normally, use the ignition switch. This will remind you to take your keys with you when parking. It could also prevent starting problems if you forget you've left the cut-out switch in the 'off' position. When returning to your motorcycle make sure someone has not done this as a trick.

3.55
*Mark **one** answer*

R-ES 15

You have adjusted the tension on your drive chain. You should check the

- ⊙ rear wheel alignment
- ⊙ tyre pressures
- ⊙ valve clearances
- ⊙ sidelights

⊙ **rear wheel alignment**

Drive chains wear and need frequent adjustment and lubrication. If the drive chain is worn or slack it can jump off the sprocket and lock the rear wheel. When you have adjusted the chain tension, you need to check the rear wheel alignment. Marks by the chain adjusters may be provided to make this easier.

3.56
*Mark **one** answer*

R-ES 4

A friend offers you a second-hand safety helmet for you to use. Why may this be a bad idea?

- ⊙ It may be damaged
- ⊙ You will be breaking the law
- ⊙ You will affect your insurance cover
- ⊙ It may be a full-face type

⊙ **It may be damaged**

A second-hand helmet may look in good condition but it could have received damage that is not visible externally. A damaged helmet could be unreliable in a crash. Don't take the risk.

3.57
*Mark **four** answers*

R-ES 15

You are riding a motorcycle of more than 50 cc. Which FOUR would make a tyre illegal?

- ⊙ Tread less than 1.6 mm deep
- ⊙ Tread less than 1 mm deep
- ⊙ A large bulge in the wall
- ⊙ A recut tread
- ⊙ Exposed ply or cord
- ⊙ A stone wedged in the tread

⊙ **Tread less than 1 mm deep**

⊙ **A large bulge in the wall**

⊙ **A recut tread**

⊙ **Exposed ply or cord**

When checking tyres make sure there are no bulges or cuts in the side walls. Always buy your tyres from a reputable dealer to ensure quality and value for money.

3.58　　Mark **two** answers　　R-ES 15 & 17

You should maintain cable operated brakes

- ⊙ by regular adjustment when necessary
- ⊙ at normal service times only
- ⊙ yearly, before taking the motorcycle for its MOT
- ⊙ by oiling cables and pivots regularly

- ⊙ **by regular adjustment when necessary**
- ⊙ **by oiling cables and pivots regularly**

Keeping your brakes in good working order is vital for safety. Cables will stretch with use and need checking and adjusting regularly. They will also need lubricating to prevent friction and wear of the cables and pivots.

3.59　　Mark **two** answers　　R-ES 15 & 17

A properly serviced motorcycle will give

- ⊙ lower insurance premiums
- ⊙ a refund on your road tax
- ⊙ better fuel economy
- ⊙ cleaner exhaust emissions

- ⊙ **better fuel economy**
- ⊙ **cleaner exhaust emissions**

When you purchase your motorcycle, check at what intervals you should have it serviced. This can vary depending on model or manufacturer. Use the service manual and keep it up to date.

3.60　　Mark **one** answer　　R-ES 15

A loosely adjusted drive chain could

- ⊙ lock the rear wheel
- ⊙ make wheels wobble
- ⊙ cause a braking fault
- ⊙ affect your headlight beam

- ⊙ **lock the rear wheel**

A motorcycle chain will stretch as it wears. It needs frequent checking, and adjustment if necessary, to keep the tension correct. In extreme cases a loose chain can jump off the sprocket and become wedged in the rear wheel. This could cause serious loss of control and result in a crash.

3.61   *Mark **one** answer*   **R-ES 4, HC r113**

Your motorcycle is NOT fitted with daytime running lights. When MUST you use a dipped headlight during the day?

- ⊙ On country roads
- ⊙ In poor visibility
- ⊙ Along narrow streets
- ⊙ When parking

⊙ **In poor visibility**

It's important that other road users can see you clearly at all times. It will help other road users to see you if you use a dipped headlight during the day. You MUST use a dipped headlight during the day if visibility is seriously reduced, that is, when you can't see for more than 100 metres (328 feet).

3.62   *Mark **one** answer*   **R-ES 15**

Tyre pressures should usually be increased on your motorcycle when

- ⊙ riding on a wet road
- ⊙ carrying a pillion passenger
- ⊙ travelling on an uneven surface
- ⊙ riding on twisty roads

⊙ **carrying a pillion passenger**

Sometimes manufacturers advise you to increase your tyre pressures for high-speed riding and when carrying extra weight. This information can be found in the handbook.

3.63   *Mark **one** answer*   **R-ES 15**

You have too much oil in your engine. What could this cause?

- ⊙ Low oil pressure
- ⊙ Engine overheating
- ⊙ Chain wear
- ⊙ Oil leaks

⊙ **Oil leaks**

Too much oil in the engine will create excess pressure and could damage engine seals and cause oil leaks. Any excess oil should be drained off.

3.64

*Mark **one** answer*

HC r123

You are leaving your motorcycle unattended on a road. When may you leave the engine running?

- ⊙ When parking for less than five minutes
- ⊙ If the battery is flat
- ⊙ When in a 20 mph zone
- ⊙ Not on any occasion

⊙ **Not on any occasion**

When you leave your motorcycle parked and unattended on a road, switch off the engine, use the steering lock and remove the ignition key. Also take any tank bags, panniers or loose luggage with you, set the alarm if it has one, and use an additional lock and chain or cable lock.

3.65

*Mark **one** answer*

R-ES 5

You are involved in a crash. To reduce the risk of fire what is the best thing to do?

- ⊙ Keep the engine running
- ⊙ Open the choke
- ⊙ Turn the fuel tap to reserve
- ⊙ Use the engine cut-out switch

⊙ **Use the engine cut-out switch**

The engine cut-out switch is used to stop the engine in an emergency. In the event of a crash this may help to reduce any fire risk.

3.66

*Mark **two** answers*

R-ES 4, HC r87

When riding at night you should

- ⊙ ride with your headlight on
- ⊙ wear reflective clothing
- ⊙ wear a tinted visor
- ⊙ ride in the centre of the road
- ⊙ give arm signals

⊙ **ride with your headlight on**

⊙ **wear reflective clothing**

At night you should wear clothing that includes reflective material to help other road users see you. This could be a vest, tabard or reflective body strap. Use your headlight on dipped or main beam as appropriate without dazzling other road users.

3.67 *Mark **two** answers* R-ES 12 & 15, HC p129

Which TWO are badly affected if the tyres are under-inflated?

⊙ Braking

⊙ Steering

⊙ Changing gear

⊙ Parking

⊙ **Braking**

⊙ **Steering**

Your tyres are your only contact with the road so it is very important to ensure that they are free from defects, have sufficient tread depth and are correctly inflated. Correct tyre pressures help reduce the risk of skidding and provide a safer and more comfortable drive or ride.

3.68 *Mark **one** answer* R-ES 5, HC r112

You must NOT sound your horn

⊙ between 10 pm and 6 am in a built-up area

⊙ at any time in a built-up area

⊙ between 11.30 pm and 7 am in a built-up area

⊙ between 11.30 pm and 6 am on any road

⊙ **between 11.30 pm and 7 am in a built-up area**

Vehicles can be noisy. Every effort must be made to prevent excessive noise, especially in built-up areas at night. Don't

• rev the engine

• sound the horn

unnecessarily.

It is illegal to sound your horn in a built-up area between 11.30 pm and 7 am, except when another vehicle poses a danger.

3.69 *Mark **one** answer* R-ES 12 & 15, HC p129

It is essential that tyre pressures are checked regularly. When should this be done?

⊙ After any lengthy journey

⊙ After travelling at high speed

⊙ When tyres are hot

⊙ When tyres are cold

⊙ **When tyres are cold**

When you check the tyre pressures do so when the tyres are cold. This will give you a more accurate reading. The heat generated from a long journey will raise the pressure inside the tyre.

*Mark **one** answer*

Supertrams or Light Rapid Transit (LRT) systems are environmentally friendly because

⊙ they use diesel power

⊙ they use quieter roads

⊙ they use electric power

⊙ they do not operate during rush hour

⊙ **they use electric power**

This means that they do not emit toxic fumes, which add to city pollution problems. They are also a lot quieter and smoother to ride on.

*Mark **one** answer*

'Red routes' in major cities have been introduced to

⊙ raise the speed limits

⊙ help the traffic flow

⊙ provide better parking

⊙ allow lorries to load more freely

⊙ **help the traffic flow**

Traffic jams today are often caused by the volume of traffic. However, inconsiderate parking can lead to the closure of an inside lane or traffic having to wait for oncoming vehicles. Driving slowly in traffic increases fuel consumption and causes a build-up of exhaust fumes.

*Mark **one** answer*

Road humps, chicanes, and narrowings are

⊙ always at major road works

⊙ used to increase traffic speed

⊙ at toll-bridge approaches only

⊙ traffic calming measures

⊙ **traffic calming measures**

Traffic calming measures help keep vehicle speeds low in congested areas where there are pedestrians and children. A pedestrian is much more likely to survive a collision with a vehicle travelling at 20 mph than at 40 mph.

3.73   *Mark **one** answer*   **R-ES 17**

The purpose of a catalytic converter is to reduce

- fuel consumption
- the risk of fire
- toxic exhaust gases
- engine wear

⊙ **toxic exhaust gases**

Catalytic converters are designed to reduce a large percentage of toxic emissions. They work more efficiently when the engine has reached its normal working temperature.

3.74   *Mark **one** answer*   **R-ES 17**

Catalytic converters are fitted to make the

- engine produce more power
- exhaust system easier to replace
- engine run quietly
- exhaust fumes cleaner

⊙ **exhaust fumes cleaner**

Harmful gases in the exhaust system pollute the atmosphere. These gases are reduced by up to 90% if a catalytic converter is fitted. Cleaner air benefits everyone, especially people who live or work near congested roads.

3.75   *Mark **three** answers*   **R-ES 17**

The pictured vehicle is 'environmentally friendly' because it

- reduces noise pollution
- uses diesel fuel
- uses electricity
- uses unleaded fuel
- reduces parking spaces
- reduces town traffic

⊙ **reduces noise pollution**

⊙ **uses electricity**

⊙ **reduces town traffic**

Trams are powered by electricity and therefore do not emit exhaust fumes. They are also much quieter than petrol or diesel engined vehicles and can carry a large number of passengers.

When should you NOT use your horn in a built-up area?

⊙ Between 8 pm and 8 am

⊙ Between 9 pm and dawn

⊙ Between dusk and 8 am

⊙ Between 11.30 pm and 7 am

⊙ **Between 11.30 pm and 7 am**

By law you must not sound your horn in a built-up area between 11.30 pm and 7.00 am. The exception to this is when another road user poses a danger.

You will use more fuel if your tyres are

⊙ under-inflated

⊙ of different makes

⊙ over-inflated

⊙ new and hardly used

⊙ **under-inflated**

Check your tyre pressures frequently – normally once a week. If pressures are lower than those recommended by the manufacturer, there will be more 'rolling resistance'. The engine will have to work harder to overcome this, leading to increased fuel consumption.

How should you dispose of a used battery?

⊙ Take it to a local authority site

⊙ Put it in the dustbin

⊙ Break it up into pieces

⊙ Leave it on waste land

⊙ Take it to a garage

⊙ Burn it on a fire

⊙ **Take it to a local authority site**

⊙ **Take it to a garage**

Batteries contain acid which is hazardous and must be disposed of safely.

3.79 *Mark one answer* **R-ES 17, HC r123**

What is most likely to cause high fuel consumption?

- ⊙ Poor steering control
- ⊙ Accelerating around bends
- ⊙ Staying in high gears
- ⊙ Harsh braking and accelerating

⊙ **Harsh braking and accelerating**

Accelerating and braking gently and smoothly will help to save fuel, reduce wear on your vehicle and is better for the environment.

3.80 *Mark one answer* **R-ES 15**

The fluid level in your battery is low. What should you top it up with?

- ⊙ Battery acid
- ⊙ Distilled water
- ⊙ Engine oil
- ⊙ Engine coolant

⊙ **Distilled water**

Some modern batteries are maintenance-free. Check your vehicle handbook and, if necessary, make sure that the plates in each battery cell are covered.

3.81 *Mark one answer* **R-ES 12**

You are parked on the road at night. Where must you use parking lights?

- ⊙ Where there are continuous white lines in the middle of the road
- ⊙ Where the speed limit exceeds 30 mph
- ⊙ Where you are facing oncoming traffic
- ⊙ Where you are near a bus stop

⊙ **Where the speed limit exceeds 30 mph**

When parking at night, park in the direction of the traffic. This will enable other road users to see the reflectors on the rear of your vehicle. Use your parking lights if the speed limit is over 30 mph.

3.82

Mark **three** answers — R-ES 17

Motor vehicles can harm the environment. This has resulted in

- air pollution
- damage to buildings
- less risk to health
- improved public transport
- less use of electrical vehicles
- using up of natural resources

- ⊙ **air pollution**
- ⊙ **damage to buildings**
- ⊙ **using up of natural resources**

Exhaust emissions are harmful to health. Together with vibration from heavy traffic this can result in damage to buildings. Most petrol and diesel fuels come from a finite and non-renewable source. Anything you can do to reduce your use of these fuels will help the environment.

3.83

Mark **three** answers — R-ES 15

Excessive or uneven tyre wear can be caused by faults in which THREE of the following?

- The gearbox
- The braking system
- The accelerator
- The exhaust system
- Wheel alignment
- The suspension

- ⊙ **The braking system**
- ⊙ **Wheel alignment**
- ⊙ **The suspension**

Regular servicing will help to detect faults at an early stage and this will avoid the risk of minor faults becoming serious or even dangerous.

3.84

Mark **one** answer — R-ES 15

You need to top up your battery. What level should you fill to?

- The top of the battery
- Half-way up the battery
- Just below the cell plates
- Just above the cell plates

- ⊙ **Just above the cell plates**

Top up the battery with distilled water and make sure each cell plate is covered.

94

3.85 Mark *one* answer **R-ES 12**

You are parking on a two-way road at night. The speed limit is 40 mph. You should park on the

- ⊙ left with parking lights on
- ⊙ left with no lights on
- ⊙ right with parking lights on
- ⊙ right with dipped headlights on

⊙ **left with parking lights on**

At night all vehicles must display parking lights when parked on a road with a speed limit greater than 30 mph. They should be close to the kerb, facing in the direction of the traffic flow and not within a distance as specified in The Highway Code.

3.86 Mark *one* answer **R-ES 18**

Before starting a journey it is wise to plan your route. How can you do this?

- ⊙ Look at a map
- ⊙ Contact your local garage
- ⊙ Look in your vehicle handbook
- ⊙ Check your vehicle registration document

⊙ **Look at a map**

Planning your journey before you set out can help to make it much easier, more pleasant and may help to ease traffic congestion. Look at a map to help you to do this. You may need different scale maps depending on where and how far you're going. Printing or writing out the route can also help.

3.87 NI EXEMPT Mark *one* answer **R-ES 18**

It can help to plan your route before starting a journey. You can do this by contacting

- ⊙ your local filling station
- ⊙ a motoring organisation
- ⊙ the Driver Vehicle Licensing Agency
- ⊙ your vehicle manufacturer

⊙ **a motoring organisation**

Most motoring organisations will give you a detailed plan of your trip showing directions and distance. Some will also include advice on rest and fuel stops. The Highways Agency website will also give you information on roadworks and incidents and gives expected delay times.

How can you plan your route before starting a long journey?

- Check your vehicle's workshop manual
- Ask your local garage
- Use a route planner on the internet
- Consult your travel agents

⊙ **Use a route planner on the internet**

Various route planners are available on the internet. Most of them give you various options allowing you to choose the most direct, quickest or scenic route. They can also include rest and fuel stops and distances. Print them off and take them with you.

Planning your route before setting out can be helpful. How can you do this?

- Look in a motoring magazine
- Only visit places you know
- Try to travel at busy times
- Print or write down the route

⊙ **Print or write down the route**

Print or write down your route before setting out. Some places are not well signed so using place names and road numbers may help you avoid problems en route. Try to get an idea of how far you're going before you leave. You can also use it to re-check the next stage at each rest stop.

Why is it a good idea to plan your journey to avoid busy times?

- You will have an easier journey
- You will have a more stressful journey
- Your journey time will be longer
- It will cause more traffic congestion

⊙ **You will have an easier journey**

No one likes to spend time in traffic queues. Try to avoid busy times related to school or work travel. As well as moving vehicles you should also consider congestion caused by parked cars, buses and coaches around schools.

3.91 *Mark one answer* **R-ES 18**

Planning your journey to avoid busy times has a number of advantages. One of these is

⊙ your journey will take longer

⊙ you will have a more pleasant journey

⊙ you will cause more pollution

⊙ your stress level will be greater

⊙ **you will have a more pleasant journey**

Having a pleasant journey can have safety benefits. You will be less tired and stressed and this will allow you to concentrate more on your driving or riding.

3.92 *Mark one answer* **R-ES 18**

It is a good idea to plan your journey to avoid busy times. This is because

⊙ your vehicle will use more fuel

⊙ you will see less road works

⊙ it will help to ease congestion

⊙ you will travel a much shorter distance

⊙ **it will help to ease congestion**

Avoiding busy times means that you are not adding needlessly to traffic congestion. Other advantages are that you will use less fuel and feel less stressed.

3.93 *Mark one answer* **R-ES 18**

By avoiding busy times when travelling

⊙ you are more likely to be held up

⊙ your journey time will be longer

⊙ you will travel a much shorter distance

⊙ you are less likely to be delayed

⊙ **you are less likely to be delayed**

If possible, avoid the early morning and, late afternoon and early evening 'rush hour'. Doing this should allow you to travel in a more relaxed frame of mind, concentrate solely on what you're doing and arrive at your destination feeling less stressed.

It can help to plan your route before starting a journey. Why should you also plan an alternative route?

- ⊙ Your original route may be blocked
- ⊙ Your maps may have different scales
- ⊙ You may find you have to pay a congestion charge
- ⊙ Because you may get held up by a tractor

⊙ **Your original route may be blocked**

It can be frustrating and worrying to find your planned route is blocked by roadworks or diversions. If you have planned an alternative you will feel less stressed and more able to concentrate fully on your driving or riding. If your original route is mostly on motorways it's a good idea to plan an alternative using non-motorway roads. Always carry a map with you just in case you need to refer to it.

As well as planning your route before starting a journey, you should also plan an alternative route. Why is this?

- ⊙ To let another driver overtake
- ⊙ Your first route may be blocked
- ⊙ To avoid a railway level crossing
- ⊙ In case you have to avoid emergency vehicles

⊙ **Your first route may be blocked**

It's a good idea to plan an alternative route in case your original route is blocked for any reason. You're less likely to feel worried and stressed if you've got an alternative in mind. This will enable you to concentrate fully on your driving or riding. Always carry a map that covers the area you will travel in.

You are making an appointment and will have to travel a long distance. You should

- ⊙ allow plenty of time for your journey
- ⊙ plan to go at busy times
- ⊙ avoid all national speed limit roads
- ⊙ prevent other drivers from overtaking

⊙ **allow plenty of time for your journey**

Always allow plenty of time for your journey in case of unforeseen problems. Anything can happen, punctures, breakdowns, road closures, diversions etc. You will feel less stressed and less inclined to take risks if you are not 'pushed for time'.

3.97   *Mark **one** answer*   **R-ES 17**

Rapid acceleration and heavy braking can lead to

- ⊙ reduced pollution
- ⊙ increased fuel consumption
- ⊙ reduced exhaust emissions
- ⊙ increased road safety

⊙ **increased fuel consumption**

Using the controls smoothly can reduce fuel consumption by about 15% as well as reducing wear and tear on your vehicle. Plan ahead and anticipate changes of speed well in advance. This will reduce the need to accelerate rapidly or brake sharply.

3.98   *Mark **one** answer*   **R-ES 17**

What percentage of all emissions does road transport account for?

- ⊙ 10%
- ⊙ 20%
- ⊙ 30%
- ⊙ 40%

⊙ **20%**

Transport is an essential part of modern life but it does have environmental effects. In heavily populated areas traffic is the biggest source of air pollution. Eco-safe driving and riding will reduce emissions and can make a surprising difference to local air quality.

3.99   *Mark **one** answer*   **R-ES 15**

Which of these, if allowed to get low, could cause you to crash?

- ⊙ Anti-freeze level
- ⊙ Brake fluid level
- ⊙ Battery water level
- ⊙ Radiator coolant level

⊙ **Brake fluid level**

You should carry out frequent checks on all fluid levels but particularly brake fluid. As the brake pads or shoes wear down the brake fluid level will drop. If it drops below the minimum mark on the fluid reservoir, air could enter the hydraulic system and lead to a loss of braking efficiency or complete brake failure.

Case study practice 3 – Safety and your motorcycle

Julia is riding her motorcycle to work. The weather is dry but chilly. Julia wears leather riding gear, boots and gauntlets, helmet and a fluorescent reflective jacket. She makes herself as visible as possible. At the service station, she buys fuel and cleans both handlebar mirrors, which have longer stems. She also makes her weekly check of tyre pressures and tread depths. The depth is well above the legal limit.

3.1 What should Julia do about protective clothing in warmer weather?

*Mark **one** answer*

⊙ Wear some summer clothing.

⊙ Continue using protective gear.

⊙ Use boots and trousers only.

⊙ Discard the gloves and boots.

R-ES 12

3.2 What colour and type of helmet are recommended for maximum visibility and safety?

*Mark **one** answer*

⊙ Black with a full-face visor.

⊙ Black without a full-face visor.

⊙ . White with a full-face visor.

⊙ White without a full-face visor.

R-ES 4

3.3 How can Julia's reflective clothing help her while riding?

*Mark **one** answer*

- ⊙ With braking and stopping.
- ⊙ With speed and gears.
- ⊙ With signalling and turning.
- ⊙ With visibility and safety.

R-ES 4, HC r86 & 87

3.4 Why might Julia have this sort of mirror?

*Mark **one** answer*

- ⊙ Because they look very cool and fashionable.
- ⊙ So that her view is completely unobstructed.
- ⊙ Because other vehicles then allow more room.
- ⊙ They help to balance and control the motorcycle.

R-ES 5

3.5 What is the minimum legal tread depth for motorcycle tyres?

*Mark **one** answer*

- ⊙ At least 1mm over three-quarters of the tread breadth and all around.
- ⊙ At least 2mm over the entire surface of tread breadth and all around.
- ⊙ At least 2mm over three-quarters of the tread breadth and all around.
- ⊙ At least 1mm over the entire surface of tread breadth and all around.

R-ES 15, HC p129

section **four**
SAFETY MARGINS

This section covers
- Stopping distances
- Road surfaces
- Skidding
- Weather conditions

Safety margins

It's essential that you always keep in mind the safety of not only yourself, but your passenger (once you've passed your test) and other road users as well.

Reduce your chances of being involved in a road traffic incident by knowing safety margins and the risk caused by not adhering to them. Never take unnecessary risks. Keep control of your motorcycle by using the correct procedures. For instance, when you're travelling downhill, control your speed by

• selecting a lower gear
• braking gently.

Don't 'coast' (ie travel in neutral or with the clutch disengaged) as this reduces your control.

R-ES 6 & 8, HC r122 & r180

Stopping distance

Leave enough room between you and the vehicle in front so you can pull up safely if it slows down or stops suddenly. Your overall stopping distance is the distance your motorcycle travels from the moment you realise you must brake to the moment the vehicle stops. This is made up of thinking distance and braking distance.

R-ES 8, HC r126

Study the typical thinking, braking and stopping distances given in *The Highway Code*. The figures given are the stopping distances if you're travelling in a vehicle or

on a motorcycle with good tyres and brakes

• on a dry road
• in good conditions.

Don't just learn the figures – you need to be able to judge the distance. A useful method is to leave a two-second time gap between yourself and the vehicle in front.

R-ES 12, HC r126 & p42-3

In other conditions you need to increase these distances:

• when it's raining or the road is wet – double the distance
• when it's icy – ten times the distance.

In faster conditions such as on motorways, increasing the distance between vehicles helps to lower the risk of collision. If any driver or rider overtakes you and pulls into the gap in front, drop back to regain a safe distance.

Your overall stopping distance will be longer when carrying a passenger.

R-ES 12 & 14, HC r126

Weather conditions

Weather conditions have a great effect on your safety margins. If the weather's really bad, such as snow, ice or thick fog, consider whether your journey's really necessary. Never underestimate the dangers, and always wear suitable clothing.

Before starting a journey in freezing weather, clear any ice and snow from your windscreen, lights, mirrors and number plates. When riding, use the highest gear you can. Also, brake gently and in plenty of time.

When there's heavy rain or the road is wet, take extra care and use both brakes. It's important to ensure your motorcycle is straight when braking, to avoid skidding.

R-ES 12, HC r227-231

When it's foggy

- allow more time for your journey
- slow down as your visibility is reduced
- increase the gap between your vehicle and the one in front of you
- keep your visor or goggles clear
- beware of others not using their headlights
- use dipped headlights even in daylight. If visibility falls below 100 metres (328 feet), use fog lights if you've got them. Remember to switch them off when the fog lifts.

Aquaplaning may happen in heavy rain. The tyres lift off the road surface and skate on a film of water. The steering becomes light. If this happens, ease off the throttle smoothly and don't brake until your steering feels normal again.

R-ES 12, HC r121, r227, r234-236

If you've driven through deep water such as a ford or a flood, test your brakes. If necessary, dry them out by applying them lightly as you go along. Use a low gear when riding through a ford or flood water.

R-ES 12, HC r121

Take care to avoid painted areas such as bus stop markings and mini-roundabouts as they may be slippery. At bus stops particularly, there may be oil on the road surface. At night, the reflection from wet roads can make it hard to see unlit objects.

Hot weather can also pose a danger. The road surface could become soft or slippery and your tyres might not grip so well. This may affect your braking as well as your steering. If it rains after a long dry spell, the road surface can become unusually slippery so take extra care.

Bright sunlight can dazzle. Other drivers might not be able to see your indicators flashing if they are dazzled. Consider giving an arm signal as well.

R-ES 12, HC r93 & r237

High winds can blow you off course, especially on an open stretch of road. They have an even greater effect on high-sided vehicles, motorcyclists and cyclists. Take care if you pass these road users as they may be blown off course by a sudden gust. Allow extra room and then check your left side as you pass them.

R-ES 12, HC r232-233

At night

When riding at night, you should NOT use tinted glasses, lenses or visors. You SHOULD wear reflective clothing and use dipped headlights. Also, using dipped headlights during the day can help you be more easily seen by others.

R-ES 12, HC r87 & r94

Skidding

Skidding is mainly caused by the driver or rider. You need to adjust your control of the vehicle to the road, weather and traffic conditions.

There's most risk of skidding in wet or icy conditions. Black ice isn't obvious until you feel the steering becoming light. Be aware that in very cold weather it could be a hazard. Skidding can be caused by

- heavy/uncoordinated braking (locking one or both wheels)
- excessive acceleration (causing rear wheel spin)
- swerving (a change of direction)
- leaning over too far when cornering (tyres may lose grip).

Scan the road ahead for clues such as road signs and markings, and hazards like potholes, debris, drain covers, oil patches or loose gravel. You shouldn't then be taken by surprise. You can

- slow down gradually before you reach the hazard, such as a bend
- avoid sudden steering movements.

R-ES 6, 8 & 12, HC r119 & r231

If you do start skidding

- ease off the throttle to regain control
- steer smoothly in the direction of the skid – if the back of the motorcycle skids to the right, steer carefully to the right, and vice versa.

If the skid is caused by braking, release the brakes to allow the wheels to turn again, then reapply the brakes as firmly as conditions will permit.

R-ES 8 & 12, HC r119 & r231

Anti-lock braking systems (ABS) are designed to prevent wheel lock caused by excessive braking. The sensor will keep the wheel at the point of lock-up for as long as the rider continues to brake hard enough to activate the system or until the motorcycle stops. Refer to the owner's handbook for details of the manufacturer's recommended method of use.

ABS doesn't necessarily reduce your stopping distance but you can continue to steer while braking because the wheels are prevented from locking. It may not work as effectively where there's surface water or a loose road surface.

R-ES 5, HC r120

Contraflow systems

Where a temporary contraflow system is in operation, you will be travelling close to oncoming traffic, sometimes in narrow lanes. When you enter a contraflow system you should

- reduce speed in good time
- choose an appropriate lane in good time
- keep the correct separation distance.

R-ES 11, HC r290

FAQs

Why does my CBT Instructor tell me to keep well to the left before a right-hand bend?

Keeping well to the left improves your view of the road ahead and gives you an earlier indication of any hazards.

R-ES 9 & 10, HC r252

How can I park my motorcycle safely on a downhill slope?

Leave it in a low gear and block the wheel or wedge it against the kerb. This will help stop your vehicle falling over or rolling downhill.

R-ES 8, HC r252

I know overtaking is a dangerous manoeuvre – are there any places that I definitely need to avoid?

Always ensure you've enough time to complete the manoeuvre safely. In particular don't overtake

- *where your view ahead is blocked (eg on a bend or near the brow of a hill)*
- *when approaching a junction*
- *if you're intending to turn off the road shortly afterwards.*

R-ES 8, HC r162-169

Why are there so many speed humps around?

These traffic-calming measures are normally found in built-up areas to improve the safety of the area. Slow right down as you approach and ride over them.

R-ES 7, HC r153

When filtering through queuing traffic, why should I be more cautious when approaching a 'keep clear' road marking?

Traffic could be emerging from a junction or side road, and may not see you. Always take care when filtering through traffic.

R-ES 7, HC p116, KYTS p63

4.1 *Mark one answer* **R-ES 8, HC r126 & p42**

Your overall stopping distance will be longer when riding

- at night
- in the fog
- with a passenger
- up a hill

⊙ **with a passenger**

When carrying a passenger on a motorcycle the overall weight will be much more than when riding alone. This additional weight will make it harder for you to stop quickly in an emergency.

4.2 *Mark one answer* **R-ES 12**

On a wet road what is the safest way to stop?

- Change gear without braking
- Use the back brake only
- Use the front brake only
- Use both brakes

⊙ **Use both brakes**

Motorcyclists need to take extra care when stopping on wet road surfaces. Plan well ahead so that you're able to brake in good time. You should ensure your motorcycle is upright and brake when travelling in a straight line.

4.3 *Mark one answer* **R-ES 12, HC r119**

You are riding in heavy rain when your rear wheel skids as you accelerate. To get control again you must

- change down to a lower gear
- ease off the throttle
- brake to reduce speed
- put your feet down

⊙ **ease off the throttle**

If you feel your back wheel beginning to skid as you pull away, ease off the throttle. This will give your rear tyre the chance to grip the road and stop the skid.

*Mark **one** answer*

It is snowing. Before starting your journey you should

⊙ think if you need to ride at all
⊙ try to avoid taking a passenger
⊙ plan a route avoiding towns
⊙ take a hot drink before setting out

⊙ **think if you need to ride at all**

Do not ride in snowy or icy conditions unless your journey is essential. If you must go out, try and keep to main roads which are more likely to be treated and clear.

*Mark **one** answer*

Why should you ride with a dipped headlight on in the daytime?

⊙ It helps other road users to see you
⊙ It means that you can ride faster
⊙ Other vehicles will get out of the way
⊙ So that it is already on when it gets dark

⊙ **It helps other road users to see you**

Make yourself as visible as possible, from the side as well as from the front and rear. Having your headlight on, even in good daylight, can help make you more conspicuous.

*Mark **one** answer*

Motorcyclists are only allowed to use high-intensity rear fog lights when

⊙ a pillion passenger is being carried
⊙ they ride a large touring machine
⊙ visibility is 100 metres (328 feet) or less
⊙ they are riding on the road for the first time

⊙ **visibility is 100 metres (328 feet) or less**

If your motorcycle is fitted with high-intensity rear fog lights you must only use them when visibility is seriously reduced, that is, when you can see no further than 100 metres (328 feet). This rule also applies to all other motor vehicles using these lights.

4.7   *Mark **three** answers*   R-ES 13, HC r113-114

You MUST use your headlight

- when riding in a group
- at night when street lighting is poor
- when carrying a passenger
- on motorways during darkness
- at times of poor visibility
- when parked on an unlit road

- ⊙ **at night when street lighting is poor**
- ⊙ **on motorways during darkness**
- ⊙ **at times of poor visibility**

Your headlight helps you to see in the dark and helps other road users to see you. You must also use your headlight at any time when visibility is seriously reduced.

4.8   *Mark **one** answer*   R-ES 10 & 12

You are riding in town at night. The roads are wet after rain. The reflections from wet surfaces will

- affect your stopping distance
- affect your road holding
- make it easy to see unlit objects
- make it hard to see unlit objects

- ⊙ **make it hard to see unlit objects**

If you can't see clearly, slow down and stop. Make sure that your visor or goggles are clean. Be extra-cautious in these conditions and allow twice the normal separation distance.

4.9   *Mark **two** answers*   R-ES 12, HC r121

You are riding through a flood. Which TWO should you do?

- Keep in a high gear and stand up on the footrests
- Keep the engine running fast to keep water out of the exhaust
- Ride slowly and test your brakes when you are out of the water
- Turn your headlight off to avoid any electrical damage

- ⊙ **Keep the engine running fast to keep water out of the exhaust**
- ⊙ **Ride slowly and test your brakes when you are out of the water**

Take extra care when riding through flood water or fords. Ride through with high engine revs while partly slipping the clutch to prevent water entering the exhaust system. Try your brakes as soon as you are clear.

4.10

Mark *one* answer

R-ES 12, HC r121

You have just ridden through a flood. When clear of the water you should test your

- ⊙ starter motor
- ⊙ headlight
- ⊙ steering
- ⊙ brakes

⊙ **brakes**

If you have ridden through deep water your brakes may be less effective. If they have been affected, ride slowly while gently applying both brakes until normal braking is restored.

4.11

Mark *one* answer

R-ES 12, HC r121

When going through flood water you should ride

- ⊙ quickly in a high gear
- ⊙ slowly in a high gear
- ⊙ quickly in a low gear
- ⊙ slowly in a low gear

⊙ **slowly in a low gear**

If you have to go through a flood, ride slowly in a low gear. Keep the engine running fast enough to keep water out of the exhaust. You may need to slip the clutch to do this.

4.12

Mark *one* answer

R-ES 13, HC r94

When riding at night you should NOT

- ⊙ switch on full beam headlights
- ⊙ overtake slower vehicles in front
- ⊙ use dipped beam headlights
- ⊙ use tinted glasses, lenses or visors

⊙ **use tinted glasses, lenses or visors**

Do not use tinted glasses, lenses or visors at night because they reduce the amount of available light reaching your eyes. It's also important to keep your visor or goggles clean to give a clear view of the road at all times.

4.13 *Mark **two** answers* **R-ES 12, HC r114-115**

Which of the following should you do when riding in fog?

- ⊙ Keep close to the vehicle in front
- ⊙ Use your dipped headlight
- ⊙ Ride close to the centre of the road
- ⊙ Keep your visor or goggles clear
- ⊙ Keep the vehicle in front in view

⊙ **Use your dipped headlight**

⊙ **Keep your visor or goggles clear**

You must use your dipped headlight when visibility is seriously reduced. In fog a film of mist can form over the outside of your visor or goggles. This can further reduce your ability to see. Be aware of this hazard and keep your visor or goggles clear.

4.14 *Mark **one** answer* **R-ES 12**

You are riding in heavy rain. Why should you try to avoid this marked area?

[BUS STOP sign]

- ⊙ It is illegal to ride over bus stops
- ⊙ The painted lines may be slippery
- ⊙ Cyclists may be using the bus stop
- ⊙ Only emergency vehicles may drive over bus stops

⊙ **The painted lines may be slippery**

Painted lines and road markings can be very slippery, especially for motorcyclists. Try to avoid them if you can do so safely.

4.15 *Mark **one** answer* **R-ES 4, HC r87**

When riding at night you should

- ⊙ wear reflective clothing
- ⊙ wear a tinted visor
- ⊙ ride in the middle of the road
- ⊙ always give arm signals

⊙ **wear reflective clothing**

You need to make yourself as visible as possible, from the front and rear and also from the side. Don't just rely on your headlight and tail light. Wear clothing that uses reflective material as this stands out in other vehicles' headlights.

4.16 — *Mark four answers* — R-ES 12

The road surface is very important to motorcyclists. Which FOUR of these are more likely to reduce the stability of your motorcycle?

- Potholes
- Drain covers
- Concrete
- Oil patches
- Tarmac
- Loose gravel

- ⊙ **Potholes**
- ⊙ **Drain covers**
- ⊙ **Oil patches**
- ⊙ **Loose gravel**

Apart from the weather conditions, the road surface and any changes in it can affect the stability of your motorcycle. Be on the lookout for poor road surfaces and be aware of any traffic around you, in case you need to take avoiding action.

4.17 — *Mark two answers* — R-ES 4, HC r87 & r114

You are riding at night. To be seen more easily you should

- ride with your headlight on dipped beam
- wear reflective clothing
- keep the motorcycle clean
- stay well out to the right
- wear waterproof clothing

- ⊙ **ride with your headlight on dipped beam**
- ⊙ **wear reflective clothing**

Reflective clothing works by reflecting light from the headlights of the other vehicles. This will make it easier for you to be seen.

Fluorescent clothing, although effective during the day, won't show up as well as reflective clothing at night.

4.18 — *Mark one answer* — R-ES 12

Your overall stopping distance will be much longer when riding

- in the rain
- in fog
- at night
- in strong winds

- ⊙ **in the rain**

Extra care should be taken in wet weather. Wet roads will affect the time it takes you to stop. Your stopping distance could be at least doubled.

4.19 — Mark **one** answer — R-ES 4

When riding in extremely cold conditions what can you do to keep warm?

- ⊙ Stay close to the vehicles in front
- ⊙ Wear suitable clothing
- ⊙ Lie flat on the tank
- ⊙ Put one hand on the exhaust pipe

⊙ **Wear suitable clothing**

Motorcyclists are exposed to the elements and can become very cold when riding in wintry conditions. It's important to keep warm or your concentration could be affected. The only way to stay warm is to wear suitable clothing. If you do find yourself getting cold then stop at a suitable place to warm up.

4.20 — Mark **two** answers — R-ES 12

You are riding in very hot weather. What are TWO effects that melting tar has on the control of your motorcycle?

- ⊙ It can make the surface slippery
- ⊙ It can reduce tyre grip
- ⊙ It can reduce stopping distances
- ⊙ It can improve braking efficiency

⊙ **It can make the surface slippery**

⊙ **It can reduce tyre grip**

If the tarmac road surface has softened in the heat, take extra care when braking and cornering. You should also look out for loose chippings where roads have been resurfaced. These will reduce your tyres' grip and can fly up, causing injury and damage.

4.21 — Mark **one** answer — R-ES 9, HC r167

You are riding past queuing traffic. Why should you be more cautious when approaching this road marking?

- ⊙ Lorries will be unloading here
- ⊙ School children will be crossing here
- ⊙ Pedestrians will be standing in the road
- ⊙ Traffic could be emerging and may not see you

⊙ **Traffic could be emerging and may not see you**

When riding past queuing traffic look out for 'keep clear' road markings that will indicate a side road or entrance on the left. Vehicles may emerge between gaps in the traffic.

113

What can cause your tyres to skid and lose their grip on the road surface?

⊙ Giving hand signals

⊙ Riding one handed

⊙ Looking over your shoulder

⊙ Heavy braking

⊙ **Heavy braking**

You can cause your motorcycle to skid by heavy or uncoordinated braking, as well as excessive acceleration, swerving or changing direction too sharply, and leaning over too far.

When riding in heavy rain a film of water can build up between your tyres and the road surface. This may result in loss of control. What can you do to avoid this happening?

⊙ Keep your speed down

⊙ Increase your tyre pressures

⊙ Decrease your tyre pressures

⊙ Keep trying your brakes

⊙ **Keep your speed down**

There is a greater risk of aquaplaning when riding at speed. Keeping your speed down will help prevent aquaplaning.

If you can do so safely, try to avoid pools of water on the road.

When riding in heavy rain a film of water can build up between your tyres and the road. This is known as aquaplaning. What should you do to keep control?

⊙ Use your rear brakes gently

⊙ Steer to the crown of the road

⊙ Ease off the throttle smoothly

⊙ Change up into a higher gear.

⊙ **Ease off the throttle smoothly**

If your vehicle starts to aquaplane ease off the throttle smoothly. Do not brake or turn the steering until tyre grip has been restored.

4.25 *Mark one answer* R-ES 12, HC r121

After riding through deep water you notice your scooter brakes do not work properly. What would be the best way to dry them out?

- ⊙ Ride slowly, braking lightly
- ⊙ Ride quickly, braking harshly
- ⊙ Stop and dry them with a cloth
- ⊙ Stop and wait for a few minutes

⊙ **Ride slowly, braking lightly**

You can help to dry out brakes by riding slowly and applying light pressure to the brake pedal/lever. DO NOT ride at normal speeds until they are working normally again.

4.26 *Mark two answers* R-ES 12, HC r234-236

You have to ride in foggy weather. You should

- ⊙ stay close to the centre of the road
- ⊙ switch only your sidelights on
- ⊙ switch on your dipped headlights
- ⊙ be aware of others not using their headlights
- ⊙ always ride in the gutter to see the kerb

⊙ **switch on your dipped headlights**

⊙ **be aware of others not using their headlights**

Only travel in fog if your journey is absolutely necessary. Fog is often patchy and visibility can suddenly reduce without warning.

4.27 *Mark one answer* R-ES 10, HC r126

Only a fool breaks the two-second rule refers to

- ⊙ the time recommended when using the choke
- ⊙ the separation distance when riding in good conditions
- ⊙ restarting a stalled engine in busy traffic
- ⊙ the time you should keep your foot down at a junction

⊙ **the separation distance when riding in good conditions**

It is very important that you always leave a safe gap between yourself and any vehicle you're following. In good conditions you need to leave at least one metre for every mile per hour of your speed or a two-second time interval.

*Mark **one** answer*

At a mini roundabout it is important that a motorcyclist should avoid

- ⊙ turning right
- ⊙ using signals
- ⊙ taking 'lifesavers'
- ⊙ the painted area

⊙ **the painted area**

Avoid riding over the painted area as these can become very slippery, especially when wet. Even on dry roads only a small part of the motorcycle's tyre makes contact with the road. Any reduction in grip can therefore affect the stability of your machine.

*Mark **two** answers*

You are riding on a motorway in a crosswind. You should take extra care when

- ⊙ approaching service areas
- ⊙ overtaking a large vehicle
- ⊙ riding in slow-moving traffic
- ⊙ approaching an exit
- ⊙ riding in exposed places

⊙ **overtaking a large vehicle**

⊙ **riding in exposed places**

Take extra care when overtaking large vehicles as they can cause air turbulence and buffeting. Beware of crosswinds when riding on exposed stretches of road, which can suddenly blow you off course. Bear in mind that strong winds can also affect the stability of other road users.

*Mark **one** answer*

Why should you try to avoid riding over this marked area?

- ⊙ It is illegal to ride over bus stops
- ⊙ It will alter your machine's centre of gravity
- ⊙ Pedestrians may be waiting at the bus stop
- ⊙ A bus may have left patches of oil

⊙ **A bus may have left patches of oil**

Try to anticipate slippery road surfaces. Watch out for oil patches at places where vehicles stop for some time, such as bus stops, lay-bys and busy junctions.

4.31   Mark **one** answer   R-ES 8, HC r126 & p40

Your overall stopping distance comprises thinking and braking distance. You are on a good, dry road surface with good brakes and tyres. What is the typical BRAKING distance at 50 mph?

- ⊙ 14 metres (46 feet)
- ⊙ 24 metres (79 feet)
- ⊙ 38 metres (125 feet)
- ⊙ 55 metres (180 feet)

⊙ **38 metres (125 feet)**

Different factors can affect how long it takes you to stop, such as weather and road conditions, vehicle condition and loading. You also need to add reaction time to this. The overall stopping distance at 50 mph includes 15 metres thinking distance (the reaction time before braking starts) plus your braking distance of 38 metres', giving a typical overall stopping distance of 53 metres (175 feet) in good conditions.

4.32   Mark **one** answer   R-ES 12, HC r121

You are riding at speed through surface water. A thin film of water has built up between your tyres and the road surface. To keep control what should you do?

- ⊙ Turn the steering quickly
- ⊙ Use the rear brake gently
- ⊙ Use both brakes gently
- ⊙ Ease off the throttle

⊙ **Ease off the throttle**

Riding at speed where there is surface water can cause it to build up between your tyres and the road. This is known as aquaplaning and results in serious loss of steering and braking control, and can cause you to crash. The faster you are going, the more likely it is to happen. If it does, ease off the throttle smoothly.

4.33   Mark **one** answer   R-ES 12, HC r126

Braking distances on ice can be

- ⊙ twice the normal distance
- ⊙ five times the normal distance
- ⊙ seven times the normal distance
- ⊙ ten times the normal distance

⊙ **ten times the normal distance**

In icy and snowy weather, your stopping distance will increase by up to ten times compared to good, dry conditions.

Take extra care when braking, accelerating and steering, to cut down the risk of skidding.

Freezing conditions will affect the distance it takes you to come to a stop. You should expect stopping distances to increase by up to

⊙ two times

⊙ three times

⊙ five times

⊙ ten times

⊙ **ten times**

Your tyre grip is greatly reduced on icy roads and you need to allow up to ten times the normal stopping distance.

In windy conditions you need to take extra care when

⊙ using the brakes

⊙ making a hill start

⊙ turning into a narrow road

⊙ passing pedal cyclists

⊙ **passing pedal cyclists**

You should always give cyclists plenty of room when overtaking. When it's windy, a sudden gust could blow them off course.

When approaching a right-hand bend you should keep well to the left. Why is this?

⊙ To improve your view of the road

⊙ To overcome the effect of the road's slope

⊙ To let faster traffic from behind overtake

⊙ To be positioned safely if you skid

⊙ **To improve your view of the road**

Doing this will give you an earlier view around the bend and enable you to see any hazards sooner.

It also reduces the risk of collision with an oncoming vehicle that may have drifted over the centre line while taking the bend.

4.37   *Mark one answer*   **R-ES 12, HC r121**

You have just gone through deep water. To dry off the brakes you should

- ⊙ accelerate and keep to a high speed for a short time
- ⊙ go slowly while gently applying the brakes
- ⊙ avoid using the brakes at all for a few miles
- ⊙ stop for at least an hour to allow them time to dry

⊙ **go slowly while gently applying the brakes**

Water on the brakes will act as a lubricant, causing them to work less efficiently. Using the brakes lightly as you go along will dry them out.

4.38   *Mark two answers*   **R-ES 12, HC r237**

In very hot weather the road surface can become soft. Which TWO of the following will be most affected?

- ⊙ The suspension
- ⊙ The grip of the tyres
- ⊙ The braking
- ⊙ The exhaust

⊙ **The grip of the tyres**

⊙ **The braking**

Only a small part of your tyres is in contact with the road. This is why you must consider the surface on which you're travelling, and alter your speed to suit the road conditions.

4.39   *Mark one answer*   **R-ES 12, HC r232-233**

Where are you most likely to be affected by a side wind?

- ⊙ On a narrow country lane
- ⊙ On an open stretch of road
- ⊙ On a busy stretch of road
- ⊙ On a long, straight road

⊙ **On an open stretch of road**

In windy conditions, care must be taken on exposed roads. A strong gust of wind can blow you off course. Watch out for other road users who are particularly likely to be affected, such as cyclists, motorcyclists, high-sided lorries and vehicles towing trailers.

In good conditions, what is the typical stopping distance at 70 mph?

- ⊙ 53 metres (175 feet)
- ⊙ 60 metres (197 feet)
- ⊙ 73 metres (240 feet)
- ⊙ 96 metres (315 feet)

⊙ **96 metres (315 feet)**

Note that this is the typical stopping distance. It will take at least this distance to think, brake and stop in good conditions. In poor conditions it will take much longer.

What is the shortest overall stopping distance on a dry road at 60 mph?

- ⊙ 53 metres (175 feet)
- ⊙ 58 metres (190 feet)
- ⊙ 73 metres (240 feet)
- ⊙ 96 metres (315 feet)

⊙ **73 metres (240 feet)**

This distance is the equivalent of 18 car lengths. Try pacing out 73 metres and then look back. It's probably further than you think.

In heavy motorway traffic the vehicle behind you is following too closely. How can you lower the risk of a collision?

- ⊙ Increase your distance from the vehicle in front
- ⊙ Operate the brakes sharply
- ⊙ Switch on your hazard lights
- ⊙ Move onto the hard shoulder and stop

⊙ **Increase your distance from the vehicle in front**

On busy roads traffic may still travel at high speeds despite being close together. Don't follow too closely to the vehicle in front. If a driver behind seems to be 'pushing' you, gradually increase your distance from the vehicle in front by slowing down gently. This will give you more space in front if you have to brake, and lessen the risk of a collision involving several vehicles.

4.43 *Mark **one** answer* HC p42-43

You are travelling at 50 mph on a good, dry road. What is your typical overall stopping distance?

⊙ 36 metres (118 feet)

⊙ 53 metres (175 feet)

⊙ 75 metres (245 feet)

⊙ 96 metres (315 feet)

⊙ **53 metres (175 feet)**

Even in good conditions it will usually take you further than you think to stop. Don't just learn the figures, make sure you understand how far the distance is.

4.44 *Mark **one** answer* HC p42-43

You are on a good, dry, road surface. Your brakes and tyres are good. What is the typical overall stopping distance at 40 mph?

⊙ 23 metres (75 feet)

⊙ 36 metres (118 feet)

⊙ 53 metres (175 feet)

⊙ 96 metres (315 feet)

⊙ **36 metres (118 feet)**

Stopping distances are affected by a number of variable factors. These include the type, model and condition of your vehicle, road and weather conditions, and your reaction time. Look well ahead for hazards and leave enough space between you and the vehicle in front. This should allow you to pull up safely if you have to, without braking sharply.

4.45 *Mark **one** answer* R-ES 12, HC r232-233

What should you do when overtaking a motorcyclist in strong winds?

⊙ Pass close

⊙ Pass quickly

⊙ Pass wide

⊙ Pass immediately

⊙ **Pass wide**

In strong winds riders of two-wheeled vehicles are particularly vulnerable. When you overtake them allow plenty of room. Always check to the left as you pass.

4.46   *Mark **one** answer*   R-ES 12, HC r232-233

You are overtaking a motorcyclist in strong winds. What should you do?

- ⊙ Allow extra room
- ⊙ Give a thank you wave
- ⊙ Move back early
- ⊙ Sound your horn

⊙ **Allow extra room**

It is easy for motorcyclists to be blown off course. Always give them plenty of room if you decide to overtake, especially in strong winds. Decide whether you need to overtake at all. Always check to the left as you pass.

4.47   *Mark **one** answer*   HC p42-43

Overall stopping distance is made up of thinking and braking distance. You are on a good, dry road surface with good brakes and tyres. What is the typical BRAKING distance from 50 mph?

- ⊙ 14 metres (46 feet)
- ⊙ 24 metres (80 feet)
- ⊙ 38 metres (125 feet)
- ⊙ 55 metres (180 feet)

⊙ **38 metres (125 feet)**

Be aware this is just the braking distance. You need to add the thinking distance to this to give the OVERALL STOPPING DISTANCE. At 50 mph the typical thinking distance will be 15 metres (50 feet), plus a braking distance of 38 metres (125 feet), giving an overall stopping distance of 53 metres (175 feet). The distance could be greater than this depending on your attention and response to any hazards. These figures are a general guide.

4.48   *Mark **one** answer*   HC r126 & 268

You are following a vehicle at a safe distance on a wet road. Another driver overtakes you and pulls into the gap you have left. What should you do?

- ⊙ Flash your headlights as a warning
- ⊙ Try to overtake safely as soon as you can
- ⊙ Drop back to regain a safe distance
- ⊙ Stay close to the other vehicle until it moves on

⊙ **Drop back to regain a safe distance**

Wet weather will affect the time it takes for you to stop and can affect your control. Your speed should allow you to stop safely and in good time. If another vehicle pulls into the gap you've left, ease back until you've regained your stopping distance.

4.49   *Mark **one** answer*   R-ES 12, HC r234-236

You are following other vehicles in fog. You have your lights on. What else can you do to reduce the chances of being in a collision?

- ⊙ Keep close to the vehicle in front
- ⊙ Use your main beam instead of dipped headlights
- ⊙ Keep up with the faster vehicles
- ⊙ Reduce your speed and increase the gap in front

⊙ **Reduce your speed and increase the gap in front**

When it's foggy use dipped headlights. This will help you see and be seen by other road users. If visibility is seriously reduced consider using front and rear fog lights. Keep a sensible speed and don't follow the vehicle in front too closely. If the road is wet and slippery you'll need to allow twice the normal stopping distance.

4.50   *Mark **three** answers*   R-ES 8 & 11, HC r290

To avoid a collision when entering a contraflow system, you should

- ⊙ reduce speed in good time
- ⊙ switch lanes at any time to make progress
- ⊙ choose an appropriate lane in good time
- ⊙ keep the correct separation distance
- ⊙ increase speed to pass through quickly
- ⊙ follow other motorists closely to avoid long queues

⊙ **reduce speed in good time**

⊙ **choose an appropriate lane in good time**

⊙ **keep the correct separation distance**

In a contraflow system you will be travelling close to oncoming traffic and sometimes in narrow lanes. You should obey the temporary speed limit signs, get into the correct lane at the proper time and keep a safe separation distance from the vehicle ahead. When traffic is at a very low speed, merging in turn is recommended if it's safe and appropriate.

Case study practice 4 – Safety margins

Kim is collecting her new motorcycle. Steve is taking her as a passenger on his machine. The weather is fine with a strong crosswind. There is a cyclist in front of Steve. The road surface is cracked and in need of repair. There are also areas of loose and crumbled tarmac. Further on, the traffic is heavier. On reaching their destination, they turn right into the dealer's forecourt.

4.1 What might Steve need to adjust on his motorcycle before the journey?

*Mark **one** answer*

⊙ Tyre pressures and headlight angle.
⊙ Front forks and handlebar height.
⊙ Pillion seating and wheel alignment.
⊙ Passenger footrests and brake linings.

R-ES 8

4.2 How could crosswinds affect Steve and Kim?

*Mark **one** answer*

⊙ Speed up their journey.
⊙ Increase fuel consumption.
⊙ Blow them off-course.
⊙ Make them feel colder.

R-ES 12, HC r232

4.3 How might the cyclist react on the road surface described?

*Mark **one** answer*

⊙   Make a U-turn and go back home.

⊙   Get off and walk along the road.

⊙   Swerve to avoid cracks and holes.

⊙   Ride faster over the uneven surface.

R-ES 10, HC r213

4.4 How would Steve need to ride on this road surface?

*Mark **one** answer*

⊙   With more care.

⊙   With lights on.

⊙   With more speed.

⊙   With brakes on.

R-ES 8, HC r288

4.5 What should Steve do just before turning right?

*Mark **one** answer*

⊙   Check over his right shoulder for overtaking vehicles.

⊙   A U-turn, to pull up on the other side of the road.

⊙   Sound the horn and flash headlights at other traffic.

⊙   Get off the motorcycle and wheel it across the road.

R-ES 3, HC r180

section **five**

HAZARD AWARENESS

This section covers
- Anticipation
- Attention
- Speed and distance
- Reaction time
- Alcohol and drugs
- Tiredness

Hazard awareness

When you start your Compulsory Basic Training (CBT) in order to learn to ride, you'll be concentrating on the basic controls of the motorcycle. As your skill improves so will your ability to recognise hazards on the road.

A hazard is a situation which may require you as a rider to respond by taking action such as braking or steering. These can be

- static hazards – such as roundabouts and junctions
- moving hazards – other road users
- road and weather conditions.

R-ES 10

Static hazards

There are numerous types of static hazard, including bends, junctions, roundabouts, shared overtaking lanes, contraflow systems, parked vehicles and skips in the road, roadworks, traffic calming, different types of crossings and traffic lights. All of these may require you to respond in some way, so

- take a mental note of their existence
- slow down and get ready to stop if necessary.

At light-controlled level crossings, you **MUST** stop before the barrier when the red lights are flashing, even if the barrier is not yet down.

R-ES 8, 9 & 10, HC r153, r293

Road signs and markings are there to give you clues. Learn their meanings. Watch out for them so that you can reduce your speed in good time and prepare yourself for any action you may need to take. The same applies to traffic lights, other light signals and signals from police or traffic officers.

If you see a sign for a bend, ask yourself, 'What if there was a pedestrian or obstruction just around the bend, could I stop in time? Could I do it safely?'

R-ES 7, HC r102-117, KYTS 10-71 & 77-93

In busy areas, parked cars can cause a hazard, especially if parked illegally – for example on the zigzag lines by a pedestrian crossing. Watch out for

- children dashing out from between the cars
- car doors opening
- cars moving away.

Would you be able to stop?

R-ES 8 & 10, HC r205-206

There's often reduced visibility at junctions, especially in built-up areas. Take extra care and pull forward slowly until you can see down the road. You may also be able to see reflections of traffic in shop windows. Don't block a junction; leave it clear to allow vehicles to enter and emerge.

R-ES 10, HC r151

127

Where lanes are closed, be ready for vehicles cutting in front of you and keep a safe distance from the vehicle in front.

If you are driving on a motorway or dual carriageway and see a hazard or obstruction ahead, briefly use your hazard warning lights to warn the traffic behind.

If your vehicle has broken down and is causing an obstruction, switch on your hazard warning lights to warn other road users.

R-ES 9 & 11, HC r116

Moving hazards

You need to look out for other types of road user: pedestrians, cyclists, horse riders, drivers of large vehicles, other motorcyclists, disabled people using a powered vehicle, other slow-moving vehicles (eg refuse lorries) and car drivers.

In built-up areas you may come across pedestrians in the road; be patient and wait for them to finish crossing. Near schools, there are often flashing amber lights warning that children may be crossing. Slow down and be ready to stop if necessary. Hand signals can help pedestrians understand your intention.

R-ES 8 & 10, HC r205-206

On country roads, there may be no pavement, so look out for pedestrians in the road. They may be walking towards you on your side of the road.

Be aware of cyclists and give them plenty of room:

- they may wobble or swerve to avoid drains or potholes
- at junctions or traffic lights, give them time to turn or pull away
- before you turn left, check for cyclists filtering on your left.

R-ES 10, HC r211-214

If you see a bus at a bus stop, think

- people may get off the bus and move across the road
- the bus may be about to move off.

School buses might stop at places other than bus stops.

R-ES 10, HC r223

At some bridges, high vehicles may need to use the centre of the road to be able to pass underneath – be prepared to give way to them.

R-ES 10, HC r221

Watch out for other vehicles, especially other motorcyclists, overtaking and cutting in front of you. If you need to, drop back to retain a safe separation distance. When turning right, don't forget the 'lifesaver look' to your right to check for overtaking vehicles before making the turn.

R-ES 8, HC r168, r179-180

Elderly drivers may not react very quickly, so be patient with them.

Some vehicles have signs on the back; for example, those with arrows, large goods vehicles over 13 metres long and vehicles carrying hazardous chemicals. Learn what they mean.

HC r117 & r216

At light-controlled junctions where the lights are not working, treat them as an unmarked junction and be prepared to stop. There may be police officers controlling traffic in these circumstances – make sure you know and understand their signals.

R-ES 10, HC r105, r176 & p105

Yourself

Don't allow yourself to become a hazard on the road. You need to be alert at all times. Make sure you use your mirrors so you are aware of what is going on around you at all times. These may be convex to give a wider field of vision.

Don't ride if you're tired. Plan your journey so that you've enough rest and refreshment breaks. Try to stop at least once every two hours.

R-ES 1 & 11, HC r91 & r161

If you feel tired, pull over at a safe and legal place to rest. When on a motorway, leave at the next exit or services.

Your concentration can also be affected by

- using a hands-free phone headset
- listening to loud music
- looking at satellite navigation equipment.

If you've had an argument, or another road-user's action has upset you, calm down before starting or continuing your journey.

When riding long distances at speed, noise can contribute to fatigue and can damage your hearing. Consider wearing ear plugs to protect your hearing when you ride.

R-ES 1, HC r148-150

Never ride if you've been drinking. It's not worth taking a chance. If you're riding, don't drink alcohol. If you've had a drink, go home by public transport. If you ride to a social event, stick to non-alcoholic drinks.

Alcohol

- reduces concentration, coordination and control
- gives a false sense of confidence
- reduces your judgement of speed
- slows down your reactions.

You must be fit to ride. Certain medicines can make you drowsy; check the label or ask your doctor or pharmacist if it's safe for you to ride your motorcycle after taking medication that may affect your riding.

R-ES 1, HC r90, r95 & r96

Using illegal drugs is highly dangerous and the effects of some can last up to 72 hours. Never take them before riding. If you've been convicted of riding whilst unfit through drink or drugs, the cost of your insurance will rise considerably. Riding while under the influence of drink or drugs may even invalidate your insurance.

R-ES 1

Your eyesight should be of a safe standard. If you need glasses to drive, wear them every time you ride. If you can't, don't ride – find another means of transport. Don't wear tinted glasses, visors or goggles at night.

You must tell the licensing authority if

• your eyesight deteriorates

• you suffer from an illness which may affect your riding.

R-ES 1, HC r90, r92-94

Road and weather conditions

Different types of weather can change a normal stretch of road into a hazard. Rain, ice, fog and even bright sunlight can have an effect on safety. Ride accordingly and be aware of the added dangers. In wet weather

• double your separation distance to four seconds

• spray may reduce your vision.

R-ES 12, HC r227

Remember that if you are wet and cold you could lose concentration and your reaction time may be slower. Always wear proper protective clothing and footwear when riding.

FAQs

How do I deal with inconsiderate road users?

There are occasions when we all make misjudgements or mistakes. Be aware that other drivers might not always follow the rules. Try not to react – ignore the error and stay calm. Don't shout or make rude gestures; this won't help the situation at all.

• *Wait if necessary to allow the other road user to move out of the way.*

• *If you feel upset, stop and take a break if you can.*

Good anticipation skills can help to prevent these incidents becoming accidents.

R-ES 1, HC r146-147

What restrictions are there on provisional licence holders?

You must not

• *ride on public roads until you have passed Compulsory Basic Training (CBT)*

• *carry a pillion passenger*

• *tow a trailer*

• *ride on a motorway.*

Until you have passed your test, you can only ride a machine with an engine capacity lower than 125 cc, unless you are accompanied by a Direct Access Scheme (DAS) instructor.

HC r253 & p123

What do I do if it looks like the driver in front has forgotten to cancel their right indicator?

Be cautious. Stay behind and don't overtake – they may be unsure of the position of a junction and turn suddenly.

HC r104

How do you prevent the vehicle behind driving too closely?

Move over and let the vehicle through if you can. If there's no room and the driver behind seems to be 'pushing' you, increase your distance from the car in front. This will lessen the risk of an incident involving several vehicles.

R-ES 10

What do I do if a car is about to reverse out in front of me?

Reduce your speed and be prepared to stop. Sound your horn to warn them you're there (in built-up areas between 11.30 pm and 7.00 am, flash your headlights instead).

R-ES 6, HC r110 & r112

What do I do if I take the wrong route and find myself in a one-way street?

Don't try to turn round in a one-way street. Continue to the end of the road and then find a safe place to turn round.

HC r143

Are there any moving picture questions in the theory test?

Yes, the hazard perception part of the theory test consists of a series of video clips. The training material for this is in DVD format.

5.1 — Mark **one** answer — **R-ES 1**

A driver's behaviour has upset you. It may help if you

- ⊙ stop and take a break
- ⊙ shout abusive language
- ⊙ gesture to them with your hand
- ⊙ follow their car, flashing your headlights

⊙ **stop and take a break**

Tiredness may make you more irritable than you would be normally. You might react differently to situations because of it. If you feel yourself becoming tense, take a break.

5.2 — Mark **one** answer — **R-ES 6, HC p103**

You are riding up to a zebra crossing. You intend to stop for waiting pedestrians. How could you let them know you are stopping?

- ⊙ By signalling with your left arm
- ⊙ By waving them across
- ⊙ By flashing your headlight
- ⊙ By signalling with your right arm

⊙ **By signalling with your right arm**

Giving the correct arm signal would indicate to approaching vehicles, as well as pedestrians, that you are stopping at the pedestrian crossing.

5.3 — Mark **one** answer — **R-ES 4, HC r92**

You are about to ride home. You cannot find the glasses you need to wear. You should

- ⊙ ride home slowly, keeping to quiet roads
- ⊙ borrow a friend's glasses and use those
- ⊙ ride home at night, so that the lights will help you
- ⊙ find a way of getting home without riding

⊙ **find a way of getting home without riding**

Don't be tempted to ride if you've lost or forgotten your glasses. You must be able to see clearly when riding. If you can't you will be endangering yourself and other road users.

5.4 — Mark **two** answers — **R-ES 1, HC r95-96**

You are not sure if your cough medicine will affect you. What TWO things should you do?

- ⊙ Ask your doctor
- ⊙ Check the medicine label
- ⊙ Ride if you feel alright
- ⊙ Ask a friend or relative for advice

⊙ **Ask your doctor**

⊙ **Check the medicine label**

If you're taking medicine or drugs prescribed by your doctor, check to ensure that they won't make you drowsy. If you forget to ask when you're at the surgery, check with your pharmacist.

5.5

*Mark **three** answers*

R-ES 1, HC r95-96

Which THREE of these are likely effects of drinking alcohol?

- Reduced co-ordination
- Increased confidence
- Poor judgement
- Increased concentration
- Faster reactions
- Colour blindness

⊙ **Reduced co-ordination**

⊙ **Increased confidence**

⊙ **Poor judgement**

Alcohol can increase confidence to a point where a rider's behaviour might become 'out of character'. Someone who normally behaves sensibly suddenly takes risks and could endanger themselves and others. Never drink and ride, or accept a ride from anyone who's been drinking.

5.6

*Mark **one** answer*

R-ES 4, HC r92

You find that you need glasses to read vehicle number plates at the required distance. When MUST you wear them?

- Only in bad weather conditions
- At all times when riding
- Only when you think it necessary
- Only in bad light or at night time

⊙ **At all times when riding**

Have your eyesight tested before you start your practical training. Then, throughout your riding life, have periodical checks to ensure that your eyesight hasn't deteriorated.

5.7

*Mark **three** answers*

R-ES 1, HC r95-96

Drinking any amount of alcohol is likely to

- slow down your reactions to hazards
- increase the speed of your reactions
- worsen your judgement of speed
- improve your awareness of danger
- give a false sense of confidence

⊙ **slow down your reactions to hazards**

⊙ **worsen your judgement of speed**

⊙ **give a false sense of confidence**

Never drink if you are going to ride. It's always the safest option not to drink at all. Don't take risks, it's not worth it.

5.8
*Mark **one** answer*

R-ES 4, HC r94

Which of the following types of glasses should NOT be worn when riding at night?

- ⊙ Half-moon
- ⊙ Round
- ⊙ Bi-focal
- ⊙ Tinted

⊙ **Tinted**

If you are riding at night or in poor visibility, tinted lenses or a tinted visor will reduce the amount of available light reaching your eyes, making you less able to see clearly.

5.9
*Mark **one** answer*

HC r116

For which of these may you use hazard warning lights?

- ⊙ When riding on a motorway to warn traffic behind of a hazard ahead
- ⊙ When you are double parked on a two way road
- ⊙ When your direction indicators are not working
- ⊙ When warning oncoming traffic that you intend to stop

⊙ **When riding on a motorway to warn traffic behind of a hazard ahead**

Hazard warning lights are an important safety feature. Use them when riding on a motorway to warn following traffic of danger ahead. You should also use them if your motorcycle has broken down and is causing an obstruction.

5.10
*Mark **two** answers*

R-ES 10, HC r223

Why should you be especially cautious when going past this stationary bus?

- ⊙ There is traffic approaching in the distance
- ⊙ The driver may open the door
- ⊙ It may suddenly move off
- ⊙ People may cross the road in front of it
- ⊙ There are bicycles parked on the pavement

⊙ **It may suddenly move off**

⊙ **People may cross the road in front of it**

A stationary bus at a bus stop can hide pedestrians just in front of it who might be about to cross the road. Only go past at a speed that will enable you to stop safely if you need to.

5.11

5.11   Mark *one* answer   R-ES 1, HC r84

When riding long distances at speed, noise can cause fatigue. What can you do to help reduce this?

⊙ Vary your speed

⊙ Wear ear plugs

⊙ Use an open-face helmet

⊙ Ride in an upright position

⊙ **Wear ear plugs**

Wearing ear plugs can help prevent hearing damage and also fatigue caused by noise.

5.12   Mark *one* answer   R-ES 1, HC r84

Why should you wear ear plugs when riding a motorcycle?

⊙ To help to prevent ear damage

⊙ To make you less aware of traffic

⊙ To help to keep you warm

⊙ To make your helmet fit better

⊙ **To help to prevent ear damage**

The use of ear plugs is recommended to reduce the effect of noise levels and protect your hearing.

5.13   Mark *one* answer   R-ES 8 & 9

Why should you check over your shoulder before turning right into a side road?

⊙ To make sure the side road is clear

⊙ To check for emerging traffic

⊙ To check for overtaking vehicles

⊙ To confirm your intention to turn

⊙ **To check for overtaking vehicles**

Take a last check over your shoulder before committing yourself to a manoeuvre. This is especially important when turning right, as other road users may not have seen your signal or may not understand your intentions.

5.14   Mark *one* answer   R-ES 1, HC r84

When riding how can you help to reduce the risk of hearing damage?

⊙ Wearing goggles

⊙ Using ear plugs

⊙ Wearing a scarf

⊙ Keeping the visor up

⊙ **Using ear plugs**

Using ear plugs can help prevent hearing damage and fatigue caused by noise.

5.15 — Mark **one** answer — HC r95

You are convicted of riding after drinking too much alcohol. How could this affect your insurance?

⊙ Your insurance may become invalid

⊙ The amount of excess you pay will be reduced

⊙ You will only be able to get third party cover

⊙ Cover will only be given for riding smaller motorcycles

⊙ **Your insurance may become invalid**

Riding while under the influence of drink or drugs can invalidate your insurance. This also endangers yourself and others. It's not a risk worth taking.

5.16 — Mark **one** answer — HC r95

You are going out to a social event and alcohol will be available. You will be riding your motorcycle shortly afterwards. What is the safest thing to do?

⊙ Stay just below the legal limit

⊙ Have soft drinks and alcohol in turn

⊙ Don't go beyond the legal limit

⊙ Stick to non-alcoholic drinks

⊙ **Stick to non-alcoholic drinks**

The legal limit of alcohol is 80 milligrams per 100 millilitres of blood. However, drinking even the smallest amount of alcohol can affect your judgement and reactions. The safest and best option is to avoid any alcohol at all when riding or driving.

5.17 — Mark **three** answers — R-ES 7 & 8, HC r162-167, KYTS p18

Overtaking is a major cause of collisions. In which THREE of these situations should you NOT overtake?

⊙ If you are turning left shortly afterwards

⊙ When you are in a one-way street

⊙ When you are approaching a junction

⊙ If you are travelling up a long hill

⊙ When your view ahead is blocked

⊙ **If you are turning left shortly afterwards**

⊙ **When you are approaching a junction**

⊙ **When your view ahead is blocked**

You should not overtake unless it is really necessary. Arriving safely is more important than taking risks. Also look out for road signs and markings that show it is illegal or would be unsafe to overtake. In many cases overtaking is unlikely to significantly improve journey times.

*Mark **one** answer*

When should you use hazard warning lights?

- When you are double-parked on a two-way road
- When your direction indicators are not working
- When warning oncoming traffic that you intend to stop
- When your motorcycle has broken down and is causing an obstruction

⊙ **When your motorcycle has broken down and is causing an obstruction**

Hazard warning lights are an important safety feature and should be used if you have broken down and are causing an obstruction. Don't use them as an excuse to park illegally, such as when using a cash machine or post box. You may also use them on motorways to warn following traffic of danger ahead.

*Mark **one** answer*

It is a very hot day. What would you expect to find?

- Mud on the road
- A soft road surface
- Roadworks ahead
- Banks of fog

⊙ **A soft road surface**

In very hot weather the road surface can become soft and may melt. Take care when braking and cornering on soft tarmac, as this can lead to reduced grip and cause skidding.

*Mark **one** answer*

You see this road marking in between queuing traffic. What should you look out for?

- Overhanging trees
- Roadworks
- Traffic wardens
- Traffic emerging

⊙ **Traffic emerging**

'Keep clear' markings should not be obstructed. They can be found in congested areas to help traffic waiting to emerge onto a busy road.

5.21   Mark **two** answers   **HC p117**

Where would you expect to see these markers?

⊙ On a motorway sign

⊙ At the entrance to a narrow bridge

⊙ On a large goods vehicle

⊙ On a builder's skip placed on the road

⊙ **On a large goods vehicle**

⊙ **On a builder's skip placed on the road**

These markers must be fitted to vehicles over 13 metres long, large goods vehicles, and rubbish skips placed in the road. They are reflective to make them easier to see in the dark.

5.22   Mark **one** answer   **R-ES 10, HC r211-214**

What is the main hazard shown in this picture?

⊙ Vehicles turning right

⊙ Vehicles doing U-turns

⊙ The cyclist crossing the road

⊙ Parked cars around the corner

⊙ **The cyclist crossing the road**

Look at the picture carefully and try to imagine you're there. The cyclist in this picture appears to be trying to cross the road. You must be able to deal with the unexpected, especially when you're approaching a hazardous junction. Look well ahead to give yourself time to deal with any hazards.

5.23   Mark **one** answer   **HC r220**

You are on a dual carriageway. Ahead you see a vehicle with an amber flashing light. What could this be?

⊙ An ambulance

⊙ A fire engine

⊙ A doctor on call

⊙ A disabled person's vehicle

⊙ **A disabled person's vehicle**

An amber flashing light on a vehicle indicates that it is slow-moving. Battery powered vehicles used by disabled people are limited to 8 mph. It's not advisable for them to be used on dual carriageways where the speed limit exceeds 50 mph. If they are then an amber flashing light must be used.

Which road user has caused a hazard?

- ⊙ The parked car (arrowed A)
- ⊙ The pedestrian waiting to cross (arrowed B)
- ⊙ The moving car (arrowed C)
- ⊙ The car turning (arrowed D)

⊙ **The parked car (arrowed A)**

The car arrowed A is parked within the area marked by zigzag lines at the pedestrian crossing. Parking here is illegal. It also

- blocks the view for pedestrians wishing to cross the road
- restricts the view of the crossing for approaching traffic.

What should the driver of the car approaching the crossing do?

- ⊙ Continue at the same speed
- ⊙ Sound the horn
- ⊙ Drive through quickly
- ⊙ Slow down and get ready to stop

⊙ **Slow down and get ready to stop**

Look well ahead to see if any hazards are developing. This will give you more time to deal with them in the correct way. The man in the picture is clearly intending to cross the road. You should be travelling at a speed that allows you to check your mirror, slow down and stop in good time. You shouldn't have to brake harshly.

A driver pulls out of a side road in front of you. You have to brake hard. You should

- ⊙ ignore the error and stay calm
- ⊙ flash your lights to show your annoyance
- ⊙ sound your horn to show your annoyance
- ⊙ overtake as soon as possible

⊙ **ignore the error and stay calm**

Where there are a number of side roads, be alert. Be especially careful if there are a lot of parked vehicles because they can make it more difficult for drivers emerging to see you. Try to be tolerant if a vehicle does emerge and you have to brake quickly. Don't react aggressively.

5.27   *Mark **three** answers*   **R-ES 8 & 10, HC r205-206**

What THREE things should the driver of the grey car (arrowed) be especially aware of?

- ⊙ Pedestrians stepping out between cars
- ⊙ Other cars behind the grey car
- ⊙ Doors opening on parked cars
- ⊙ The bumpy road surface
- ⊙ Cars leaving parking spaces
- ⊙ Empty parking spaces

- ⊙ **Pedestrians stepping out between cars**

- ⊙ **Doors opening on parked cars**

- ⊙ **Cars leaving parking spaces**

You need to be aware that other road users may not have seen you. Always be on the lookout for hazards that may develop suddenly and need you to take avoiding action.

5.28   *Mark **one** answer*   **R-ES 8, 9, 10, HC r154**

You see this sign ahead. You should expect the road to

- ⊙ go steeply uphill
- ⊙ go steeply downhill
- ⊙ bend sharply to the left
- ⊙ bend sharply to the right

- ⊙ **bend sharply to the left**

Adjust your speed in good time and select the correct gear for your speed. Going too fast into the bend could cause you to lose control.

Braking late and harshly while changing direction reduces your vehicle's grip on the road, and is likely to cause a skid.

5.29   *Mark **one** answer*   **HC r216**

An elderly person's driving ability could be affected because they may be unable to

- ⊙ obtain car insurance
- ⊙ understand road signs
- ⊙ react very quickly
- ⊙ give signals correctly

- ⊙ **react very quickly**

Be tolerant of older drivers. Poor eyesight and hearing could affect the speed with which they react to a hazard and may cause them to be hesitant.

*Mark **one** answer*

You are approaching this cyclist. You should

⊙ overtake before the cyclist gets to the junction

⊙ flash your headlights at the cyclist

⊙ slow down and allow the cyclist to turn

⊙ overtake the cyclist on the left-hand side

⊙ **slow down and allow the cyclist to turn**

Keep well back and allow the cyclist room to take up the correct position for the turn. Don't get too close behind or try to squeeze past.

*Mark **one** answer*

Why must you take extra care when turning right at this junction?

⊙ Road surface is poor

⊙ Footpaths are narrow

⊙ Road markings are faint

⊙ There is reduced visibility

⊙ **There is reduced visibility**

You may have to pull forward slowly until you can see up and down the road. Be aware that the traffic approaching the junction can't see you either. If you don't know that it's clear, don't go.

*Mark **one** answer*

A driver does something that upsets you. You should

⊙ try not to react

⊙ let them know how you feel

⊙ flash your headlights several times

⊙ sound your horn

⊙ **try not to react**

There are times when other road users make a misjudgement or mistake. When this happens try not to get annoyed and don't react by showing anger. Sounding your horn, flashing your headlights or shouting won't help the situation. Good anticipation will help to prevent these incidents becoming collisions.

5.33   Mark *one* answer   R-ES 10, HC r223

When approaching this bridge you should give way to

- ⊙ bicycles
- ⊙ buses
- ⊙ motorcycles
- ⊙ cars

⊙ **buses**

A double-deck bus or high-sided lorry will have to take up a position in the centre of the road so that it can clear the bridge. There is normally a sign to indicate this.

Look well down the road, through the bridge and be aware you may have to stop and give way to an oncoming large vehicle.

5.34   Mark *one* answer   R-ES 10

What type of vehicle could you expect to meet in the middle of the road?

- ⊙ Lorry
- ⊙ Bicycle
- ⊙ Car
- ⊙ Motorcycle

⊙ **Lorry**

The highest point of the bridge is in the centre so a large vehicle might have to move to the centre of the road to allow it enough room to pass under the bridge.

5.35   Mark *one* answer   R-ES 1 & 11, HC r91

You are planning a long journey. Do you need to plan rest stops?

- ⊙ Yes, you should plan to stop every half an hour
- ⊙ Yes, regular stops help concentration
- ⊙ No, you will be less tired if you get there as soon as possible
- ⊙ No, only fuel stops will be needed

⊙ **Yes, regular stops help concentration**

Try to plan your journey so that you can take rest stops. It's recommended that you take a break of at least 15 minutes after every two hours of driving. This should help to maintain your concentration.

*Mark **one** answer* **R-ES 10, HC r146 & r151**

At this blind junction you must stop

⊙ behind the line, then edge forward to see clearly

⊙ beyond the line at a point where you can see clearly

⊙ only if there is traffic on the main road

⊙ only if you are turning to the right

⊙ **behind the line, then edge forward to see clearly**

The 'stop' sign has been put here because there is a poor view into the main road. You must stop because it will not be possible to assess the situation on the move, however slowly you are travelling.

*Mark **one** answer* **R-ES 7, HC r291-299**

The red lights are flashing. What should you do when approaching this level crossing?

⊙ Go through quickly

⊙ Go through carefully

⊙ Stop before the barrier

⊙ Switch on hazard warning lights

⊙ **Stop before the barrier**

At level crossings the red lights flash before and when the barrier is down. At most crossings an amber light will precede the red lights. You must stop behind the white line unless you have already crossed it when the amber light comes on. NEVER zigzag around half-barriers.

*Mark **one** answer* **R-ES 9, HC r176**

You are approaching crossroads. The traffic lights have failed. What should you do?

⊙ Brake and stop only for large vehicles

⊙ Brake sharply to a stop before looking

⊙ Be prepared to brake sharply to a stop

⊙ Be prepared to stop for any traffic.

⊙ **Be prepared to stop for any traffic.**

When approaching a junction where the traffic lights have failed, you should proceed with caution. Treat the situation as an unmarked junction and be prepared to stop.

5.39 Mark *one* answer   R-ES 7, HC r105 & 208

You have just passed these warning lights. What hazard would you expect to see next?

⊙ A level crossing with no barrier

⊙ An ambulance station

⊙ A school crossing patrol

⊙ An opening bridge

⊙ **A school crossing patrol**

These lights warn that children may be crossing the road to a nearby school. Slow down so that you're ready to stop if necessary.

5.40 Mark *one* answer   HC r206-207

What should the driver of the red car (arrowed) do?

⊙ Wave the pedestrians who are waiting to cross

⊙ Wait for the pedestrian in the road to cross

⊙ Quickly drive behind the pedestrian in the road

⊙ Tell the pedestrian in the road she should not have crossed

⊙ **Wait for the pedestrian in the road to cross**

Some people might take longer to cross the road. They may be older or have a disability. Be patient and don't hurry them by showing your impatience. They might have poor eyesight or not be able to hear traffic approaching. If pedestrians are standing at the side of the road, don't signal or wave them to cross. Other road users may not have seen your signal and this could lead the pedestrians into a hazardous situation.

*Mark **one** answer*

What should you do as you approach this overhead bridge?

- Move out to the centre of the road before going through
- Find another route, this is only for high vehicles
- Be prepared to give way to large vehicles in the middle of the road
- Move across to the right hand side before going through

⊙ **Be prepared to give way to large vehicles in the middle of the road**

Oncoming large vehicles may need to move to the middle of the road so that they can pass safely under the bridge. There will not be enough room for you to continue and you should be ready to stop and wait.

*Mark **one** answer*

Why are mirrors often slightly curved (convex)?

- They give a wider field of vision
- They totally cover blind spots
- They make it easier to judge the speed of following traffic
- They make following traffic look bigger

⊙ **They give a wider field of vision**

Although a convex mirror gives a wide view of the scene behind, you should be aware that it will not show you everything behind or to the side of the vehicle. Before you move off you will need to check over your shoulder to look for anything not visible in the mirrors.

*Mark **one** answer*

You think the driver of the vehicle in front has forgotten to cancel their right indicator. You should

- flash your lights to alert the driver
- sound your horn before overtaking
- overtake on the left if there is room
- stay behind and not overtake

⊙ **stay behind and not overtake**

The driver may be unsure of the location of a junction and turn suddenly. Be cautious and don't attempt to overtake.

5.44   *Mark **one** answer*   **R-ES 11, HC r167, r225, r289 & p113**

You see this sign on the rear of a slow-moving lorry that you want to pass. It is travelling in the middle lane of a three-lane motorway. You should

⊙ cautiously approach the lorry then pass on either side

⊙ follow the lorry until you can leave the motorway

⊙ wait on the hard shoulder until the lorry has stopped

⊙ approach with care and keep to the left of the lorry

⊙ **approach with care and keep to the left of the lorry**

This sign is found on slow-moving or stationary works vehicles. If you wish to overtake, do so on the left, as indicated. Be aware that there might be workmen in the area.

5.45   *Mark **one** answer*   **HC r154**

You are following a slower-moving vehicle on a narrow country road. There is a junction just ahead on the right. What should you do?

⊙ Overtake after checking your mirrors and signalling

⊙ Stay behind until you are past the junction

⊙ Accelerate quickly to pass before the junction

⊙ Slow down and prepare to overtake on the left

⊙ **Stay behind until you are past the junction**

You should never overtake as you approach a junction. If a vehicle emerged from the junction while you were overtaking, a dangerous situation could develop very quickly.

What is the main hazard the driver of the red car (arrowed) should be aware of?

- ⊙ Glare from the sun may affect the driver's vision
- ⊙ The black car may stop suddenly
- ⊙ The bus may move out into the road
- ⊙ Oncoming vehicles will assume the driver is turning right

⊙ **The bus may move out into the road**

If you can do so safely give way to buses signalling to move off at bus stops. Try to anticipate the actions of other road users around you. The driver of the red car should be prepared for the bus pulling out. As you approach a bus stop look to see how many passengers are waiting to board. If the last one has just got on, the bus is likely to move off.

This yellow sign on a vehicle indicates this is

- ⊙ a broken-down vehicle
- ⊙ a school bus
- ⊙ an ice cream van
- ⊙ a private ambulance

⊙ **a school bus**

Buses which carry children to and from school may stop at places other than scheduled bus stops. Be aware that they might pull over at any time to allow children to get on or off. This will normally be when traffic is heavy during rush hour.

Why are place names painted on the road surface?

- ⊙ To restrict the flow of traffic
- ⊙ To warn you of oncoming traffic
- ⊙ To enable you to change lanes early
- ⊙ To prevent you changing lanes

⊙ **To enable you to change lanes early**

The names of towns and cities may be painted on the road at busy junctions and complex road systems. Their purpose is to let you move into the correct lane in good time, allowing traffic to flow more freely.

5.49   *Mark **two** answers*   **R-ES 8 & 10, HC r205-206**

What TWO main hazards should you be aware of when going along this street?

- ⊙ Glare from the sun
- ⊙ Car doors opening suddenly
- ⊙ Lack of road markings
- ⊙ The headlights on parked cars being switched on
- ⊙ Large goods vehicles
- ⊙ Children running out from between vehicles

⊙ **Car doors opening suddenly**

⊙ **Children running out from between vehicles**

On roads where there are many parked vehicles you should take extra care. You might not be able to see children between parked cars and they may run out into the road without looking.

People may open car doors without realising the hazard this can create. You will also need to look well down the road for oncoming traffic.

5.50   *Mark **one** answer*   **R-ES 10, HC r211-214**

What is the main hazard you should be aware of when following this cyclist?

- ⊙ The cyclist may move to the left and dismount
- ⊙ The cyclist may swerve out into the road
- ⊙ The contents of the cyclist's carrier may fall onto the road
- ⊙ The cyclist may wish to turn right at the end of the road

⊙ **The cyclist may swerve out into the road**

When following a cyclist be aware that they have to deal with the hazards around them. They may wobble or swerve to avoid a pothole in the road or see a potential hazard and change direction suddenly. Don't follow them too closely or rev your engine impatiently.

5.51 — Mark *two* answers — R-ES 4

You get cold and wet when riding. Which TWO are likely to happen?

- You may lose concentration
- You may slide off the seat
- Your visor may freeze up
- Your reaction times may be slower
- Your helmet may loosen

⊙ **You may lose concentration**

⊙ **Your reaction times may be slower**

When you're riding a motorcycle make sure you're wearing suitable clothing. If you become cold and uncomfortable this could cause you to lose concentration and could slow down your reaction time.

5.52 — Mark *one* answer — R-ES 8, 9, 10, HC r153

In areas where there are 'traffic calming' measures you should

- travel at a reduced speed
- always travel at the speed limit
- position in the centre of the road
- only slow down if pedestrians are near

⊙ **travel at a reduced speed**

Traffic calming measures such as road humps, chicanes and narrowings are intended to slow you down. Maintain a reduced speed until you reach the end of these features. They are there to protect pedestrians. Kill your speed!

5.53 — Mark *two* answers — R-ES 10, HC r291-299 & p108-9

When approaching this hazard why should you slow down?

- Because of the bend
- Because it's hard to see to the right
- Because of approaching traffic
- Because of animals crossing
- Because of the level crossing

⊙ **Because of the bend**

⊙ **Because of the level crossing**

There are two hazards clearly signed in this picture. You should be preparing for the bend by slowing down and selecting the correct gear. You might also have to stop at the level crossing, so be alert and be prepared to stop if necessary.

5.54 *Mark **one** answer* **HC p104**

What does this signal from a police officer mean to oncoming traffic?

- ⊙ Go ahead
- ⊙ Stop
- ⊙ Turn left
- ⊙ Turn right

⊙ **Stop**

Police officers may need to direct traffic, for example, at a junction where the traffic lights have broken down. Check your copy of The Highway Code for the signals that they use.

5.55 *Mark **one** answer* **HC r135**

Some two-way roads are divided into three lanes. Why are these particularly dangerous?

- ⊙ Traffic in both directions can use the middle lane to overtake
- ⊙ Traffic can travel faster in poor weather conditions
- ⊙ Traffic can overtake on the left
- ⊙ Traffic uses the middle lane for emergencies only

⊙ **Traffic in both directions can use the middle lane to overtake**

If you intend to overtake you must consider that approaching traffic could be planning the same manoeuvre. When you have considered the situation and have decided it is safe, indicate your intentions early. This will show the approaching traffic that you intend to pull out.

5.56 *Mark **three** answers* **HC r95**

Which THREE result from drinking alcohol?

- ⊙ Less control
- ⊙ A false sense of confidence
- ⊙ Faster reactions
- ⊙ Poor judgement of speed
- ⊙ Greater awareness of danger

⊙ **Less control**

⊙ **A false sense of confidence**

⊙ **Poor judgement of speed**

You must understand the serious dangers of mixing alcohol with driving or riding. Alcohol will severely reduce your ability to drive or ride safely. Just one drink could put you over the limit. Don't risk people's lives – DON'T DRINK AND DRIVE OR RIDE!

Case study practice 5 – Hazard awareness

You have had new mirrors fitted to your motorcycle. They are slightly curved and give a wider field of vision. You are travelling to a local pub to see some friends and stay for several hours. At the end of the evening, you ride home. The weather has changed and it is raining steadily. There is a skip parked on the road ahead, showing parking lights and hazard warning plates.

5.1 What word describes these slightly curved mirrors?

*Mark **one** answer*

- ⊙ Convenient.
- ⊙ Concourse.
- ⊙ Convex.
- ⊙ Concentric.

R-ES 5

5.2 What is the safest thing to do, during your stay at the pub?

*Mark **one** answer*

- ⊙ Only drink pints of shandy.
- ⊙ Alternate soft drinks with alcohol.
- ⊙ Drink shorts with lots of water.
- ⊙ Stick to soft drinks the whole time.

R-ES 1, HC r95

5.3 How could the conditions affect your visibility during your journey home?

*Mark **one** answer*

⊙ By making you less visible to others.

⊙ By making it easier for you to see others.

⊙ By making the street lights seem brighter.

⊙ By making other road users take care.

R-ES 10, HC r227

5.4 What colour hazard warning plates would you see on skips and long vehicles?

*Mark **one** answer*

⊙ Red and yellow.

⊙ Blue and yellow.

⊙ Green and yellow.

⊙ White and yellow.

HC p117

5.5 In this weather, how much time should you leave between your vehicle and the one in front?

*Mark **one** answer*

⊙ Two seconds.

⊙ Three seconds.

⊙ Four seconds.

⊙ Five seconds.

R-ES 11, HC r227

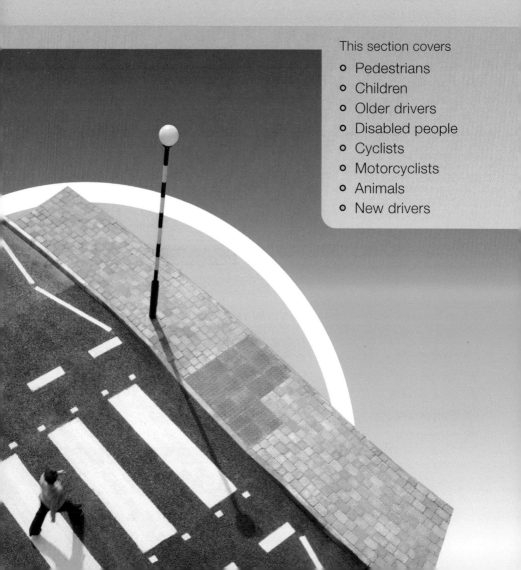

section **six**
VULNERABLE ROAD USERS

This section covers
- Pedestrians
- Children
- Older drivers
- Disabled people
- Cyclists
- Motorcyclists
- Animals
- New drivers

Vulnerable road users

The most vulnerable road users are cyclists, pedestrians, motorcyclists and horse riders. Always be aware of their presence and treat them with respect. It's particularly important to show consideration to children, elderly and disabled people.

The most vulnerable types of driver are those who are still learning, inexperienced or older. Keep calm and be patient around them.

Pedestrians

Pedestrians normally use a pavement or footpath. Take extra care if they have to walk in the road when the pavement is closed due to street repairs or on country roads where there's no pavement. Always check for road signs which might indicate that people may be walking in the road.

R-ES 10, HC r2 & r206

On country roads, pedestrians are advised to walk on the right-hand side of the road so they are facing oncoming traffic. Signs may warn you of people walking in the road. A large group of people, such as those on an organised walk, may walk on the left-hand side. At night the person at the rear should carry a bright red light to warn approaching vehicles of their presence.

HC r5, KYTS p13

Watch out for pedestrians already crossing when you're turning into a side road. They have priority, so wait for them to cross.

R-ES 9, HC r170

Be ready to slow down and stop as you approach a pedestrian crossing.

- Zebra crossings – slow down and prepare to stop if someone is waiting to cross.
- Pelican crossings are light-controlled. During the flashing amber phase, give way to pedestrians on the crossing. If the lights change to green while someone is still crossing, be patient and wait until they have finished crossing.
- Puffin crossings have sensors to detect when people are on the crossing. The lights don't change from red until the crossing is clear.
- Toucan crossings – cyclists can cross at the same time as pedestrians. There's no flashing amber phase.

Remember also that you should never park on or near a pedestrian crossing; for example, on the zigzag lines either side of a zebra crossing.

R-ES 8, HC r195-199

Children

Children cause particular problems because they can be unpredictable. They are less likely than other pedestrians to look before stepping into the road. Ride carefully near schools.

- There may be flashing amber lights under a school warning sign. Reduce your speed until you're clear of the area.

- Be prepared for a school crossing patrol to stop the traffic by stepping out into the road with a stop sign.

R-ES 10, HC r208-210

Don't wait or park on yellow zigzag lines outside a school. A clear view of the crossing area outside the school is needed by

- drivers on the road
- pedestrians on the pavement.

R-ES 7, HC r208 & r238, KYTS p56

Buses and coaches carrying schoolchildren show a special sign in the back. This indicates that they may stop frequently and not just at normal bus stops.

R-ES 10, HC r207

Elderly and disabled pedestrians

If you see elderly people about to cross the road ahead, be careful, as they may have misjudged your speed.

If they are crossing, be patient and allow them to cross in their own time. Treat disabled pedestrians as you would able-bodied, but be patient as they may need extra time to cross the road.

A pedestrian with hearing difficulties may have a dog with a

- distinctive yellow or burgundy-coloured coat or

- distinctive orange lead and collar.

Take extra care as they may not be aware of vehicles approaching.

A person carrying a white stick with a red band is both deaf and blind. They may also be accompanied by a guide dog with a red and white checked harness.

R-ES 10, HC r207

Cyclists

Cyclists should normally follow the same rules as drivers and riders, but they are slower and more vulnerable. In some areas signs may indicate special cycle or shared cycle and pedestrian routes.

Advanced stop lines are provided to allow cyclists to position themselves in front of other traffic. When the lights are red or about to become red you should stop at the first white line. If you're overtaking a cyclist, give them as much room as you would a car. They may need to swerve

- to avoid an uneven road surface
- if they're affected by the wind.

R-ES 8 &10, HC r107, KYTS p35-36

A cyclist going slowly, or glancing over their shoulder to check for traffic, may be planning to turn right. Stay behind and give them plenty of room. Never overtake a cyclist (or moped) just before you turn left. Hold back and wait until they have passed the junction before you turn.

When you're emerging from a junction, look carefully for cyclists. They're not as easy to see as larger vehicles. Also look out for cyclists emerging from junctions.

R-ES 9, HC r77 & r187

Be aware of cyclists at a roundabout. They are slower and more vulnerable than other road users, and may decide to stay in the left-hand lane whatever direction they're planning to take. Hold back and allow plenty of room.

Other motorcyclists

When you're moving in queues of traffic, be aware that other motorcyclists may also

- filter between lanes
- cut in just in front of you
- pass very close to you.

Before you turn right, always check for other traffic, especially motorcyclists, who may be overtaking. Always use the 'lifesaver' look before making your manoeuvre.

If there's a slow-moving motorcyclist ahead and you're unsure what the rider is going to do, stay behind them in case they need to change direction suddenly.

R-ES 9, HC r180

Animals

Always ride carefully if there are horses or other animals on the road. Stay well back and don't rev your engine or sound your horn near horses as this may startle them. Go very slowly

and be ready to stop. When it's safe to overtake, drive slowly and leave plenty of room.

Take particular care when approaching a roundabout. Horse riders, like cyclists, may keep to the left, even if they're signalling right.

R-ES 9 & 10, HC r187 & r214-215

Other drivers

The reactions of other drivers, especially inexperienced or older drivers, may be slower than yours. Learner drivers may make a mistake such as stalling at a junction. Try to be patient and be ready to slow down or stop if necessary.

In fast-flowing traffic, if you find another vehicle is following you too closely, slow down gradually to increase the distance in front.

R-ES 1, HC r216-217

Statistics show that 17- to 25-year-olds are the most likely to be involved in a road traffic incident. Overconfidence and lack of experience and judgement are the main causes of incidents for young and new drivers and motorcyclists.

Newly qualified riders can decrease their risk of road traffic incidents, particularly on the motorway, by taking further training; for example, under the Enhanced Rider Scheme (ERS).

R-ES 11, HC p134

FAQs

What should I do if parked vehicles restrict my view when emerging from a junction?

Stop, then creep forward slowly until you've a clear view.

R-ES 10

How can I tell if someone is going to cross the road between parked cars?

You can't, but look for tell-tale signs such as a ball bouncing out into the road or a bicycle wheel sticking out between cars. Slow down and be prepared to stop.

R-ES 10, HC r205

Who is most vulnerable at road junctions?

Junctions are dangerous places, especially for those who can't be seen as easily, eg pedestrians, cyclists and other motorcyclists. Always take extra care.

R-ES 10, HC r170 & r211

What does a flashing amber beacon on the top of a vehicle mean?

This indicates a slow-moving vehicle. A powered vehicle used by a disabled person must have a flashing amber light when travelling on a dual carriageway. Take care when overtaking.

HC r225

Why do I need to be careful if a bus has stopped on the other side of the road?

Pedestrians may come from behind the bus and cross the road, or dash across from your left.

R-ES 10, HC r223

If I have a collision, what's the first thing I have to do?

Stop. By law, you must stop at the scene of the incident if damage or injury is caused to any other person, vehicle, animal or property.

R-ES 16, HC r286

6.1

*Mark **one** answer*

R-ES 9, HC r221

You should not ride too closely behind a lorry because

- ⊙ you will breathe in the lorry's exhaust fumes
- ⊙ wind from the lorry will slow you down
- ⊙ drivers behind you may not be able to see you
- ⊙ it will reduce your view ahead

⊙ **it will reduce your view ahead**

If you're following too close behind a large vehicle your view beyond it will be restricted. Drop back. This will help you to see more of the road ahead. It will also help the driver of the large vehicle to see you in the mirror and gives you a safe separation distance in which to take avoiding action if a hazardous situation arises.

6.2

*Mark **three** answers*

R-ES 10, HC r58

You are riding on a country lane. You see cattle on the road. You should

- ⊙ slow down
- ⊙ stop if necessary
- ⊙ give plenty of room
- ⊙ rev your engine
- ⊙ sound your horn
- ⊙ ride up close behind them

⊙ **slow down**

⊙ **stop if necessary**

⊙ **give plenty of room**

Try not to startle the animals. They can be easily frightened by noise or by traffic passing too closely.

6.3

*Mark **one** answer*

R-ES 9

A learner driver has begun to emerge into your path from a side road on the left. You should

- ⊙ be ready to slow down and stop
- ⊙ let them emerge then ride close behind
- ⊙ turn into the side road
- ⊙ brake hard, then wave them out

⊙ **be ready to slow down and stop**

If you see another vehicle begin to emerge into your path you should ride defensively. Always be ready to slow down or stop if necessary.

6.4

R-ES 1 & 10, HC r204 & r207

The vehicle ahead is being driven by a learner. You should

- ⊙ keep calm and be patient
- ⊙ ride up close behind
- ⊙ put your headlight on full beam
- ⊙ sound your horn and overtake

⊙ **keep calm and be patient**

Learners might take longer to react to traffic situations. Don't unnerve them by riding up close behind or showing signs of impatience.

6.5

R-ES 10, HC r126

You are riding in fast-flowing traffic. The vehicle behind is following too closely. You should·

- ⊙ slow down gradually to increase the gap in front of you
- ⊙ slow down as quickly as possible by braking
- ⊙ accelerate to get away from the vehicle behind you
- ⊙ apply the brakes sharply to warn the driver behind

⊙ **slow down gradually to increase the gap in front of you**

It is dangerous for vehicles to travel too close together. Visibility is reduced and there is a higher risk of collision if a vehicle brakes suddenly to avoid a hazard. By increasing the separation distance between you and the vehicle in front, you have a greater safety margin. It also gives space for the vehicles behind to overtake you if they wish.

6.6

R-ES 8, HC r195

You are riding towards a zebra crossing. Waiting to cross is a person in a wheelchair. You should

- ⊙ continue on your way
- ⊙ wave to the person to cross
- ⊙ wave to the person to wait
- ⊙ be prepared to stop

⊙ **be prepared to stop**

As you would with an able-bodied person, you should prepare to slow down and stop. Don't wave them across, as other traffic may not stop.

6.7

*Mark **one** answer*

R-ES 11 & 12, HC r233

Why should you allow extra room when overtaking another motorcyclist on a windy day?

⊙ The rider may turn off suddenly to get out of the wind

⊙ The rider may be blown across in front of you

⊙ The rider may stop suddenly

⊙ The rider may be travelling faster than normal

⊙ **The rider may be blown across in front of you**

On a windy day, be aware that the blustery conditions might blow you or other motorcyclists out of position. Think about this before deciding to overtake.

6.8

*Mark **two** answers*

R-ES 8, HC r196-198

You have stopped at a pelican crossing. A disabled person is crossing slowly in front of you. The lights have now changed to green. You should

⊙ allow the person to cross

⊙ ride in front of the person

⊙ ride behind the person

⊙ sound your horn

⊙ be patient

⊙ edge forward slowly

⊙ **allow the person to cross**

⊙ **be patient**

At a pelican crossing the green light means you may proceed as long as the crossing is clear. If someone hasn't finished crossing, be patient and wait for them.

6.9

*Mark **one** answer*

R-ES 9, HC r170

Where should you take particular care to look out for other motorcyclists and cyclists?

⊙ On dual carriageways

⊙ At junctions

⊙ At zebra crossings

⊙ On one-way streets

⊙ **At junctions**

Other motorcyclists and cyclists may be difficult to see on the road, particularly at junctions. If your view is blocked by other traffic you may not be able to see them approaching.

Why is it vital for a rider to make a 'lifesaver' check before turning right?

- ⊙ To check for any overtaking traffic
- ⊙ To confirm that they are about to turn
- ⊙ To make sure the side road is clear
- ⊙ To check that the rear indicator is flashing

⊙ **To check for any overtaking traffic**

The 'lifesaver' glance makes you aware of what is happening behind and alongside you before altering your course. This glance must be timed so that you still have time to react if it isn't safe to carry out your manoeuvre.

You are about to overtake horse riders. Which TWO of the following could scare the horses?

- ⊙ Sounding your horn
- ⊙ Giving arm signals
- ⊙ Riding slowly
- ⊙ Revving your engine

⊙ **Sounding your horn**

⊙ **Revving your engine**

When passing horses allow them plenty of space and slow down. Animals can be frightened by sudden or loud noises, so don't sound your horn or rev the engine.

What is a main cause of road traffic incidents among young and new motorcyclists?

- ⊙ Using borrowed equipment
- ⊙ Lack of experience and judgement
- ⊙ Riding in bad weather conditions
- ⊙ Riding on country roads

⊙ **Lack of experience and judgement**

Young and inexperienced motorcyclists are far more likely to be involved in incidents than more experienced riders. Reasons for this include natural exuberance, showing off, competitive behaviour and over confidence. Don't overestimate your abilities and never ride too fast for the conditions.

6.13 — *Mark **one** answer* — R-ES 1

Which of the following is applicable to young motorcyclists?

- ⊙ They are normally better than experienced riders
- ⊙ They are usually less likely to have a crash
- ⊙ They are often over-confident of their own ability
- ⊙ They are more likely to get cheaper insurance

- ⊙ **They are often over-confident of their own ability**

Young and inexperienced motorcyclists often have more confidence than ability. It takes time to gain experience and become a good rider. Make sure you have the right attitude and put safety first.

6.14 — *Mark **one** answer* — HC r 208 & p116, KYTS p56

The road outside this school is marked with yellow zigzag lines. What do these lines mean?

- ⊙ You may park on the lines when dropping off school children
- ⊙ You may park on the lines when picking up school children
- ⊙ You should not wait or park your motorcycle here
- ⊙ You must stay with your motorcycle if you park here

- ⊙ **You should not wait or park your motorcycle here**

Parking here will block the view of the school gates, endangering the lives of children on their way to and from school.

Which sign means that there may be people walking along the road?

Always check the road signs. Triangular signs are warning signs and they'll keep you informed of hazards ahead and help you to anticipate any problems. There are a number of different signs showing pedestrians. Learn the meaning of each one.

You are turning left at a junction. Pedestrians have started to cross the road. You should

- go on, giving them plenty of room
- stop and wave at them to cross
- blow your horn and proceed
- give way to them

⊙ **give way to them**

If you're turning into a side road, pedestrians already crossing the road have priority and you should give way to them. Don't wave them across the road, sound your horn, flash your lights or give any other misleading signal. Other road users may misinterpret your signal and this may lead the pedestrians into a dangerous situation. If a pedestrian is slow or indecisive be patient and wait. Don't hurry them across by revving your engine.

Which THREE should you do when passing sheep on a road?

- Allow plenty of room
- Go very slowly
- Pass quickly but quietly
- Be ready to stop
- Briefly sound your horn

⊙ **Allow plenty of room**

⊙ **Go very slowly**

⊙ **Be ready to stop**

Slow down and be ready to stop if you see animals in the road ahead. Animals are easily frightened by noise and vehicles passing too close to them. Stop if signalled to do so by the person in charge.

6.18

Mark **one** answer

R-ES 9, HC r170

You are turning left from a main road into a side road. People are already crossing the road into which you are turning. You should

- ⊙ continue, as it is your right of way
- ⊙ signal to them to continue crossing
- ⊙ wait and allow them to cross
- ⊙ sound your horn to warn them of your presence

⊙ **wait and allow them to cross**

Always check the road into which you are turning. Approaching at the correct speed will allow you enough time to observe and react.

Give way to any pedestrians already crossing the road.

6.19

Mark **one** answer

R-ES 9, HC r170

You are at a road junction, turning into a minor road. There are pedestrians crossing the minor road. You should

- ⊙ stop and wave the pedestrians across
- ⊙ sound your horn to let the pedestrians know that you are there
- ⊙ give way to the pedestrians who are already crossing
- ⊙ carry on; the pedestrians should give way to you

⊙ **give way to the pedestrians who are already crossing**

Always look into the road into which you are turning. If there are pedestrians crossing, give way to them, but don't wave or signal to them to cross. Signal your intention to turn as you approach.

*Mark **one** answer*

You are turning left into a side road. What hazards should you be especially aware of?

- ⊙ One way street
- ⊙ Pedestrians
- ⊙ Traffic congestion
- ⊙ Parked vehicles

⊙ **Pedestrians**

Make sure that you have reduced your speed and are in the correct gear for the turn. Look into the road before you turn and always give way to any pedestrians who are crossing.

*Mark **one** answer*

You intend to turn right into a side road. Just before turning you should check for motorcyclists who might be

- ⊙ overtaking on your left
- ⊙ following you closely
- ⊙ emerging from the side road
- ⊙ overtaking on your right

⊙ **overtaking on your right**

Never attempt to change direction to the right without first checking your right-hand mirror. A motorcyclist might not have seen your signal and could be hidden by the car behind you. This action should become a matter of routine.

*Mark **one** answer*

A toucan crossing is different from other crossings because

- ⊙ moped riders can use it
- ⊙ it is controlled by a traffic warden
- ⊙ it is controlled by two flashing lights
- ⊙ cyclists can use it

⊙ **cyclists can use it**

Toucan crossings are shared by pedestrians and cyclists and they are shown the green light together. Cyclists are permitted to cycle across.

The signals are push-button operated and there is no flashing amber phase.

6.23   *Mark one answer*   **R-ES 10, HC r208-210**

How will a school crossing patrol signal you to stop?

⊙ By pointing to children on the opposite pavement

⊙ By displaying a red light

⊙ By displaying a stop sign

⊙ By giving you an arm signal

⊙ **By displaying a stop sign**

If a school crossing patrol steps out into the road with a stop sign you must stop. Don't wave anyone across the road and don't get impatient or rev your engine.

6.24   *Mark one answer*   **HC r209 & p117**

Where would you see this sign?

⊙ In the window of a car taking children to school

⊙ At the side of the road

⊙ At playground areas

⊙ On the rear of a school bus or coach

⊙ **On the rear of a school bus or coach**

Vehicles that are used to carry children to and from school will be travelling at busy times of the day. If you're following a vehicle with this sign be prepared for it to make frequent stops. It might pick up or set down passengers in places other than normal bus stops.

6.25   *Mark one answer*   **HC p109, KYTS p13**

Which sign tells you that pedestrians may be walking in the road as there is no pavement?

    ⊙

⊙   ⊙

⊙

Give pedestrians who are walking at the side of the road plenty of room when you pass them. They may turn around when they hear your engine and unintentionally step into the path of your vehicle.

What does this sign mean?

⊙ No route for pedestrians and cyclists

⊙ A route for pedestrians only

⊙ A route for cyclists only

⊙ A route for pedestrians and cyclists

⊙ **A route for pedestrians and cyclists**

This sign shows a shared route for pedestrians and cyclists: when it ends, the cyclists will be rejoining the main road.

You see a pedestrian with a white stick and red band. This means that the person is

⊙ physically disabled

⊙ deaf only

⊙ blind only

⊙ deaf and blind

⊙ **deaf and blind**

If someone is deaf as well as blind, they may be carrying a white stick with a red reflective band. You can't see if a pedestrian is deaf. Don't assume everyone can hear you approaching.

What action would you take when elderly people are crossing the road?

⊙ Wave them across so they know that you have seen them

⊙ Be patient and allow them to cross in their own time

⊙ Rev the engine to let them know that you are waiting

⊙ Tap the horn in case they are hard of hearing

⊙ **Be patient and allow them to cross in their own time**

Be aware that older people might take a long time to cross the road. They might also be hard of hearing and not hear you approaching. Don't hurry older people across the road by getting too close to them or revving your engine.

6.29   *Mark one answer*   **R-ES 10, HC r207**

You see two elderly pedestrians about to cross the road ahead. You should

⊙ expect them to wait for you to pass

⊙ speed up to get past them quickly

⊙ stop and wave them across the road

⊙ be careful, they may misjudge your speed

⊙ **be careful, they may misjudge your speed**

Older people may have impaired hearing, vision, concentration and judgement. They may also walk slowly and so could take a long time to cross the road.

6.30   *Mark one answer*   **HC r187**

You are coming up to a roundabout. A cyclist is signalling to turn right. What should you do?

⊙ Overtake on the right

⊙ Give a horn warning

⊙ Signal the cyclist to move across

⊙ Give the cyclist plenty of room

⊙ **Give the cyclist plenty of room**

If you're following a cyclist who's signalling to turn right at a roundabout leave plenty of room. Give them space and time to get into the correct lane.

6.31   *Mark two answers*   **HC r213**

Which TWO should you allow extra room when overtaking?

⊙ Motorcycles

⊙ Tractors

⊙ Bicycles

⊙ Road-sweeping vehicles

⊙ **Motorcycles**

⊙ **Bicycles**

Don't pass riders too closely as this may cause them to lose balance. Always leave as much room as you would for a car, and don't cut in.

6.32   *Mark **one** answer*   R-ES 9, HC r211-212

Why should you look particularly for motorcyclists and cyclists at junctions?

- ⊙ They may want to turn into the side road
- ⊙ They may slow down to let you turn
- ⊙ They are harder to see
- ⊙ They might not see you turn

⊙ **They are harder to see**

Cyclists and motorcyclists are smaller than other vehicles and so are more difficult to see. They can easily become hidden from your view by cars parked near a junction.

6.33   *Mark **one** answer*   R-ES 9, HC r211

You are waiting to come out of a side road. Why should you watch carefully for motorcycles?

- ⊙ Motorcycles are usually faster than cars
- ⊙ Police patrols often use motorcycles
- ⊙ Motorcycles are small and hard to see
- ⊙ Motorcycles have right of way

⊙ **Motorcycles are small and hard to see**

If you're waiting to emerge from a side road watch out for motorcycles: they're small and can be difficult to see. Be especially careful if there are parked vehicles restricting your view, there might be a motorcycle approaching.

IF YOU DON'T KNOW, DON'T GO.

6.34   *Mark **one** answer*   R-ES 9, HC r86-87

In daylight, an approaching motorcyclist is using a dipped headlight. Why?

- ⊙ So that the rider can be seen more easily
- ⊙ To stop the battery overcharging
- ⊙ To improve the rider's vision
- ⊙ The rider is inviting you to proceed

⊙ **So that the rider can be seen more easily**

A motorcycle can be lost from sight behind another vehicle. The use of the headlight helps to make it more conspicuous and therefore more easily seen.

6.35 *Mark one answer* R-ES 1 & 10, HC r86-87

Motorcyclists should wear bright clothing mainly because

⊙ they must do so by law

⊙ it helps keep them cool in summer

⊙ the colours are popular

⊙ drivers often do not see them

⊙ **drivers often do not see them**

Motorcycles are small vehicles and can be difficult to see. If the rider wears bright clothing it can make it easier for other road users to see them approaching, especially at junctions.

6.36 *Mark one answer* R-ES 10, HC r180

There is a slow-moving motorcyclist ahead of you. You are unsure what the rider is going to do. You should

⊙ pass on the left

⊙ pass on the right

⊙ stay behind

⊙ move closer

⊙ **stay behind**

If a motorcyclist is travelling slowly it may be that they are looking for a turning or entrance. Be patient and stay behind them in case they need to make a sudden change of direction.

6.37 *Mark one answer* R-ES 9 & 10, HC r212

Motorcyclists will often look round over their right shoulder just before turning right. This is because

⊙ they need to listen for following traffic

⊙ motorcycles do not have mirrors

⊙ looking around helps them balance as they turn

⊙ they need to check for traffic in their blind area

⊙ **they need to check for traffic in their blind area**

If you see a motorcyclist take a quick glance over their shoulder, this could mean they are about to change direction. Recognising a clue like this helps you to be prepared and take appropriate action, making you safer on the road.

*Mark **three** answers*

At road junctions which of the following are most vulnerable?

- ☉ Cyclists
- ☉ Motorcyclists
- ☉ Pedestrians
- ☉ Car drivers
- ☉ Lorry drivers

☉ **Cyclists**

☉ **Motorcyclists**

☉ **Pedestrians**

Pedestrians and riders on two wheels can be harder to see than other road users. Make sure you keep a look-out for them, especially at junctions. Good effective observation, coupled with appropriate action, can save lives.

---

*Mark **one** answer*

Motorcyclists are particularly vulnerable

- ☉ when moving off
- ☉ on dual carriageways
- ☉ when approaching junctions
- ☉ on motorways

☉ **when approaching junctions**

Another road user failing to see a motorcyclist is a major cause of collisions at junctions. Wherever streams of traffic join or cross there's the potential for this type of incident to occur.

---

*Mark **two** answers*

You are approaching a roundabout. There are horses just ahead of you. You should

- ☉ be prepared to stop
- ☉ treat them like any other vehicle
- ☉ give them plenty of room
- ☉ accelerate past as quickly as possible
- ☉ sound your horn as a warning

☉ **be prepared to stop**

☉ **give them plenty of room**

Horse riders often keep to the outside of the roundabout even if they are turning right. Give them plenty of room and remember that they may have to cross lanes of traffic.

6.41   Mark **one** answer   R-ES 8 & 10

As you approach a pelican crossing the lights change to green. Elderly people are halfway across. You should

⊙ wave them to cross as quickly as they can

⊙ rev your engine to make them hurry

⊙ flash your lights in case they have not heard you

⊙ wait because they will take longer to cross

⊙ **wait because they will take longer to cross**

Even if the lights turn to green, wait for them to clear the crossing. Allow them to cross the road in their own time, and don't try to hurry them by revving your engine.

6.42   Mark **one** answer   R-ES 8 & 10, HC r208 & 210

There are flashing amber lights under a school warning sign. What action should you take?

⊙ Reduce speed until you are clear of the area

⊙ Keep up your speed and sound the horn

⊙ Increase your speed to clear the area quickly

⊙ Wait at the lights until they change to green

⊙ **Reduce speed until you are clear of the area**

The flashing amber lights are switched on to warn you that children may be crossing near a school. Slow down and take extra care as you may have to stop.

6.43   Mark **one** answer   R-ES 7, HC r208 & 238, KYTS p56

These road markings must be kept clear to allow

Ⓦ-SCHOOL KEEP CLEAR-Ⓦ

⊙ school children to be dropped off

⊙ for teachers to park

⊙ school children to be picked up

⊙ a clear view of the crossing area

⊙ **a clear view of the crossing area**

The markings are there to show that the area must be kept clear to allow an unrestricted view for

• approaching drivers and riders

• children wanting to cross the road.

*Mark **one** answer*

Where would you see this sign?

- ⊙ Near a school crossing
- ⊙ At a playground entrance
- ⊙ On a school bus
- ⊙ At a 'pedestrians only' area

⊙ **On a school bus**

Watch out for children crossing the road from the other side of the bus.

---

*Mark **one** answer*

You are following two cyclists. They approach a roundabout in the left-hand lane. In which direction should you expect the cyclists to go?

- ⊙ Left
- ⊙ Right
- ⊙ Any direction
- ⊙ Straight ahead

⊙ **Any direction**

Cyclists approaching a roundabout in the left-hand lane may be turning right but may not have been able to get into the correct lane due to the heavy traffic. They may also feel safer keeping to the left all the way round the roundabout. Be aware of them and give them plenty of room.

---

*Mark **one** answer*

You are travelling behind a moped. You want to turn left just ahead. You should

- ⊙ overtake the moped before the junction
- ⊙ pull alongside the moped and stay level until just before the junction
- ⊙ sound your horn as a warning and pull in front of the moped
- ⊙ stay behind until the moped has passed the junction

⊙ **stay behind until the moped has passed the junction**

Passing the moped and turning into the junction could mean that you cut across the front of the rider. This might force them to slow down, stop or even lose control. Slow down and stay behind the moped until it has passed the junction and you can then turn safely.

6.47   Mark **one** answer   **R-ES 8 & 10 HC r76 & 187**

You see a horse rider as you approach a roundabout. They are signalling right but keeping well to the left. You should

- ⊙ proceed as normal
- ⊙ keep close to them
- ⊙ cut in front of them
- ⊙ stay well back

⊙ **stay well back**

Allow the horse rider to enter and exit the roundabout in their own time. They may feel safer keeping to the left all the way around the roundabout. Don't get up close behind or alongside them. This is very likely to upset the horse and create a dangerous situation.

6.48   Mark **one** answer   **R-ES 1 & 10, HC r216-217**

How would you react to drivers who appear to be inexperienced?

- ⊙ Sound your horn to warn them of your presence
- ⊙ Be patient and prepare for them to react more slowly
- ⊙ Flash your headlights to indicate that it is safe for them to proceed
- ⊙ Overtake them as soon as possible

⊙ **Be patient and prepare for them to react more slowly**

Learners might not have confidence when they first start to drive. Allow them plenty of room and don't react adversely to their hesitation. We all learn from experience, but new drivers will have had less practice in dealing with all the situations that might occur.

6.49   Mark **one** answer   **HC r5, KYTS p13**

At night you see a pedestrian wearing reflective clothing and carrying a bright red light. What does this mean?

- ⊙ You are approaching roadworks
- ⊙ You are approaching an organised walk
- ⊙ You are approaching a slow-moving vehicle
- ⊙ You are approaching a traffic danger spot

⊙ **You are approaching an organised walk**

The people on the walk should be keeping to the left, but don't assume this. Pass slowly, make sure you have time to do so safely. Be aware that the pedestrians have their backs to you and may not know that you're there.

6.50 *Mark one answer*   R-ES 1, HC r216-217

You are following a learner driver who stalls at a junction. You should

- be patient as you expect them to make mistakes
- stay very close behind and flash your headlights
- start to rev your engine if they take too long to restart
- immediately steer around them and drive on

⊙ **be patient as you expect them to make mistakes**

Learning is a process of practice and experience. Try to understand this and tolerate those who are at the beginning of this process.

6.51 *Mark one answer*   HC r5 & r154, KYTS p13

You are on a country road. What should you expect to see coming towards you on YOUR side of the road?

- Motorcycles
- Bicycles
- Pedestrians
- Horse riders

⊙ **Pedestrians**

On a quiet country road always be aware that there may be a hazard just around the next bend, such as a slow-moving vehicle or pedestrians. Pedestrians are advised to walk on the right-hand side of the road if there is no pavement, so they may be walking towards you on your side of the road.

6.52 *Mark one answer*   R-ES 8 & 10, HC r170

You are turning left into a side road. Pedestrians are crossing the road near the junction. You must

- wave them on
- sound your horn
- switch on your hazard lights
- wait for them to cross

⊙ **wait for them to cross**

Check that it's clear before you turn into a junction. If there are pedestrians crossing they have priority, so let them cross in their own time.

6.53   *Mark **one** answer*   R-ES 1, HC r216-217

You are following a car driven by an elderly driver. You should

⊙ expect the driver to drive badly

⊙ flash your lights and overtake

⊙ be aware that the driver's reactions may not be as fast as yours

⊙ stay very close behind but be careful

⊙ **be aware that the driver's reactions may not be as fast as yours**

You must show consideration to other road users. The reactions of older drivers may be slower and they might need more time to deal with a situation. Be tolerant and don't lose patience or show your annoyance.

6.54   *Mark **one** answer*   R-ES 9 & 10, HC r72 & 187

You are following a cyclist. You wish to turn left just ahead. You should

⊙ overtake the cyclist before the junction

⊙ pull alongside the cyclist and stay level until after the junction

⊙ hold back until the cyclist has passed the junction

⊙ go around the cyclist on the junction

⊙ **hold back until the cyclist has passed the junction**

Make allowances for cyclists. Allow them plenty of room. Don't try to overtake and then immediately turn left. Be patient and stay behind them until they have passed the junction.

6.55   *Mark **one** answer*   HC r76 & 187

A horse rider is in the left-hand lane approaching a roundabout. You should expect the rider to

⊙ go in any direction

⊙ turn right

⊙ turn left

⊙ go ahead

⊙ **go in any direction**

Horses and their riders will move more slowly than other road users. They might not have time to cut across heavy traffic to take up positions in the offside lane. For this reason a horse and rider may approach a roundabout in the left-hand lane, even though they're turning right.

6.56   *Mark **one** answer*   **HC r225**

Powered vehicles used by disabled people are small and hard to see. How do they give early warning when on a dual carriageway?

- They will have a flashing red light
- They will have a flashing green light
- They will have a flashing blue light
- They will have a flashing amber light.

⊙ **They will have a flashing amber light.**

Powered vehicles used by disabled people are small, low, hard to see and travel very slowly. On a dual carriageway a flashing amber light will warn other road users.

6.57   *Mark **one** answer*   **R-ES 9 & 10, HC r77 & 187**

You should never attempt to overtake a cyclist

- just before you turn left
- on a left hand bend
- on a one-way street
- on a dual carriageway

⊙ **just before you turn left**

If you want to turn left and there's a cyclist in front of you, hold back. Wait until the cyclist has passed the junction and then turn left behind them.

6.58   *Mark **one** answer*   **HC r225**

Ahead of you there is a moving vehicle with a flashing amber beacon. This means it is

- slow moving
- broken down
- a doctor's car
- a school crossing patrol

⊙ **slow moving**

As you approach the vehicle, assess the situation. Due to its slow progress you will need to judge whether it is safe to overtake.

6.59 *Mark **one** answer*   **HC r77**

You are approaching this roundabout and see the cyclist signal right. Why is the cyclist keeping to the left?

⊙ It is a quicker route for the cyclist

⊙ The cyclist is going to turn left instead

⊙ The cyclist thinks The Highway Code does not apply to bicycles

⊙ The cyclist is slower and more vulnerable

⊙ **The cyclist is slower and more vulnerable**

Cycling in today's heavy traffic can be hazardous. Some cyclists may not feel happy about crossing the path of traffic to take up a position in an outside lane. Be aware of this and understand that, although in the left-hand lane, the cyclist might be turning right.

6.60 *Mark **one** answer*   **R-ES 8 & 10, HC r214-215**

You notice horse riders in front. What should you do FIRST?

⊙ Pull out to the middle of the road

⊙ Slow down and be ready to stop

⊙ Accelerate around them

⊙ Signal right

⊙ **Slow down and be ready to stop**

Be particularly careful when approaching horse riders – slow down and be prepared to stop. Always pass wide and slowly and look out for signals given by horse riders. Horses are unpredictable: always treat them as potential hazards and take great care when passing them.

*Mark **one** answer*

You must not stop on these road markings because you may obstruct

⦿ children's view of the crossing area

/\\─SCHOOL KEEP CLEAR─\\/

These markings are found on the road outside schools. DO NOT stop (even to set down or pick up children) or park on them. The markings are to make sure that drivers, riders, children and other pedestrians have a clear view.

⦿ children's view of the crossing area

⦿ teachers' access to the school

⦿ delivery vehicles' access to the school

⦿ emergency vehicles' access to the school

---

*Mark **one** answer*

The left-hand pavement is closed due to street repairs. What should you do?

⦿ Watch out for pedestrians walking in the road

Where street repairs have closed off pavements, proceed carefully and slowly as pedestrians might have to walk in the road.

⦿ Watch out for pedestrians walking in the road

⦿ Use your right-hand mirror more often

⦿ Speed up to get past the roadworks quicker

⦿ Position close to the left-hand kerb

---

*Mark **one** answer*

You are following a motorcyclist on an uneven road. You should

⦿ allow extra room in case they swerve to avoid potholes

Potholes and bumps in the road can unbalance a motorcyclist. For this reason the rider might swerve to avoid an uneven road surface. Watch out at places where this is likely to occur.

⦿ allow less room so you can be seen in their mirrors

⦿ overtake immediately

⦿ allow extra room in case they swerve to avoid potholes

⦿ allow the same room as normal because road surfaces do not affect motorcyclists

6.64

*Mark **one** answer*

HC p109, KYTS p36

What does this sign tell you?

⊙ No cycling

⊙ Cycle route ahead

⊙ Cycle parking only

⊙ End of cycle route

⊙ **Cycle route ahead**

With people's concern today for the environment, cycle routes are being created in our towns and cities. These are usually defined by road markings and signs.

Respect the presence of cyclists on the road and give them plenty of room if you need to pass.

6.65

*Mark **one** answer*

HC r63 & 140, KYTS p38

What does this sign mean?

⊙ Contraflow pedal cycle lane

⊙ With-flow pedal cycle lane

⊙ Pedal cycles and buses only

⊙ No pedal cycles or buses

⊙ **With-flow pedal cycle lane**

The picture of a cycle will also usually be painted on the road, sometimes with a different coloured surface. Leave these clear for cyclists and don't pass too closely when you overtake.

6.66

*Mark **one** answer*

HC p134

You have just passed your test. How can you reduce your risk of being involved in a collision?

⊙ By always staying close to the vehicle in front

⊙ By never going over 40 mph

⊙ By staying only in the left-hand lane on all roads

⊙ By taking further training

⊙ **By taking further training**

New drivers and riders are often involved in a collision or incident early in their driving career. Due to a lack of experience they may not react to hazards as quickly as more experienced road users. Approved training courses are offered by driver and rider training schools. The Pass Plus scheme has been created by DSA for new drivers who would like to improve their basic skills and safely widen their driving experience.

6.67

*Mark **one** answer*

R-ES 8, HC r195-199

You are approaching this crossing. You should

- ⊙ prepare to slow down and stop
- ⊙ stop and wave the pedestrians across
- ⊙ speed up and pass by quickly
- ⊙ continue unless the pedestrians step out

⊙ **prepare to slow down and stop**

Be courteous and prepare to stop. Do not wave people across as this could be dangerous if another vehicle is approaching the crossing.

6.68

*Mark **one** answer*

R-ES 10, HC r207

You see a pedestrian with a dog. The dog has a yellow or burgundy coat. This especially warns you that the pedestrian is

- ⊙ elderly
- ⊙ dog training
- ⊙ colour blind
- ⊙ deaf

⊙ **deaf**

Take extra care as the pedestrian may not be aware of vehicles approaching.

6.69

*Mark **one** answer*

R-ES 8 & 10, HC r191-199

At toucan crossings

- ⊙ you only stop if someone is waiting to cross
- ⊙ cyclists are not permitted
- ⊙ there is a continuously flashing amber beacon
- ⊙ pedestrians and cyclists may cross

⊙ **pedestrians and cyclists may cross**

There are some crossings where cycle routes lead the cyclists to cross at the same place as pedestrians. These are called toucan crossings. Always look out for cyclists, as they're likely to be approaching faster than pedestrians.

6.70 *Mark **one** answer* **R-ES 7, HC r178**

Some junctions controlled by traffic lights have a marked area between two stop lines. What is this for?

- To allow taxis to position in front of other traffic
- To allow people with disabilities to cross the road
- To allow cyclists and pedestrians to cross the road together
- To allow cyclists to position in front of other traffic

⊙ **To allow cyclists to position in front of other traffic**

These are known as advanced stop lines. When the lights are red (or about to become red) you should stop at the first white line. However if you have crossed that line as the lights change you must stop at the second line even if it means you are in the area reserved for cyclists.

6.71 *Mark **one** answer* **R-ES 7, HC r178**

At some traffic lights there are advance stop lines and a marked area. What are these for?

- To allow cyclists to position in front of other traffic
- To let pedestrians cross when the lights change
- To prevent traffic from jumping the lights
- To let passengers get off a bus which is queuing

⊙ **To allow cyclists to position in front of other traffic**

You should always stop at the first white line. Avoid going into the marked area which is reserved for cyclists only. However if you have crossed the first white line at the time the signal changes to red you must stop at the second line even if you are in the marked area.

6.72 *Mark **one** answer* **R-ES 8 & 10, HC r211-213**

When you are overtaking a cyclist you should leave as much room as you would give to a car. What is the main reason for this?

- The cyclist might speed up
- The cyclist might get off the bike
- The cyclist might swerve
- The cyclist might have to make a left turn

⊙ **The cyclist might swerve**

Before overtaking assess the situation. Look well ahead to see if the cyclist will need to change direction. Be especially aware of the cyclist approaching parked vehicles as they will need to alter course. Do not pass too closely or cut in sharply.

Case study practice 6 – Vulnerable road users

Daniel lives in a village and is riding his motorcycle to town. Sheep are being herded across the road ahead. Once in town, traffic is heavy. At a Pelican crossing, amber lights are flashing and people are still crossing. Later, Daniel needs to turn left into a side road where pedestrians are just beginning to cross. Further along on Daniel's side of the road, there is a refuse collection vehicle with flashing amber beacons.

6.1 How should Daniel act while the sheep are crossing?

*Mark **one** answer*

- ⊙ Turn the engine off and wait until the animals have crossed.
- ⊙ Get off the motorcycle and wheel it past the animals.
- ⊙ Move slowly forward and sound the horn until they move.
- ⊙ Flash the headlights and rev the engine to hurry them across.

R-ES 10, HC r214

6.2 At the Pelican crossing, how should Daniel act?

*Mark **one** answer*

- ⊙ Stop but keep revving the engine to hurry them up.
- ⊙ Stop and wait patiently until they have crossed.
- ⊙ Keep moving slowly forward with lights flashing.
- ⊙ Keep going and ride slowly past the pedestrians.

HC r196

6.3 What should Daniel do at this left turn?

*Mark **one** answer*

⊙   Get off and wheel the motorcycle on the pavement.

⊙   Indicate then ride slowly round the pedestrians.

⊙   Flash his headlights and use the horn before turning.

⊙   Wait until the pedestrians have crossed safely.

R-ES 9, HC r170

6.4 Which of these vehicles might have an amber beacon?

*Mark **one** answer*

⊙   A vehicle which is slow-moving.

⊙   A vehicle which is reversing.

⊙   A vehicle which has a puncture.

⊙   A vehicle which is pulling out.

HC r225

6.5 How should Daniel overtake the vehicle?

*Mark **one** answer*

⊙   By dismounting and wheeling the motorcycle.

⊙   By revving the engine until the vehicle moves over.

⊙   By waiting until the road is clear of oncoming traffic.

⊙   By riding quickly past, whilst sounding the horn.

R-ES 8, HC r162 & 163

section **seven**
OTHER TYPES OF VEHICLE

This section covers
- Other motorcyclists
- Lorries
- Buses
- Trams

Other types of vehicle

You need to take extra care when meeting or following different types of vehicle, both smaller and larger vehicles.

Other motorcycles

Other motorcyclists can be blown sideways and may veer into your path more easily, so

- if you're overtaking another motorcyclist allow extra room
- if a motorcyclist in front of you is overtaking a high-sided vehicle, keep well back as they could be blown off course.

R-ES 12, HC r232-233

Watch out for signs warning you that the road is particularly susceptible to side winds.

Metal drain covers can become very slippery in wet weather and are particularly hazardous for two-wheeled vehicles. Take care to avoid uneven or slippery surfaces and watch for other motorcyclists having to do so.

R-ES 10, HC r109 & r213

Large vehicles

Large vehicles reduce your view of the road ahead. Keep well back if you're following a large vehicle, especially if you're hoping to overtake. If another vehicle fills the gap you've left, drop back further. This will improve your view of the road ahead.

R-ES 8, HC r164 & r222

Overtaking a large or slow-moving vehicle is more risky because of the length of the vehicle – it takes longer to overtake. Keep well back until you can see that it is clear. This also helps the driver see you in their mirrors. Never begin to overtake unless you're sure that you can complete the manoeuvre safely.

R-ES 8 & 12, HC r232-233

In wet weather large vehicles throw up a lot of spray. This can affect your visibility, and your vision if your visor becomes smeared or dirty. You should drop back further until you can see better. If the spray makes it difficult for you to see or be seen

- use dipped headlights
- use rear fog lights (if fitted) when visibility is seriously reduced, ie less than 100 metres (328 feet)
- stop and clean your visor to make sure you can see properly again before continuing.

R-ES 11 & 12, HC r227

Stay well back and give lorries plenty of room as they approach or emerge from

- road junctions
- crossroads
- mini-roundabouts.

To get round a corner, they may need to move in the opposite direction to which they're indicating. This is because of the length of their vehicle. If they want to turn left,

187

they may indicate left but move over to the right, and vice versa.

If you're waiting to emerge left from a minor road and a large vehicle is approaching from the right, wait. It may seem as if there's time to turn but the large vehicle could easily hide an overtaking vehicle.

R-ES 9, HC r221

Buses

Bus drivers need to make frequent stops. If a bus pulls up at a bus stop, watch carefully for pedestrians who may get off and cross the road in front of or behind the bus. Be prepared to give way to a bus which is trying to move off from a bus stop, as long as it's safe to do so.

R-ES 9, HC r223

Trams

Trams operate in some cities. Take extra care around them – they are silent, move quickly and can't steer to avoid you. Also in these cities, there may be additional white light signals at some traffic lights. These are especially for tram drivers. When riding in tram areas, take care when crossing tram tracks, particularly in bad weather, as they can become very slippery.

R-ES 8 & 10, HC r223-224

FAQs

If I'm driving downhill and a lorry coming uphill needs to move out to pass a parked car, should I stop for it?

Slow down and give way if possible. It's much more difficult for large vehicles to stop and then start up again if they are going uphill.

R-ES 11 & 12, HC r227

Which vehicles are most affected by crosswinds?

Crosswinds are much more likely to affect cyclists, motorcyclists and high-sided vehicles than they are cars. If you're following or overtaking, be aware that they might swerve suddenly and allow extra room.

R-ES 11 & 12, HC r227

Why are two-way roads divided into three lanes more dangerous?

Traffic in both directions can use the middle lane to overtake, so approaching traffic could be intending to make the same manoeuvre at the same time.

R-ES 11 & 12, HC r227

Is there a speed limit for powered vehicles used by disabled people?

Powered vehicles used by disabled people, such as wheelchairs and scooters, have a maximum speed limit of 8 mph (12 km/h) when used on the road.

R-ES 11 & 12, HC r227

7.1 *Mark **one** answer* R-ES 9, HC r221

You are riding behind a long vehicle. There is a mini-roundabout ahead. The vehicle is signalling left, but positioned to the right. You should

- ⊙ sound your horn
- ⊙ overtake on the left
- ⊙ keep well back
- ⊙ flash your headlights

⊙ **keep well back**

The long vehicle needs more room than other vehicles in order to make the left turn. Don't overtake on the left – the driver will not expect you to be there and may not see you. Staying well back will also give you a better view around the vehicle.

7.2 *Mark **two** answers* R-ES 7, HC r302

Why should you be careful when riding on roads where electric trams operate?

- ⊙ They cannot steer to avoid you
- ⊙ They move quickly and quietly
- ⊙ They are noisy and slow
- ⊙ They can steer to avoid you
- ⊙ They give off harmful exhaust fumes

⊙ **They cannot steer to avoid you**

⊙ **They move quickly and quietly**

Electric trams run on rails and cannot steer to avoid you. Keep a lookout for trams as they move very quietly and can appear suddenly.

7.3 *Mark **one** answer* R-ES 7, 8 & 10, HC r232-233

You are about to overtake a slow-moving motorcyclist. Which one of these signs would make you take special care?

⊙   ⊙

⊙   ⊙

⊙

In windy weather, watch out for motorcyclists and also cyclists as they can be blown sideways into your path. When you pass them, leave plenty of room and check their position in your mirror before pulling back in.

*Mark **one** answer*

You are following a long vehicle approaching a crossroads. The driver signals right but moves close to the left-hand kerb. What should you do?

- ⊙ Warn the driver of the wrong signal
- ⊙ Wait behind the long vehicle
- ⊙ Report the driver to the police
- ⊙ Overtake on the right-hand side

⊙ **Wait behind the long vehicle**

When a long vehicle is going to turn right it may need to keep close to the left-hand kerb. This is to prevent the rear end of the trailer cutting the corner. You need to be aware of how long vehicles behave in such situations. Don't overtake the lorry because it could turn as you're alongside. Stay behind and wait for it to turn.

*Mark **one** answer*

You are following a long vehicle. It approaches a crossroads and signals left, but moves out to the right. You should

- ⊙ get closer in order to pass it quickly
- ⊙ stay well back and give it room
- ⊙ assume the signal is wrong and it is really turning right
- ⊙ overtake as it starts to slow down

⊙ **stay well back and give it room**

A lorry may swing out to the right as it approaches a left turn. This is to allow the rear wheels to clear the kerb as it turns. Don't try to filter through if you see a gap on the nearside.

7.6   *Mark one answer*   **R-ES 8, HC r164 & 222**

You are waiting to emerge left from a minor road. A large vehicle is approaching from the right. You have time to turn, but you should wait. Why?

⊙ The large vehicle can easily hide an overtaking vehicle

⊙ The large vehicle can turn suddenly

⊙ The large vehicle is difficult to steer in a straight line

⊙ The large vehicle can easily hide vehicles from the left

⊙ **The large vehicle can easily hide an overtaking vehicle**

Large vehicles can hide other vehicles that are overtaking, especially motorcycles which may be filtering past queuing traffic. You need to be aware of the possibility of hidden vehicles and not assume that it is safe to emerge.

7.7   *Mark one answer*   **R-ES 9, HC r221**

You are approaching a mini-roundabout. The long vehicle in front is signalling left but positioned over to the right. You should

⊙ sound your horn

⊙ overtake on the left

⊙ follow the same course as the lorry

⊙ keep well back

⊙ **keep well back**

At mini-roundabouts there isn't much room for a long vehicle to manoeuvre. It will have to swing out wide so that it can complete the turn safely. Keep well back and don't try to move up alongside it.

7.8   *Mark one answer*   **R-ES 8 & 12, HC r164, r232-233**

Why is it more difficult to overtake a large vehicle than a car?

⊙ It takes longer to pass one

⊙ They may suddenly pull up

⊙ Their brakes are not as good

⊙ They climb hills more slowly

⊙ **It takes longer to pass one**

Depending on relevant speed, it will usually take you longer to pass a lorry than other vehicles. Some hazards to watch for include oncoming traffic, junctions ahead, bends or dips which could restrict your view, and signs or road markings that prohibit overtaking. Make sure you can see that it's safe to complete the manoeuvre before you start to overtake.

191

Before overtaking a large vehicle you should keep well back. Why is this?

- ◉ To give acceleration space to overtake quickly on blind bends
- ◉ To get the best view of the road ahead
- ◉ To leave a gap in case the vehicle stops and rolls back
- ◉ To offer other drivers a safe gap if they want to overtake you

◉ **To get the best view of the road ahead**

When following a large vehicle keep well back. If you're too close you won't be able to see the road ahead and the driver of the long vehicle might not be able to see you in their mirrors.

You are travelling behind a bus that pulls up at a bus stop. What should you do?

- ◉ Accelerate past the bus sounding your horn
- ◉ Watch carefully for pedestrians
- ◉ Be ready to give way to the bus
- ◉ Pull in closely behind the bus

◉ **Watch carefully for pedestrians**

◉ **Be ready to give way to the bus**

There might be pedestrians crossing from in front of the bus. Look out for them if you intend to pass. Consider staying back and waiting.

How many people are waiting to get on the bus? Check the queue if you can. The bus might move off straight away if there is no one waiting to get on.

If a bus is signalling to pull out, give it priority as long as it is safe to do so.

In front of you is a class 3 powered vehicle (powered wheelchair) driven by a disabled person. These vehicles have a maximum speed of

- ◉ 8 mph (12 km/h)
- ◉ 18 mph (29 km/h)
- ◉ 28 mph (45 km/h)
- ◉ 38 mph (61 km/h)

◉ **8 mph (12 km/h)**

These vehicles are battery powered and very vulnerable due to their slow speed, small size and low height. Some are designed for pavement and road use and have a maximum speed of 8 mph (12 km/h). Others are for pavement use only and are restricted to 4 mph (6 km/h). Take extra care and be patient if you are following one. Allow plenty of room when overtaking and do not go past unless you can do so safely.

7.12
*Mark **one** answer*
R-ES 10, 11 & 12, HC r227

You are following a large lorry on a wet road. Spray makes it difficult to see. You should

⊙ drop back until you can see better

⊙ put your headlights on full beam

⊙ keep close to the lorry, away from the spray

⊙ speed up and overtake quickly

⊙ **drop back until you can see better**

Large vehicles may throw up a lot of spray when the roads are wet. This will make it difficult for you to see ahead. Dropping back further will

• move you out of the spray and allow you to see further

• increase your separation distance. It takes longer to stop when the roads are wet and you need to allow more room.

Don't

• follow the vehicle in front too closely

• overtake, unless you can see and are sure that the way ahead is clear.

7.13
*Mark **one** answer*
R-ES 9, HC r221

You are following a large articulated vehicle. It is going to turn left into a narrow road. What action should you take?

⊙ Move out and overtake on the right

⊙ Pass on the left as the vehicle moves out

⊙ Be prepared to stop behind

⊙ Overtake quickly before the lorry moves out

⊙ **Be prepared to stop behind**

Lorries are larger and longer than other vehicles and this can affect their position when approaching junctions. When turning left they may move out to the right so that they don't cut in and mount the kerb with the rear wheels.

You keep well back while waiting to overtake a large vehicle. A car fills the gap. You should

- ⊙ sound your horn
- ⊙ drop back further
- ⊙ flash your headlights
- ⊙ start to overtake

⊙ **drop back further**

It's very frustrating when your separation distance is shortened by another vehicle. React positively, stay calm and drop further back.

You are following a long lorry. The driver signals to turn left into a narrow road. What should you do?

- ⊙ Overtake on the left before the lorry reaches the junction
- ⊙ Overtake on the right as soon as the lorry slows down
- ⊙ Do not overtake unless you can see there is no oncoming traffic
- ⊙ Do not overtake, stay well back and be prepared to stop.

⊙ **Do not overtake, stay well back and be prepared to stop.**

When turning into narrow roads articulated and long vehicles will need more room. Initially they will need to swing out in the opposite direction to which they intend to turn. They could mask another vehicle turning out of the same junction. DON'T be tempted to overtake them or pass on the inside.

When you approach a bus signalling to move off from a bus stop you should

- ⊙ get past before it moves
- ⊙ allow it to pull away, if it is safe to do so
- ⊙ flash your headlights as you approach
- ⊙ signal left and wave the bus on

⊙ **allow it to pull away, if it is safe to do so**

Try to give way to buses if you can do so safely, especially when they signal to pull away from bus stops. Look out for people who've stepped off the bus or are running to catch it, and may try to cross the road without looking. Don't try to accelerate past before it moves away or flash your lights as other road users may be misled by this signal.

7.17
*Mark **one** answer*

R-ES 9, 10 & 11, HC r162-164, r221 & r232-233

You wish to overtake a long, slow-moving vehicle on a busy road. You should

- ⊙ follow it closely and keep moving out to see the road ahead
- ⊙ flash your headlights for the oncoming traffic to give way
- ⊙ stay behind until the driver waves you past
- ⊙ keep well back until you can see that it is clear

⊙ **keep well back until you can see that it is clear**

If you want to overtake a long vehicle, stay well back so that you can get a better view of the road ahead. The closer you get the less you will be able to see of the road ahead. Be patient, overtaking calls for sound judgement. DON'T take a gamble, only overtake when you are certain that you can complete the manoeuvre safely.

7.18
*Mark **one** answer*

R-ES 11 & 12, HC r232-233

Which of these is LEAST likely to be affected by crosswinds?

- ⊙ Cyclists
- ⊙ Motorcyclists
- ⊙ High-sided vehicles
- ⊙ Cars

⊙ **Cars**

Although cars are the least likely to be affected, crosswinds can take anyone by surprise. This is most likely to happen after overtaking a large vehicle, when passing gaps between hedges or buildings, and on exposed sections of road.

7.19
*Mark **one** answer*

R-ES 9, HC r221

What should you do as you approach this lorry?

- ⊙ Slow down and be prepared to wait
- ⊙ Make the lorry wait for you
- ⊙ Flash your lights at the lorry
- ⊙ Move to the right-hand side of the road

⊙ **Slow down and be prepared to wait**

When turning, long vehicles need much more room on the road than other vehicles. At junctions they may take up the whole of the road space, so be patient and allow them the room they need.

*Mark **one** answer*

You are following a large vehicle approaching crossroads. The driver signals to turn left. What should you do?

- ⊙ Overtake if you can leave plenty of room
- ⊙ Overtake only if there are no oncoming vehicles
- ⊙ Do not overtake until the vehicle begins to turn.
- ⊙ Do not overtake when at or approaching a junction.

⊙ **Do not overtake when at or approaching a junction.**

Hold back and wait until the vehicle has turned before proceeding. Do not overtake because the vehicle turning left could hide a vehicle emerging from the same junction.

*Mark **one** answer*

Powered vehicles, such as wheelchairs or scooters, used by disabled people have a maximum speed of

- ⊙ 8 mph
- ⊙ 12 mph
- ⊙ 16 mph
- ⊙ 20 mph

⊙ **8 mph**

These are small battery powered vehicles and include wheelchairs and mobility scooters. Some are designed for use on the pavement only and have an upper speed limit of 4 mph (6 km/h). Others can go on the road as well and have a speed limit of 8 mph (12 km/h). They are now very common and are generally used by the elderly, disabled or infirm. Take great care as they are extremely vulnerable because of their low speed and small size.

Case study practice 7 – Other types of vehicle

Susan travels to work in the town centre on her motorcycle. It is a dull, wet day. There are many trams and tramlines in the town area, and a bus is indicating to pull out from a bus stop. At one junction, Susan has to cross the tramlines. On the main high street, there are specifically shaped signs for trams. Ahead, Susan sees a large vehicle indicating to turn left.

7.1 How can Susan improve her visibility in this weather?

*Mark **one** answer*

- ⊙ By using main beam headlights.
- ⊙ By using hazard warning lights.
- ⊙ By using dipped headlights.
- ⊙ By using front and rear fog lights.

R-ES 4, HC r86

7.2 How should Susan react to the bus?

*Mark **one** answer*

- ⊙ Rev the engine and sound the horn.
- ⊙ Keep going past but slow down a little.
- ⊙ Speed up quickly to get past the bus.
- ⊙ Allow it to pull out if it is safe to do so.

HC r223

7.3 Why should Susan take care when crossing the tramlines?

*Mark **one** answer*

- ⊙ The tyres could get stuck between the tracks.
- ⊙ The lines could be very slippery in wet weather.
- ⊙ The motorcycle's tyres could stick to the metal.
- ⊙ The gaps in the lines could be full of water.

R-ES 8, HC r306

7.4 What shape forms the tram signs which Susan sees?

*Mark **one** answer*

- ⊙ Triangle.
- ⊙ Diamond.
- ⊙ Hexagon.
- ⊙ Rectangle.

KYTS p31

7.5 What might this large vehicle do next?

*Mark **one** answer*

- ⊙ Pull a little over to the right.
- ⊙ Use the horn to warn others.
- ⊙ Pull a little over to the left.
- ⊙ Run over the pavement area.

R-ES 9, HC r170 & r221

section **eight**

MOTORCYCLE HANDLING

This section covers

- Weather conditions
- Road conditions
- Time of the day
- Speed
- Traffic calming

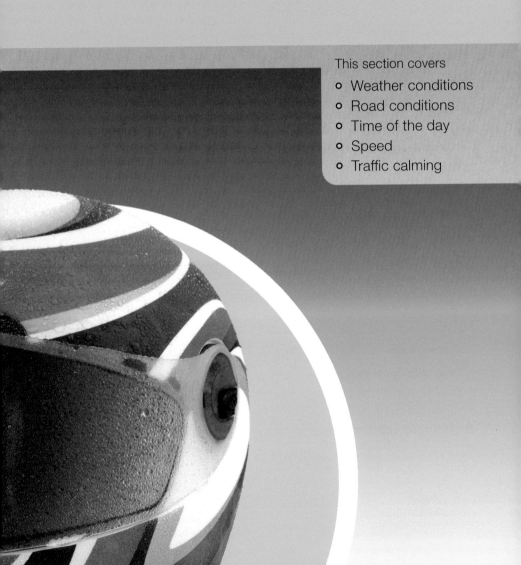

Motorcycle handling

Various conditions can affect the handling of your vehicle. These can roughly be divided into

- weather and light conditions
- control and speed
- road surfaces.

Weather conditions

Rain or wet conditions

When it's raining or the road is wet, leave at least double the normal stopping distance. If you're following a vehicle at a safe distance and another vehicle pulls into the gap you've left, drop back to regain a safe distance. During the day, use dipped headlights to help other road users to see you.

R-ES 11 & 12, HC r126 & r227

In winter a ford is more likely to flood, making it difficult to cross. There may be a depth gauge, which will help you decide whether you should go through. If you decide to continue, use a low gear and drive through slowly. Test your brakes afterwards: wet brakes are less effective.

R-ES 11 & 12, HC r121

Fog

When visibility is seriously reduced you must use headlights, or fog lights if you have them. 'Seriously reduced' generally means if you can't see for more than 100 metres (328 feet).

Never use front or rear fog lights unless visibility is seriously reduced. If you've been using them and conditions improve, remember to switch them off. Don't use fog lights when they're not needed because

- you may be breaking the law
- they can dazzle other road users
- road users behind you won't be able to see your brake lights as clearly, or they may think you're braking when you're not.

Always keep your speed down in foggy weather, as it's harder to see what is happening ahead. Increase your distance from the vehicle in front, in case it stops or slows suddenly. Always allow more time for your journey in adverse weather conditions.

R-ES 11 & 12, HC r114 & r226

Be especially careful when riding on motorways in fog; reflective studs help you to see the road ahead. In particular

- red studs mark the left-hand edge of the carriageway
- amber studs mark the central reservation.

R-ES 7, HC r122

Very bad weather

If it's very foggy or snow is falling heavily, don't travel unless your journey is essential. If you must travel, take great care and allow plenty of time.

Before you start out, make sure that your lights are working and your screen (if fitted) and visor are clean.

R-ES 11 & 12, HC r228-235

When on the road keep well back – increase the gap between yourself and the vehicle ahead in case it stops suddenly. In icy conditions it can take ten times the normal distance to stop compared to dry conditions.

If the road looks wet and your tyres are making hardly any noise, this could indicate the presence of black ice. Slow down but use the highest gear possible.

If you are parking on the road in foggy conditions, you must leave parking lights on.

Windy weather

Wind can affect all vehicles. A sudden gust may catch your motorcycle

- when passing a high-sided vehicle on the motorway
- when riding on an exposed stretch of road.

Keep your speed down and watch for gaps between buildings or hedges where gusts may suddenly occur.

R-ES 11 & 12, HC r232

Riding at night

Make sure that your headlights don't dazzle the vehicle you're following or any oncoming traffic. If you are dazzled by the headlights of an oncoming vehicle, slow down or stop to remain in full control.

Be extra careful when you overtake at night. You can't see as far ahead and there may be bends in the road.

On a motorway, use

- dipped headlights, even if the road is well-lit
- sidelights if you're broken down on the hard shoulder. This will help other road users to see you.

R-ES 11, 12 & 13, HC r114-115

Control and speed

For safety, before starting your engine, push the motorcycle forward to check that the rear wheel turns freely. Then glance at the neutral light on your instrument panel. Apply the front brake before getting on the motorcycle. If parked on a two-way road, you should get on from the left.

When astride your motorcycle, you should be able to place both feet on the ground comfortably, to support yourself and your machine. Never ride with the side stand left in the down position – this can be dangerous especially when cornering. Always fold the stand away safely before setting off.

Once moving, the normal riding position should be about central in the lane you're using. Try not to look down as this can affect your balance.

R-ES 6

Keep full control of your motorcycle at all times. Riding with the clutch disengaged or in neutral for any length of time (coasting) reduces control, especially of steering and braking. This is especially dangerous when travelling downhill as the motorcycle will pick up speed quickly when there's no engine braking.

R-ES 6 & 8, HC r122

You can use your motorcycle's engine to help control your speed. Select a lower gear when riding down a steep hill. This can be especially important as your brakes may become less effective due to overheating.

When riding up a steep hill, the engine will work harder and you'll slow down sooner. Try to avoid loss of balance or wobbling.

Take extra care on a single-track road. If you see a vehicle coming towards you, pull into, or stop opposite, a passing place.

Always ride in accordance with the conditions. Your stopping distance will be affected by

* your speed
* the condition of your tyres
* the road surface
* the weather.

R-ES 8 & 10, HC r155

When riding normally, you should brake when the motorcycle is upright and moving in a straight line. Apply both brakes smoothly. If your motorcycle has linked brakes, refer to the owner's manual.

To stop in an emergency, or on a wet road, apply the front brake just before the rear brake. Try to avoid skidding, as it can be hard to regain control once a skid has started.

The main causes of a motorcycle skidding are

* leaning over too far when cornering
* too much acceleration
* heavy or sharp braking.

If you do not have anti-lock brakes and your motorcycle begins to skid when you are braking on a wet road, the first thing you should do is release the footbrake. If both wheels skid, release both brakes together. Avoid braking suddenly or harshly, as this will make the situation worse.

R-ES 6, 8 & 10, HC r117-119

Traffic calming and road surfaces

Traffic calming is used to slow down traffic and make the roads safer for vulnerable road users, especially pedestrians. One of the most common measures is road humps (sometimes called speed humps). Stay within the speed limit and don't overtake other vehicles within these areas.

R-ES 7, HC r153

A rumble device (raised markings across the road) is often used to alert you to a hazard such as a roundabout and to encourage you to reduce speed.

In cities where trams operate, the areas used

by the trams may have a different surface texture or colour. This may be edged with white line markings.

HC r300, KYTS p31, p68 & p75

If it rains after a long dry hot spell, the road surface may be unusually slippery. Loose chippings can also contribute to skidding, so slow down and take care in these conditions.

R-ES 8 & 12, HC r237

Painted road markings, tar banding, tram rails and drain covers can all become very slippery in wet weather. Avoid riding over them if you can. If this is not possible, take great care, especially when braking or cornering.

Spilt diesel fuel can also be very slippery. If you see a rainbow pattern on the road surface, slow down in good time and avoid the area if possible.

R-ES 8 & 12, HC r213 & r 306

Some motorcycles are fitted with Traction Control Systems (TCS) which help to prevent the rear wheel spinning, especially when accelerating on a slippery surface.

FAQs

Am I allowed to wait in a box junction?

Yes, if you want to turn right and your exit's clear but you're prevented from turning by oncoming traffic.

Do I need to leave sidelights on when I park on a two-way road?

Leave your sidelights on

- *if the speed limit's more than 30 mph (48 km/h)*
- *when it's foggy.*

Always park on the left-hand side of the road.

R-ES 12 & 13, HC r248-251

I'm following a slow-moving vehicle. I want to overtake but it's been signalling right for some time. What should I do?

Wait for the signal to be cancelled before overtaking. The other driver may have misjudged the distance to a road junction or there might be a hidden hazard.

HC r167

Are there any times when I can overtake on the left?

Yes

- *if you're in a one-way street*
- *when the vehicle in front is signalling to turn right*
- *in slow-moving queues when traffic in the right-hand lane is moving more slowly than traffic in your lane.*

R-ES 8, HC r163

8.1
*Mark **two** answers*

R-ES 6

As a safety measure before starting your engine, you should

- ⊙ push the motorcycle forward to check the rear wheel turns freely
- ⊙ engage first gear and apply the rear brake
- ⊙ engage first gear and apply the front brake
- ⊙ glance at the neutral light on your instrument panel

⊙ **push the motorcycle forward to check the rear wheel turns freely**

⊙ **glance at the neutral light on your instrument panel**

Before starting the engine you should ensure the motorcycle is in neutral. This can be done by, moving the motorcycle to check that the rear wheel turns freely and making sure the neutral warning light is lit when the ignition is turned on.

8.2
*Mark **two** answers*

R-ES 9, HC r170

You are approaching this junction. As the motorcyclist you should

- ⊙ prepare to slow down
- ⊙ sound your horn
- ⊙ keep near the left kerb
- ⊙ speed up to clear the junction
- ⊙ stop, as the car has right of way

⊙ **prepare to slow down**

⊙ **sound your horn**

Look out for road signs indicating side roads, even if you aren't turning off. A driver who is emerging might not be able to see you due to parked cars or heavy traffic. Always be prepared, and stop if necessary. Remember, no one has priority at unmarked crossroads.

8.3
*Mark **one** answer*

R-ES 8

What can you do to improve your safety on the road as a motorcyclist?

- ⊙ Anticipate the actions of others
- ⊙ Stay just above the speed limits
- ⊙ Keep positioned close to the kerbs
- ⊙ Remain well below speed limits

⊙ **Anticipate the actions of others**

Always ride defensively. This means looking and planning ahead as well as anticipating the actions of other road users.

Which THREE of these can cause skidding?

- Braking too gently
- Leaning too far over when cornering
- Staying upright when cornering
- Braking too hard
- Changing direction suddenly

⊙ **Leaning too far over when cornering**

⊙ **Braking too hard**

⊙ **Changing direction suddenly**

In order to keep control of your motorcycle and prevent skidding you must plan well ahead to prevent harsh, late braking. Try o avoid braking while changing direction, as this reduces the tyres' grip on the road. Take the road and weather conditions into consideration and adjust your speed if necessary.

It is very cold and the road looks wet. You cannot hear any road noise. You should

- continue riding at the same speed
- ride slower in as high a gear as possible
- ride in as low a gear as possible
- keep revving your engine
- slow down as there may be black ice

⊙ **ride slower in as high a gear as possible**

⊙ **slow down as there may be black ice**

Rain freezing on roads is called black ice. It can be hard to see. Indications of black ice are when you can't hear tyre noise and the steering becomes very light. You need to keep your speed down and avoid harsh steering, braking and acceleration. Riding in as high a gear as possible will help to reduce the risk of wheel-spin.

When riding a motorcycle you should wear full protective clothing

- at all times
- only on faster, open roads
- just on long journeys
- only during bad weather

⊙ **at all times**

Protective clothing is designed to protect you from the cold and wet and also gives some protection from injury.

8.7 *Mark **two** answers* R-ES 12

You have to make a journey in fog. What are the TWO most important things you should do before you set out?

- Fill up with fuel
- Make sure that you have a warm drink with you
- Check that your lights are working
- Check the battery
- Make sure that your visor is clean

⊙ **Check that your lights are working**

⊙ **Make sure that your visor is clean**

When you're riding a motorcycle, keep your visor as clean as possible to give you a clear view of the road. It's a good idea to carry a clean, damp cloth in a polythene bag for this purpose.

You need to ensure that your lights are clean and can be seen clearly by other road users. This is especially important when visibility is reduced, for example in fog or heavy rain.

8.8 *Mark **one** answer* R-ES 8

The best place to park your motorcycle is

- on soft tarmac
- on bumpy ground
- on grass
- on firm, level ground

⊙ **on firm, level ground**

Parking your motorcycle on soft ground might cause the stand to sink and the bike to fall over. The ground should also be level to ensure that the bike is stable. Where off-road parking or motorcycle parking areas are available, use them.

8.9 *Mark **one** answer* R-ES 12

When riding in windy conditions, you should

- stay close to large vehicles
- keep your speed up
- keep your speed down
- stay close to the gutter

⊙ **keep your speed down**

Strong winds can blow motorcycles off course and even across the road. In windy conditions you need to, slow down, avoid riding on exposed roads and watch for gaps in buildings and hedges where you may be affected by a sudden blast of wind.

8.10

R-ES 8

In normal riding your position on the road should be

- about a foot from the kerb
- about central in your lane
- on the right of your lane
- near the centre of the road

⊙ **about central in your lane**

If you're riding a motorcycle it's very important to ride where other road users can see you. In normal weather you should ride in the centre of your lane. This will help you to avoid uneven road surfaces in the gutter and allow others to overtake on the right if they wish.

8.11

R-ES 6

Your motorcycle is parked on a two-way road. You should get on from the

- right and apply the rear brake
- left and leave the brakes alone
- left and apply the front brake
- right and leave the brakes alone

⊙ **left and apply the front brake**

When you get onto a motorcycle you should get on from the left side to avoid putting yourself in danger from passing traffic. Also apply the front brake to prevent the motorcycle rolling either forwards or backwards.

8.12

R-ES 2

To gain basic skills in how to ride a motorcycle you should

- practise off-road with an approved training body
- ride on the road on the first dry day
- practise off-road in a public park or in a quiet cul-de-sac
- ride on the road as soon as possible

⊙ **practise off-road with an approved training body**

All new motorcyclists must complete a course of basic training with an approved training body before going on the road. This training is given on a site which has been authorised by the Driving Standards Agency as being suitable for off-road training.

8.13   *Mark **one** answer*   R-ES 5

You should not ride with your clutch lever
pulled in for longer than necessary because it

- ⊙ increases wear on the gearbox
- ⊙ increases petrol consumption
- ⊙ reduces your control of the motorcycle
- ⊙ reduces the grip of the tyres

⊙ **reduces your control of the motorcycle**

Riding with the clutch lever pulled in is
known as coasting. It gives you less
steering control, reduces traction, and can
cause you to pick up speed. When you're
travelling downhill your motorcycle will pick
up speed quickly. If you are coasting the
engine won't be able to assist the braking.

8.14   *Mark **one** answer*   R-ES 7 & 12

You are approaching a road with a surface
of loose chippings. What should you do?

- ⊙ Ride normally
- ⊙ Speed up
- ⊙ Slow down
- ⊙ Stop suddenly

⊙ **Slow down**

The handling of your motorcycle will be
greatly affected by the road surface. Look
well ahead and be especially alert if the
road looks uneven or has loose chippings.
Slow down in good time as braking harshly
in these conditions will cause you to skid.
Avoid making sudden changes of direction
for the same reason.

8.15   *Mark **one** answer*   R-ES 8 & 12, HC r237

It rains after a long dry, hot spell. This may
cause the road surface to

- ⊙ be unusually slippery
- ⊙ give better grip
- ⊙ become covered in grit
- ⊙ melt and break up

⊙ **be unusually slippery**

Oil and other substances build up on the
road surface during long dry spells and
when it rains this surface becomes very
slippery.

*Mark **three** answers*

The main causes of a motorcycle skidding are

- ☉ heavy and sharp braking
- ☉ excessive acceleration
- ☉ leaning too far when cornering
- ☉ riding in wet weather
- ☉ riding in the winter

☉ **heavy and sharp braking**

☉ **excessive acceleration**

☉ **leaning too far when cornering**

Skids are a lot easier to get into than they are to get out of.

Riding at a speed that suits the conditions, looking ahead for hazards and braking in good time will all help you to avoid skidding or losing control of your vehicle.

*Mark **one** answer*

To stop your motorcycle quickly in an emergency you should apply

- ☉ the rear brake only
- ☉ the front brake only
- ☉ the front brake just before the rear
- ☉ the rear brake just before the front

☉ **the front brake just before the rear**

You should plan ahead to avoid the need to stop suddenly. But if an emergency should arise you must be able to stop safely. Applying the correct amount of braking effort to each wheel will help you to stop safely and in control.

*Mark **one** answer*

You leave the choke on for too long. This causes the engine to run too fast. When is this likely to make your motorcycle most difficult to control?

- ☉ Accelerating
- ☉ Going uphill
- ☉ Slowing down
- ☉ On motorways

☉ **Slowing down**

Forgetting to switch the choke off will cause the engine to run too fast. This makes it difficult to control the motorcycle, especially when slowing down, for example when approaching junctions and bends.

8.19

Mark one answer

R-ES 6

You should NOT look down at the front wheel when riding because it can

- make your steering lighter
- improve your balance
- use less fuel
- upset your balance

⊙ **upset your balance**

When riding look ahead and around you, but don't look down at the front wheel as this can severely upset your balance.

8.20

Mark one answer

R-ES 6

In normal riding conditions you should brake

- by using the rear brake first and then the front
- when the motorcycle is being turned or ridden through a bend
- by pulling in the clutch before using the front brake
- when the motorcycle is upright and moving in a straight line

⊙ **when the motorcycle is upright and moving in a straight line**

A motorcycle is most stable when it's upright and moving in a straight line. This is the best time to brake. Normally both brakes should be used, with the front brake being applied just before the rear.

8.21

Mark three answers

R-ES 6 & 8, HC r126 & p42-3

Which THREE of the following will affect your stopping distance?

- How fast you are going
- The tyres on your motorcycle
- The time of day
- The weather
- The street lighting

⊙ **How fast you are going**

⊙ **The tyres on your motorcycle**

⊙ **The weather**

There are several factors that can affect the distance it takes to stop your motorcycle. In wet weather you should double the separation distance from the vehicle in front. Your tyres will have less grip on the road and you therefore need to allow more time to stop. Always ride in accordance with the conditions.

211

8.22 *Mark **one** answer* **R-ES 11**

You are on a motorway at night. You MUST have your headlights switched on unless

- ⊙ there are vehicles close in front of you
- ⊙ you are travelling below 50 mph
- ⊙ the motorway is lit
- ⊙ your motorcycle is broken down on the hard shoulder

⊙ **your motorcycle is broken down on the hard shoulder**

Always use your headlights at night on a motorway unless you have stopped on the hard shoulder. If you have to use the hard shoulder, switch off the headlights but leave the parking lights on so that other road users can see your motorcycle.

8.23 *Mark **one** answer* **R-ES 12**

You have to park on the road in fog. You should

- ⊙ leave parking lights on
- ⊙ leave no lights on
- ⊙ leave dipped headlights on
- ⊙ leave main beam headlights on

⊙ **leave parking lights on**

If you have to park on the road in foggy conditions it's important that your motorcycle can be seen by other road users. Try to find a place to park off the road. If this isn't possible leave your motorcycle facing in the same direction as the traffic. Make sure that your lights are clean and that you leave your parking lights on.

8.24 *Mark **one** answer* **R-ES 15**

You ride over broken glass and get a sudden puncture. What should you do?

- ⊙ Close the throttle and roll to a stop
- ⊙ Brake to a stop as quickly as possible
- ⊙ Release your grip on the handlebars
- ⊙ Steer from side to side to keep your balance

⊙ **Close the throttle and roll to a stop**

Your motorcycle will be very unstable if a tyre bursts. Try to keep a straight course and stop as gently as possible.

8.25   *Mark **one** answer*   **R-ES 5**

Traction Control Systems (TCS) are fitted to some motorcycles. What does this help to prevent?

⊙ Wheelspin when accelerating

⊙ Skidding when braking too hard

⊙ Uneven front tyre wear

⊙ Uneven rear tyre wear

⊙ **Wheelspin when accelerating**

Traction Control Systems (TCS) help to prevent the rear wheel from spinning, especially when accelerating on a slippery surface.

8.26   *Mark **one** answer*   **R-ES 8 & 12**

Spilt fuel on the road can be very dangerous for you as a motorcyclist. How can this hazard be seen?

⊙ By a rainbow pattern on the surface

⊙ By a series of skid marks

⊙ By a pitted road surface

⊙ By a highly polished surface

⊙ **By a rainbow pattern on the surface**

This rainbow-coloured pattern can be seen much more easily on a wet road. You should avoid riding over these areas if possible. If you have to go over them do so with extreme caution.

8.27   *Mark **one** answer*   **R-ES 5**

You leave the choke on for too long. This could make the engine run faster than normal. This will make your motorcycle

⊙ handle much better

⊙ corner much safer

⊙ stop much more quickly

⊙ more difficult to control

⊙ **more difficult to control**

Leaving the choke on for longer than necessary will usually make the engine run too fast. This can lead to loss of control, which is especially dangerous when approaching junctions and bends in the road and whenever you need to slow down.

Which FOUR types of road surface increase the risk of skidding for motorcyclists?

- ⊙ White lines
- ⊙ Dry tarmac
- ⊙ Tar banding
- ⊙ Yellow grid lines
- ⊙ Loose chippings

- ⊙ **White lines**
- ⊙ **Tar banding**
- ⊙ **Yellow grid lines**
- ⊙ **Loose chippings**

When riding it's important to look out for slippery surfaces. These include, potholes, drain covers (especially in the wet), oily and greasy surfaces, road markings, tram tracks, wet mud and leaves. You will then have more time to brake or change course if you need to.

You are riding on a wet road. When braking you should

- ⊙ apply the rear brake well before the front
- ⊙ apply the front brake just before the rear
- ⊙ avoid using the front brake at all
- ⊙ avoid using the rear brake at all

- ⊙ **apply the front brake just before the rear**

On wet roads you will need to be especially careful: brake earlier and more smoothly. Always try to brake when the motorcycle is upright. This is particularly important in wet conditions.

The road is wet. You are passing a line of queuing traffic and riding on the painted road markings. You should take extra care, particularly when

- ⊙ signalling
- ⊙ braking
- ⊙ carrying a passenger
- ⊙ checking your mirrors

- ⊙ **braking**

Take extra care when braking or cornering on wet roads and try to avoid slippery objects, such as drain covers and painted road markings.

8.31   Mark **one** answer   R-ES 8

You are going ahead and will have to cross tram lines. Why should you be especially careful ?

- ⊙ Tram lines are always 'live'
- ⊙ Trams will be stopping here
- ⊙ Pedestrians will be crossing here
- ⊙ The steel rails can be slippery

⊙ **The steel rails can be slippery**

These rails can affect your steering and be a hazard when braking. The smooth surface of the rails makes them slippery and dangerous for motorcyclists, especially when wet. Try to cross them at right angles.

8.32   Mark **one** answer   R-ES 8

You have to brake sharply and your motorcycle starts to skid. You should

- ⊙ continue braking and select a low gear
- ⊙ apply the brakes harder for better grip
- ⊙ select neutral and use the front brake only
- ⊙ release the brakes and reapply

⊙ **release the brakes and reapply**

If you skid as a result of braking harshly you need to ease off the brakes to stop the skid. Then reapply them progressively to stop.

8.33   Mark **one** answer   R-ES 5

Your motorcycle does NOT have linked brakes. What should you do when braking to a normal stop?

- ⊙ Only apply the front brake
- ⊙ Rely just on the rear brake
- ⊙ Apply both brakes smoothly
- ⊙ Apply either of the brakes gently

⊙ **Apply both brakes smoothly**

In normal riding you should always use both brakes. Braking when the motorcycle is upright and travelling in a straight line helps you to keep control. If your motorcycle has linked brakes refer to the owners manual.

*Mark **one** answer*   **R-ES 8 & 12**

You are riding in wet weather. You see diesel fuel on the road. What should you do?

◉ Swerve to avoid the area

◉ Accelerate through quickly

◉ Brake sharply to a stop

◉ Slow down in good time

◉ **Slow down in good time**

Spilt diesel will show up in wet weather as a rainbow-coloured pattern on the road. You should try to avoid riding over this area if you can. Slow down in good time but don't swerve suddenly or change direction without taking proper observation.

8.35 *Mark **one** answer*   **R-ES 5 & 6**

Braking too hard has caused both wheels to skid. What should you do?

◉ Release both brakes together

◉ Release the front then the rear brake

◉ Release the front brake only

◉ Release the rear brake only

◉ **Release both brakes together**

Braking too hard will cause a skid. Release the brakes immediately to allow the wheels to turn, then reapply them as firmly as the road surface and conditions will allow.

8.36 *Mark **one** answer*   **R-ES 8 & 12**

You see a rainbow-coloured pattern across the road. What will this warn you of?

◉ A soft uneven road surface

◉ A polished road surface

◉ Fuel spilt on the road

◉ Water on the road

◉ **Fuel spilt on the road**

If fuel, especially diesel, is spilt on the road it will make the surface very slippery. In wet weather this can be seen as a rainbow-coloured pattern on the road.

8.37 *Mark **one** answer*   **R-ES 12, HC r234-235**

Why should you always reduce your speed when travelling in fog?

◉ The brakes do not work as well

◉ You will be dazzled by other headlights

◉ The engine will take longer to warm up

◉ It is more difficult to see events ahead

◉ **It is more difficult to see events ahead**

You won't be able to see as far ahead in fog as you can on a clear day. You will need to reduce your speed so that, if a hazard looms out of the fog, you have the time and space to take avoiding action.

Travelling in fog is hazardous. If you can, try and delay your journey until it has cleared.

8.38 *Mark one answer* R-ES 6

You are sitting on a stationary motorcycle and checking your riding position. You should be able to

- ⊙ just touch the ground with your toes
- ⊙ place both feet on the ground
- ⊙ operate the centre stand
- ⊙ adjust your mirrors by stretching

⊙ **place both feet on the ground**

When sitting astride a stationary motorcycle you should be able to place both feet on the ground to support yourself and your machine.

8.39 *Mark one answer* R-ES 12, HC r237

It has rained after a long dry spell. You should be very careful because the road surface will be unusually

- ⊙ rough
- ⊙ dry
- ⊙ sticky
- ⊙ slippery

⊙ **slippery**

During a long hot, dry spell the road surface will become coated with rubber and dust. When it rains after this the road surface will be unusually slippery. Take extra care, particularly at junctions, bends and roundabouts, and allow double the usual stopping distance.

8.40 *Mark one answer* R-ES 6

Riding with the side stand down could cause you to crash. This is most likely to happen when

- ⊙ going uphill
- ⊙ accelerating
- ⊙ braking
- ⊙ cornering

⊙ **cornering**

Cornering with the side stand down could lead to a serious crash. Most motorcycles have a device that stops the engine if you try to ride off with the side stand down, but don't rely on this.

You are entering a bend. Your side stand is not fully raised. This could

- ⊙ cause you to crash
- ⊙ improve your balance
- ⊙ alter the motorcycle's centre of gravity
- ⊙ make the motorcycle more stable

⊙ **cause you to crash**

If the stand isn't fully up it could dig into the road and cause a serious crash. Always check that it is fully raised before moving off. Most side stands have a safety device or cut-out switch, but do NOT rely on this. CHECK FOR YOURSELF!

In which THREE of these situations may you overtake another vehicle on the left?

- ⊙ When you are in a one-way street
- ⊙ When approaching a motorway slip road where you will be turning off
- ⊙ When the vehicle in front is signalling to turn right
- ⊙ When a slower vehicle is travelling in the right-hand lane of a dual carriageway
- ⊙ In slow-moving traffic queues when traffic in the right-hand lane is moving more slowly

⊙ **When you are in a one-way street**

⊙ **When the vehicle in front is signalling to turn right**

⊙ **In slow-moving traffic queues when traffic in the right-hand lane is moving more slowly**

At certain times of the day, traffic might be heavy. If traffic is moving slowly in queues and vehicles in the right-hand lane are moving more slowly, you may overtake on the left. Don't keep changing lanes to try and beat the queue.

You are travelling in very heavy rain. Your overall stopping distance is likely to be

- ⊙ doubled
- ⊙ halved
- ⊙ up to ten times greater
- ⊙ no different

⊙ **doubled**

As well as visibility being reduced, the road will be extremely wet. This will reduce the grip the tyres have on the road and increase the distance it takes to stop. Double your separation distance.

8.44 *Mark **two** answers* **R-ES 8 & 13**

Which TWO of the following are correct?
When overtaking at night you should

- ⊙ wait until a bend so that you can see the oncoming headlights
- ⊙ sound your horn twice before moving out
- ⊙ be careful because you can see less
- ⊙ beware of bends in the road ahead
- ⊙ put headlights on full beam

⊙ **be careful because you can see less**

⊙ **beware of bends in the road ahead**

Only overtake the vehicle in front if it's really necessary. At night the risks are increased due to the poor visibility. Don't overtake if there's a possibility of

- road junctions
- bends ahead
- the brow of a bridge or hill, except on a dual carriageway
- pedestrian crossings
- double white lines ahead
- vehicles changing direction
- any other potential hazard.

8.45 *Mark **one** answer* **R-ES 7, HC r174**

When may you wait in a box junction?

- ⊙ When you are stationary in a queue of traffic
- ⊙ When approaching a pelican crossing
- ⊙ When approaching a zebra crossing
- ⊙ When oncoming traffic prevents you turning right

⊙ **When oncoming traffic prevents you turning right**

The purpose of a box junction is to keep the junction clear by preventing vehicles from stopping in the path of crossing traffic.

You must not enter a box junction unless your exit is clear. But, you may enter the box and wait if you want to turn right and are only prevented from doing so by oncoming traffic.

Which of these plates normally appear with this road sign?

⊙ Humps for ½ mile

⊙ Hump Bridge

⊙ Low Bridge

⊙ Soft Verge

⊙ Humps for ½ mile

Road humps are used to slow down the traffic. They are found in places where there are often pedestrians, such as

- in shopping areas
- near schools
- in residential areas.

Watch out for people close to the kerb or crossing the road.

Traffic calming measures are used to

⊙ stop road rage

⊙ help overtaking

⊙ slow traffic down

⊙ help parking

⊙ **slow traffic down**

Traffic calming measures are used to make the roads safer for vulnerable road users, such as cyclists, pedestrians and children. These can be designed as chicanes, road humps or other obstacles that encourage drivers and riders to slow down.

You are on a motorway in fog. The left-hand edge of the motorway can be identified by reflective studs. What colour are they?

⊙ Green

⊙ Amber

⊙ Red

⊙ White

⊙ **Red**

Be especially careful if you're on a motorway in fog. Reflective studs are used to help you in poor visibility. Different colours are used so that you'll know which lane you are in. These are

- red on the left-hand side of the road
- white between lanes
- amber on the right-hand edge of the carriageway
- green between the carriageway and slip roads.

8.49 *Mark **two** answers* **HC r153, KYTS p68 & 75**

A rumble device is designed to

- give directions
- prevent cattle escaping
- alert you to low tyre pressure
- alert you to a hazard
- encourage you to reduce speed

◉ **alert you to a hazard**

◉ **encourage you to reduce speed**

A rumble device usually consists of raised markings or strips across the road. It gives an audible, visual and tactile warning of a hazard. These strips are found in places where traffic has constantly ignored warning or restriction signs. They are there for a good reason. Slow down and be ready to deal with a hazard.

8.50 *Mark **one** answer* **R-ES 12, HC r234-235**

You have to make a journey in foggy conditions. You should

- follow other vehicles' tail lights closely
- avoid using dipped headlights
- leave plenty of time for your journey
- keep two seconds behind other vehicles

◉ **leave plenty of time for your journey**

If you're planning to make a journey when it's foggy, listen to the weather reports on the radio or television. Don't travel if visibility is very poor or your trip isn't necessary.

If you do travel, leave plenty of time for your journey. If someone is expecting you at the other end, let them know that you'll be taking longer than normal to arrive.

8.51 *Mark **one** answer* **R-ES 13, HC r114-115**

You are overtaking a car at night. You must be sure that

- you flash your headlights before overtaking
- you select a higher gear
- you have switched your lights to full beam before overtaking
- you do not dazzle other road users

◉ **you do not dazzle other road users**

To prevent your lights from dazzling the driver of the car in front, wait until you've overtaken before switching to full beam.

You are on a road which has speed humps. A driver in front is travelling slower than you. You should

- ⊙ sound your horn
- ⊙ overtake as soon as you can
- ⊙ flash your headlights
- ⊙ slow down and stay behind

⊙ **slow down and stay behind**

Be patient and stay behind the car in front. Normally you should not overtake other vehicles in traffic-calmed areas. If you overtake here your speed may exceed that which is safe along that road, defeating the purpose of the traffic calming measures.

You see these markings on the road. Why are they there?

- ⊙ To show a safe distance between vehicles
- ⊙ To keep the area clear of traffic
- ⊙ To make you aware of your speed
- ⊙ To warn you to change direction

⊙ **To make you aware of your speed**

These lines may be painted on the road on the approach to a roundabout, village or a particular hazard. The lines are raised and painted yellow and their purpose is to make you aware of your speed. Reduce your speed in good time so that you avoid having to brake harshly over the last few metres before reaching the junction.

Areas reserved for trams may have

- ⊙ metal studs around them
- ⊙ white line markings
- ⊙ zigzag markings
- ⊙ a different coloured surface
- ⊙ yellow hatch markings
- ⊙ a different surface texture

⊙ **white line markings**

⊙ **a different coloured surface**

⊙ **a different surface texture**

Trams can run on roads used by other vehicles and pedestrians. The part of the road used by the trams is known as the reserved area and this should be kept clear. It has a coloured surface and is usually edged with white road markings. It might also have different surface texture.

8.55   *Mark one answer*   **R-ES 8 & 10, HC r155**

You see a vehicle coming towards you on a single-track road. You should

⊙ go back to the main road

⊙ do an emergency stop

⊙ stop at a passing place

⊙ put on your hazard warning lights

⊙ **stop at a passing place**

You must take extra care when on single track roads. You may not be able to see around bends due to high hedges or fences. Proceed with caution and expect to meet oncoming vehicles around the next bend. If you do, pull into or opposite a passing place.

8.56   *Mark one answer*   **R-ES 12, HC r213**

The road is wet. Why might a motorcyclist steer round drain covers on a bend?

⊙ To avoid puncturing the tyres on the edge of the drain covers

⊙ To prevent the motorcycle sliding on the metal drain covers

⊙ To help judge the bend using the drain covers as marker points

⊙ To avoid splashing pedestrians on the pavement

⊙ **To prevent the motorcycle sliding on the metal drain covers**

Other drivers or riders may have to change course due to the size or characteristics of their vehicle. Understanding this will help you to anticipate their actions. Motorcyclists and cyclists will be checking the road ahead for uneven or slippery surfaces, especially in wet weather. They may need to move across their lane to avoid surface hazards such as potholes and drain covers.

8.57   *Mark one answer*   **R-ES 12, HC r121**

After this hazard you should test your brakes. Why is this?

⊙ You will be on a slippery road

⊙ Your brakes will be soaking wet

⊙ You will be going down a long hill

⊙ You will have just crossed a long bridge

⊙ **Your brakes will be soaking wet**

A ford is a crossing over a stream that's shallow enough to go through. After you've gone through a ford or deep puddle the water will affect your brakes. To dry them out apply a light brake pressure while moving slowly. Don't travel at normal speeds until you are sure your brakes are working properly again.

Case study practice 8 – Motorcycle handling

You're carrying a pillion passenger on your motorcycle. You buy fuel at the service station, then make various checks, including on tyre pressures. You want to turn left on leaving the forecourt. There are parked cars obscuring your view. On the main road, you leave a larger gap between you and the vehicle in front.

8.1 How can the passenger affect the way you ride?

*Mark **one** answer*

⊙ The extra weight can affect your balance.

⊙ Your stopping distance would be shorter.

⊙ It would be easier for you to accelerate.

⊙ A passenger can help with observation.

R-ES 14

8.2 Other than tyre pressures, what else might need adjusting under these circumstances?

*Mark **one** answer*

⊙ Brakes.

⊙ Headlights.

⊙ Handlebars.

⊙ Seating.

R-ES 14

8.3 What should you do about your obstructed view at the junction?

*Mark **one** answer*

⊙ Stop and wait until some of the parked cars move away.

⊙ Stop and get off, then wheel the motorcycle into the road.

⊙ Stop and make your passenger signal to oncoming traffic.

⊙ Stop, then edge forward slowly until you can see clearly.

R-ES 9, HC r170-171

8.4 What is one of the things you should instruct your passenger to do before the journey?

*Mark **one** answer*

⊙ Lean to the side in order to see ahead.

⊙ Lean with you when going round bends.

⊙ Look behind and then signal for you.

⊙ Keep upright when going round bends.

R-ES 14

8.5 Why have you chosen to leave a larger gap?

*Mark **one** answer*

⊙ Your passenger will be able to see more clearly.

⊙ You are trying to keep away from exhaust fumes.

⊙ Your passenger told you to keep further back.

⊙ You might need more room in which to stop safely.

R-ES 14

section **nine**
MOTORWAY RULES

This section covers
- Speed limits
- Lane discipline
- Stopping
- Lighting
- Parking

Motorway rules

Motorways are designed to help traffic travel faster. Conditions can change more quickly than on other roads, so you need to be especially alert at all times.

Check your motorcycle thoroughly before starting a long motorway journey. Continuous high speeds may increase the risk of breaking down. Remember, to ride on a motorway, your motorcycle must have an engine capacity of 50 cc or more.

R-ES 11, HC r253

Riding on the motorway

To join the motorway

- use the slip road to adjust your speed to traffic already on the motorway
- always give way to traffic already on the motorway.

Once you've joined the motorway, keep in the left-hand lane while you get used to the higher speeds of motorway traffic.

All traffic should normally use the left-hand lane of the motorway unless overtaking, regardless of the speed they're travelling. Use the middle and right-hand lanes only for overtaking other vehicles.

R-ES 11, HC r259, r264, r267

When you overtake you should normally only overtake on the right. However, you may overtake on the left if traffic is moving slowly in queues and the queue on your right is moving more slowly than the one you're in.

Where there's a steep uphill gradient, a separate crawler lane may be provided for slow-moving vehicles. This helps the faster-moving traffic to flow more easily.

R-ES 11, HC r139, r268

If you're travelling in the left-hand lane and traffic is joining from a slip road, move to another lane if you're able to do so safely. This helps the flow of traffic joining the motorway, especially at peak times. Take care when filtering on high-speed roads.

Countdown markers on the left-hand verge indicate that you're approaching the next exit. If you want to leave the motorway, try to get into the left-hand lane in good time. If, by mistake, you go past the exit you wanted, carry on to the next one. Never try to stop or go back.

R-ES 11, HC r272

Speed limits

The national speed limit for cars and motorcycles on a motorway is 70 mph (112 km/h). The same limit applies to all lanes. Obey any signs showing a lower speed limit.

A vehicle towing a trailer

- is restricted to a lower speed limit of 60 mph (96 km/h)
- is not allowed to travel in the right-hand lane of a three-lane motorway unless there are lane closures.

In Northern Ireland, a vehicle towing a trailer should not use the right-hand lane of a three-lane motorway.

R-ES 11, HC r261 & p40

You can use your hazard lights to show following traffic that the traffic ahead is slowing down or stopping suddenly. Switch them off as soon as a queue forms behind you.

R-ES 11, HC r116

As you approach any roadworks, take extra care. There are usually lower speed limits, especially if there's a contraflow system. You should obey all speed limits and keep a good distance from the vehicle ahead.

R-ES 11, HC r289-290

Congestion relief

A scheme called Active Traffic Management (ATM) is in operation on some motorways to help reduce congestion. Where this is in force, mandatory speed limit signs will show on the gantries. If traffic speed can stay constant over a longer distance, bunching will be reduced and journey times will normally improve.

In ATM areas, the hard shoulder may be used as a running lane. You will know when you

can use this because a speed limit sign will be shown above all lanes, including the hard shoulder. A red cross showing above the hard shoulder indicates that you shouldn't travel in this lane and it should be used only in an emergency or breakdown.

R-ES 18, HC r269

Emergency Refuge Areas have also been built in these areas for use in cases of emergency or breakdown.

Highways Agency Traffic Officers operate on most motorways and some 'A' class roads throughout England. They

- are able to stop and direct anyone on a motorway or an 'A' road
- answer motorway emergency telephones which are linked to Highways Agency control centres in some areas.

R-ES 18, HC r105 & r108

Lane markings

Reflective studs help you to identify your position on the carriageway, especially at night or in fog. The different colours are as follows:

- red – between the hard shoulder and carriageway
- amber – between the edge of the carriageway and the central reservation
- white – between lanes
- green – between the carriageway and slip roads

- fluorescent green/yellow – at contraflow systems and roadworks.

R-ES 11, HC r132

Stopping and breakdowns

Only stop on the motorway

- if flashing red lights show above every lane
- when told to do so by the police
- in a traffic jam
- in an emergency or breakdown.

Move over if signals on the overhead gantries advise you to do so.

R-ES 11, HC r258 & r270, KYTS p90

Only stop on the hard shoulder in an emergency. To stop for any other reason, such as to have a rest or look at a map, either leave at the next exit or go to a service area.

If your motorcycle breaks down or has a puncture, try to get onto the hard shoulder and call for help. If you can, use one of the emergency telephones which are

- normally at one-mile intervals. Marker posts at 100-metre intervals point you in the direction of the nearest phone
- connected directly to police control or the Highways Agency. They will be able to locate you easily.

R-ES 11 & 16, HC r270 & r275

When using an emergency phone, stand and face oncoming traffic. You can then see any hazards approaching: for example, the draught from a large vehicle could unsteady you if you're taken unawares. If you decide to use your mobile phone

- check your location (the number on the nearest marker post) before you make the call
- give this information to the emergency services.

R-ES 11 & 16, HC r275

To rejoin the carriageway from the hard shoulder, wait for a safe gap and then gain speed on hard shoulder before moving out onto the main carriageway.

If you're not able to get onto the hard shoulder when you break down

- switch on your hazard warning lights
- leave your motorcycle only when you can get clear of the carriageway safely.

R-ES 11 & 16, HC r276 & r277

FAQs

Can I ride on a motorway with a provisional car or motorcycle licence?

You can't drive or ride on the motorway until you've passed your practical test, but you can drive or ride on dual carriageways.

R-ES 11, HC r253

I know that pedestrians and horse riders can't use a motorway – what vehicles aren't allowed?

The following vehicles aren't allowed on a motorway:

- *bicycles*
- *motorcycles under 50 cc*
- *most invalid carriages*
- *agricultural vehicles*
- *certain slow-moving vehicles.*

HC r253

9.1   *Mark one answer*   R-ES 11, HC r269 -271

On a motorway you may ONLY stop on the hard shoulder

⊙ in an emergency

⊙ If you feel tired and need to rest

⊙ if you go past the exit that you wanted to take

⊙ to pick up a hitchhiker

⊙ **in an emergency**

You must not stop on the hard shoulder except in an emergency. Never use it to, have a rest or a picnic, pick up hitchhikers, answer a mobile phone, or check a road map. You must not travel back along the hard shoulder if you go past your intended exit.

9.2   *Mark one answer*   R-ES 11, HC r259-260, r264 & r272

You are intending to leave the motorway at the next exit. Before you reach the exit you should normally position your motorcycle

⊙ in the middle lane

⊙ in the left-hand lane

⊙ on the hard shoulder

⊙ in any lane

⊙ **in the left-hand lane**

You'll see the first advance warning sign for a junction one mile from the exit. If you're travelling at 60 mph you'll only have about 50 seconds before you reach the countdown markers. Move in to the left-hand lane in good time if you're not there already. Don't cut across traffic at the last moment.

9.3   *Mark one answer*   R-ES 11

You are joining a motorway from a slip road. You should

⊙ adjust your speed to the speed of the traffic on the motorway

⊙ accelerate as quickly as you can and ride straight out

⊙ ride onto the hard shoulder until a gap appears

⊙ expect drivers on the motorway to give way to you

⊙ **adjust your speed to the speed of the traffic on the motorway**

Give way to the traffic already on the motorway and join it where there's a suitable gap in the traffic. Don't expect traffic on the motorway to give way to you, but try to avoid stopping at the end of the slip road.

A motorcycle is not allowed on a motorway if it has an engine size smaller than

⊙ 50 cc

⊙ 125 cc

⊙ 150 cc

⊙ 250 cc

⊙ **50 cc**

Very small motorcycles are not allowed to use motorways due to their restricted speed, as this may cause a hazard to other vehicles.

To ride on a motorway your motorcycle must be

⊙ 50 cc or more

⊙ 100 cc or more

⊙ 125 cc or more

⊙ 250 cc or more

⊙ **50 cc or more**

Traffic on motorways travels at high speeds. Vehicles need to be capable of keeping up with the flow of traffic. For this reason low-powered vehicles are prohibited.

On a three-lane motorway why should you normally ride in the left-hand lane?

⊙ The left-hand lane is only for lorries and motorcycles

⊙ The left-hand lane should only be used by smaller vehicles

⊙ The lanes on the right are for overtaking

⊙ Motorcycles are not allowed in the far right-hand lane

⊙ **The lanes on the right are for overtaking**

Change lanes only if necessary. When you do change lanes make sure you observe, signal and manoeuvre in good time. Always remember your 'lifesaver' check. This is a final, quick rearward glance before you pull out.

9.7 *Mark **one** answer* **R-ES 11, HC r264-265**

You are riding at 70 mph on a three-lane motorway. There is no traffic ahead. Which lane should you use?

- Any lane
- Middle lane
- Right-hand lane
- Left-hand lane

⊙ **Left-hand lane**

Use the left-hand lane if it's free, regardless of the speed you're travelling.

9.8 NI EXEMPT *Mark **one** answer* **R-ES 11, HC r124-125, r261 & p40**

You are riding on a motorway. Unless signs show otherwise you must NOT exceed

- 50 mph
- 60 mph
- 70 mph
- 80 mph

⊙ **70 mph**

Ride in accordance with the conditions. Bad weather or heavy traffic may mean you have to lower your speed.

9.9 *Mark **one** answer* **R-ES 11**

Why is it particularly important to carry out a check of your motorcycle before making a long motorway journey?

- You will have to do more harsh braking on motorways
- Motorway service stations do not deal with breakdowns
- The road surface will wear down the tyres faster
- Continuous high speeds may increase the risk of your motorcycle breaking down

⊙ **Continuous high speeds may increase the risk of your motorcycle breaking down**

Before starting a motorway journey, make sure your motorcycle can cope with the demands of high-speed riding. Things you need to check include, oil, water and tyres. When you're travelling a long way it's a good idea to plan rest stops in advance.

*Mark **one** answer*

When joining a motorway you must always

⊙ use the hard shoulder

⊙ stop at the end of the acceleration lane

⊙ come to a stop before joining the motorway

⊙ give way to traffic already on the motorway

⊙ **give way to traffic already on the motorway**

You should give way to traffic already on the motorway. Where possible they may move over to let you in but don't force your way into the traffic stream. The traffic may be travelling at high speed so you should match your speed to fit in.

*Mark **one** answer*

What is the national speed limit for cars and motorcycles in the centre lane of a three-lane motorway?

⊙ 40 mph

⊙ 50 mph

⊙ 60 mph

⊙ 70 mph

⊙ **70 mph**

Unless shown otherwise, the speed limit on a motorway applies to all the lanes. Look out for any signs of speed limit changes due to roadworks or traffic flow control.

*Mark **one** answer*

What is the national speed limit on motorways for cars and motorcycles?

⊙ 30 mph

⊙ 50 mph

⊙ 60 mph

⊙ 70 mph

⊙ **70 mph**

Travelling at the national speed limit doesn't allow you to hog the right-hand lane. Always use the left-hand lane whenever possible. When leaving a motorway get into the left-hand lane well before your exit. Reduce your speed on the slip road and look out for sharp bends or curves and traffic queuing at roundabouts.

9.13   Mark **one** answer   **R-ES 11**

The left-hand lane on a three-lane motorway is for use by

- any vehicle
- large vehicles only
- emergency vehicles only
- slow vehicles only

⊙ **any vehicle**

On a motorway all traffic should use the left-hand lane unless overtaking. Use the centre or right-hand lanes if you need to overtake. If you're overtaking a number of slower vehicles move back to the left-hand lane when you're safely past. Check your mirrors frequently and don't stay in the middle or right-hand lane if the left-hand lane is free.

9.14   Mark **one** answer   **R-ES 11**

Which of these IS NOT allowed to travel in the right-hand lane of a three-lane motorway?

- A small delivery van
- A motorcycle
- A vehicle towing a trailer
- A motorcycle and side-car

⊙ **A vehicle towing a trailer**

A vehicle with a trailer is restricted to 60 mph. For this reason it isn't allowed in the right-hand lane as it might hold up the faster-moving traffic that wishes to overtake in that lane.

9.15   Mark **one** answer   **R-ES 15, HC r275**

You break down on a motorway. You need to call for help. Why may it be better to use an emergency roadside telephone rather than a mobile phone?

- It connects you to a local garage
- Using a mobile phone will distract other drivers
- It allows easy location by the emergency services
- Mobile phones do not work on motorways

⊙ **It allows easy location by the emergency services**

On a motorway it is best to use a roadside emergency telephone so that the emergency services are able to locate you easily. The nearest telephone is shown by an arrow on marker posts at the edge of the hard shoulder. If you use a mobile, they will need to know your exact location. Before you call, find out the number on the nearest marker post. This number will identify your exact location.

After a breakdown you need to rejoin the main carriageway of a motorway from the hard shoulder. You should

⊙ move out onto the carriageway then build up your speed

⊙ move out onto the carriageway using your hazard lights

⊙ gain speed on the hard shoulder before moving out onto the carriageway

⊙ wait on the hard shoulder until someone flashes their headlights at you

⊙ **gain speed on the hard shoulder before moving out onto the carriageway**

Wait for a safe gap in the traffic before you move out. Indicate your intention and use the hard shoulder to gain speed but don't force your way into the traffic.

A crawler lane on a motorway is found

⊙ on a steep gradient

⊙ before a service area

⊙ before a junction

⊙ along the hard shoulder

⊙ **on a steep gradient**

Slow-moving, large vehicles might slow down the progress of other traffic. On a steep gradient this extra lane is provided for these slow-moving vehicles to allow the faster-moving traffic to flow more easily.

You are on a motorway. You become tired and decide you need to rest. What should you do?

⊙ Stop on the hard shoulder

⊙ Pull up on a slip road

⊙ Park on the central reservation

⊙ Leave at the next exit

⊙ **Leave at the next exit**

Ideally you should plan your journey so that you have regular rest stops. If you do become tired leave at the next exit, or pull in at a service area if this is sooner.

9.19 *Mark **one** answer* R-ES 11, HC r272

What do these motorway signs show?

⊙ They are countdown markers to a bridge

⊙ They are distance markers to the next telephone

⊙ They are countdown markers to the next exit

⊙ They warn of a police control ahead

⊙ **They are countdown markers to the next exit**

The exit from a motorway is indicated by countdown markers. These are positioned 90 metres (100 yards) apart, the first being 270 metres (300 yards) from the start of the slip road. Move into the left-hand lane well before you reach the start of the slip road.

9.20 *Mark **one** answer* R-ES 11, HC r132

On a motorway the amber reflective studs can be found between

⊙ the hard shoulder and the carriageway

⊙ the acceleration lane and the carriageway

⊙ the central reservation and the carriageway

⊙ each pair of the lanes

⊙ **the central reservation and the carriageway**

On motorways reflective studs are located into the road to help you in the dark and in conditions of poor visibility. Amber-coloured studs are found on the right-hand edge of the main carriageway, next to the central reservation.

9.21 *Mark **one** answer* R-ES 11, HC r270

You are travelling on a motorway. You decide you need a rest. You should

⊙ stop on the hard shoulder

⊙ pull in at the nearest service area

⊙ pull up on a slip road

⊙ park on the central reservation

⊙ **pull in at the nearest service area**

If you feel tired stop at the nearest service area. If it's too far away leave the motorway at the next exit and find a safe place to stop. You must not stop on the carriageway or hard shoulder of a motorway except in an emergency, in a traffic queue, when signalled to do so by a police or enforcement officer, or by traffic signals. Plan your journey so that you have regular rest stops.

9.22 *Mark **one** answer* R-ES 11, HC r132

What colour are the reflective studs between the lanes on a motorway?

- ⊙ Green
- ⊙ Amber
- ⊙ White
- ⊙ Red

⊙ **White**

White studs are found between the lanes on motorways. The light from your headlights is reflected back and this is especially useful in bad weather, when visibility is restricted.

9.23 *Mark **one** answer* R-ES 11, HC r132

What colour are the reflective studs between a motorway and its slip road?

- ⊙ Amber
- ⊙ White
- ⊙ Green
- ⊙ Red

⊙ **Green**

The studs between the carriageway and the hard shoulder are normally red. These change to green where there is a slip road. They will help you identify slip roads when visibility is poor or when it is dark.

9.24 *Mark **one** answer* R-ES 11, HC r275

You have broken down on a motorway. To find the nearest emergency telephone you should always walk

- ⊙ with the traffic flow
- ⊙ facing oncoming traffic
- ⊙ in the direction shown on the marker posts
- ⊙ in the direction of the nearest exit

⊙ **in the direction shown on the marker posts**

Along the hard shoulder there are marker posts at 100-metre intervals. These will direct you to the nearest emergency telephone.

9.25 Mark **one** answer R-ES 11, HC r264 & 267

You are joining a motorway. Why is it important to make full use of the slip road?

- ⊙ Because there is space available to turn round if you need to
- ⊙ To allow you direct access to the overtaking lanes
- ⊙ To build up a speed similar to traffic on the motorway
- ⊙ Because you can continue on the hard shoulder

⊙ **To build up a speed similar to traffic on the motorway**

Try to join the motorway without affecting the progress of the traffic already travelling on it. Always give way to traffic already on the motorway. At busy times you may have to slow down to merge into slow-moving traffic.

9.26 Mark **one** answer R-ES 11, HC r275

How should you use the emergency telephone on a motorway?

- ⊙ Stay close to the carriageway
- ⊙ Face the oncoming traffic
- ⊙ Keep your back to the traffic
- ⊙ Stand on the hard shoulder

⊙ **Face the oncoming traffic**

Traffic is passing you at speed. If the draught from a large lorry catches you by surprise it could blow you off balance and even onto the carriageway. By facing the oncoming traffic you can see approaching lorries and so be prepared for their draught. You are also in a position to see other hazards approaching.

9.27 Mark **one** answer R-ES 11, HC r132

You are on a motorway. What colour are the reflective studs on the left of the carriageway?

- ⊙ Green
- ⊙ Red
- ⊙ White
- ⊙ Amber

⊙ **Red**

Red studs are placed between the edge of the carriageway and the hard shoulder. Where slip roads leave or join the motorway the studs are green.

On a three-lane motorway which lane should you normally use?

⊙ Left

⊙ Right

⊙ Centre

⊙ Either the right or centre

⊙ **Left**

On a three-lane motorway you should travel in the left-hand lane unless you're overtaking. This applies regardless of the speed at which you're travelling.

When going through a contraflow system on a motorway you should

⊙ ensure that you do not exceed 30 mph

⊙ keep a good distance from the vehicle ahead

⊙ switch lanes to keep the traffic flowing

⊙ stay close to the vehicle ahead to reduce queues

⊙ **keep a good distance from the vehicle ahead**

There's likely to be a speed restriction in force. Keep to this. Don't

• switch lanes

• get too close to traffic in front of you.

Be aware there will be no permanent barrier between you and the oncoming traffic.

Which FOUR of these must NOT use motorways?

⊙ Learner car drivers

⊙ Motorcycles over 50cc

⊙ Double-deck buses

⊙ Farm tractors

⊙ Horse riders

⊙ Cyclists

⊙ **Learner car drivers**

⊙ **Farm tractors**

⊙ **Horse riders**

⊙ **Cyclists**

In addition, motorways MUST NOT be used by pedestrians, motorcycles under 50 cc, certain slow-moving vehicles without permission, and invalid carriages weighing less than 254 kg (560 lbs).

9.31   Mark *one* answer   R-ES 11, HC r288 & 290

You are approaching roadworks on a motorway. What should you do?

- ⊙ Speed up to clear the area quickly
- ⊙ Always use the hard shoulder
- ⊙ Obey all speed limits
- ⊙ Stay very close to the vehicle in front

⊙ **Obey all speed limits**

Collisions can often happen at roadworks. Be aware of the speed limits, slow down in good time and keep your distance from the vehicle in front.

9.32   Mark *one* answer   R-ES 7, HC r132

You are on a three-lane motorway. There are red reflective studs on your left and white ones to your right. Where are you?

- ⊙ In the right-hand lane
- ⊙ In the middle lane
- ⊙ On the hard shoulder
- ⊙ In the left-hand lane

⊙ **In the left-hand lane**

The colours of the reflective studs on the motorway and their locations are

- • red – between the hard shoulder and the carriageway
- • white – lane markings
- • amber – between the edge of the carriageway and the central reservation
- • green – along slip road exits and entrances
- • bright green/yellow – roadworks and contraflow systems.

9.33   Mark *one* answer   R-ES 11, HC r269 & 270

What should you use the hard shoulder of a motorway for?

- ⊙ Stopping in an emergency
- ⊙ Leaving the motorway
- ⊙ Stopping when you are tired
- ⊙ Joining the motorway

⊙ **Stopping in an emergency**

Don't use the hard shoulder for stopping unless it is an emergency. If you want to stop for any other reason go to the next exit or service station.

Immediately after joining a motorway you should normally

- ⊙ try to overtake
- ⊙ re-adjust your mirrors
- ⊙ position your vehicle in the centre lane
- ⊙ keep in the left-hand lane

⊙ **keep in the left-hand lane**

Stay in the left-hand lane long enough to get used to the higher speeds of motorway traffic.

What is the right-hand lane used for on a three-lane motorway?

- ⊙ Emergency vehicles only
- ⊙ Overtaking
- ⊙ Vehicles towing trailers
- ⊙ Coaches only

⊙ **Overtaking**

You should keep to the left and only use the right-hand lane if you're passing slower-moving traffic.

Which FOUR of these must NOT use motorways?

- ⊙ Learner car drivers
- ⊙ Motorcycles over 50cc
- ⊙ Double-deck buses
- ⊙ Farm tractors
- ⊙ Learner motorcyclists
- ⊙ Cyclists

⊙ **Learner car drivers**

⊙ **Farm tractors**

⊙ **Learner motorcyclists**

⊙ **Cyclists**

Learner car drivers and motorcyclists are not allowed on the motorway until they have passed their practical test.

Motorways have rules that you need to know before you venture out for the first time. When you've passed your practical test it's a good idea to have some lessons on motorways. Check with your instructor about this.

9.37   *Mark **one** answer*   **HC r269**

You are in the right-hand lane on a motorway. You see these overhead signs. This means

- ⊙ move to the left and reduce your speed to 50 mph
- ⊙ there are roadworks 50 metres (55 yards) ahead
- ⊙ use the hard shoulder until you have passed the hazard
- ⊙ leave the motorway at the next exit

⊙ **move to the left and reduce your speed to 50 mph**

You MUST obey this sign. There might not be any visible signs of a problem ahead. However, there might be queuing traffic or another hazard which you cannot yet see.

9.38   *Mark **one** answer*   **R-ES 18, HC r258 & 269**

You are allowed to stop on a motorway when you

- ⊙ need to walk and get fresh air
- ⊙ wish to pick up hitchhikers
- ⊙ are told to do so by flashing red lights
- ⊙ need to use a mobile telephone

⊙ **are told to do so by flashing red lights**

You MUST stop if there are red lights flashing above every lane on the motorway. However, if any of the other lanes do not show flashing red lights or red cross you may move into that lane and continue if it is safe to do so.

9.39   *Mark **one** answer*   **R-ES 11**

You are travelling along the left-hand lane of a three-lane motorway. Traffic is joining from a slip road. You should

- ⊙ race the other vehicles
- ⊙ move to another lane
- ⊙ maintain a steady speed
- ⊙ switch on your hazard flashers

⊙ **move to another lane**

You should move to another lane if it is safe to do so. This can greatly assist the flow of traffic joining the motorway, especially at peak times.

9.40

Mark **one** answer

R-ES 11, HC r264 & 267

A basic rule when on motorways is

- ⊙ use the lane that has least traffic
- ⊙ keep to the left-hand lane unless overtaking
- ⊙ overtake on the side that is clearest
- ⊙ try to keep above 50 mph to prevent congestion

⊙ **keep to the left-hand lane unless overtaking**

You should normally travel in the left-hand lane unless you are overtaking a slower-moving vehicle. When you are past that vehicle move back into the left-hand lane as soon as it's safe to do so. Don't cut across in front of the vehicle that you're overtaking.

9.41

Mark **one** answer

R-ES 11, HC r268

On motorways you should never overtake on the left unless

- ⊙ you can see well ahead that the hard shoulder is clear
- ⊙ the traffic in the right-hand lane is signalling right
- ⊙ you warn drivers behind by signalling left
- ⊙ there is a queue of slow-moving traffic to your right that is moving more slowly than you are

⊙ **there is a queue of slow-moving traffic to your right that is moving more slowly than you are**

Only overtake on the left if traffic is moving slowly in queues and the traffic on your right is moving more slowly than the traffic in your lane.

9.42

NI EXEMPT   Mark **one** answer

R-ES 18, HC r108

Highways Agency Traffic Officers

- ⊙ will not be able to assist at a breakdown or emergency
- ⊙ are not able to stop and direct anyone on a motorway
- ⊙ will tow a broken down vehicle and it's passengers home
- ⊙ are able to stop and direct anyone on a motorway

⊙ **are able to stop and direct anyone on a motorway**

Highways Agency Traffic Officers (HATOs) are able to stop and direct traffic on most motorways and some 'A' class roads. They work in partnership with the police at motorway incidents and provide a highly-trained and visible service. Their role is to help keep traffic moving and make your journey as safe and reliable as possible. They are recognised by an orange and yellow jacket and their vehicle has yellow and black markings.

9.43   *Mark **one** answer*   R-ES 18

An Emergency Refuge Area is an area

- ⊙ on a motorway for use in cases of emergency or breakdown
- ⊙ for use if you think you will be involved in a road rage incident
- ⊙ on a motorway for a police patrol to park and watch traffic
- ⊙ for construction and road workers to store emergency equipment

⊙ **on a motorway for use in cases of emergency or breakdown**

Emergency Refuge Areas may be found at the side of the hard shoulder about 500 metres apart. If you break down you should use them rather than the hard shoulder if you are able. When re-joining the motorway you must remember to take extra care especially when the hard shoulder is being used as a running lane within an Active Traffic Management area. Try to match your speed to that of traffic in the lane you are joining.

9.44   *Mark **one** answer*   R-ES 18

What is an Emergency Refuge Area on a motorway for?

- ⊙ An area to park in when you want to use a mobile phone
- ⊙ To use in cases of emergency or breakdown
- ⊙ For an emergency recovery vehicle to park in a contra-flow system
- ⊙ To drive in when there is queuing traffic ahead

⊙ **To use in cases of emergency or breakdown**

In cases of breakdown or emergency try to get your vehicle into an Emergency Refuge Area. This is safer than just stopping on the hard shoulder as it gives you greater distance from the main carriageway. If you are able to re-join the motorway you must take extra care, especially when the hard shoulder is being used as a running lane.

9.45   NI EXEMPT   *Mark **one** answer*   HC r108

Motorway emergency telephones are usually linked to the police. In some areas they are now linked to

- ⊙ the Highways Agency Control Centre
- ⊙ the Driver Vehicle Licensing Agency
- ⊙ the Driving Standards Agency
- ⊙ the local Vehicle Registration Office

⊙ **the Highways Agency Control Centre**

In some areas motorway telephones are now linked to a Highways Agency Control Centre, instead of the police. Highways Agency Traffic Officers work in partnership with the police and assist at motorway emergencies and incidents. They are recognised by a high-visibility orange and yellow jacket and high-visibility vehicle with yellow and black chequered markings.

245

You are on a motorway. A red cross is displayed above the hard shoulder. What does this mean?

⊙ Pull up in this lane to answer your mobile phone

⊙ Use this lane as a running lane

⊙ This lane can be used if you need a rest

⊙ You should not travel in this lane

⊙ **You should not travel in this lane**

Active Traffic Management schemes are being introduced on motorways. Within these areas at certain times the hard shoulder will be used as a running lane. A red cross above the hard shoulder shows that this lane should NOT be used, except for emergencies and breakdowns.

You are on a motorway in an Active Traffic Management (ATM) area. A mandatory speed limit is displayed above the hard shoulder. What does this mean?

⊙ You should not travel in this lane

⊙ The hard shoulder can be used as a running lane

⊙ You can park on the hard shoulder if you feel tired

⊙ You can pull up in this lane to answer a mobile phone

⊙ **The hard shoulder can be used as a running lane**

A mandatory speed limit sign above the hard shoulder shows that it can be used as a running lane between junctions. You must stay within the speed limit. Look out for vehicles that may have broken down and could be blocking the hard shoulder.

9.48   NI EXEMPT   *Mark **one** answer*   **R-ES 18, HC r269**

The aim of an Active Traffic Management scheme on a motorway is to

- prevent overtaking
- reduce rest stops
- prevent tailgating
- reduce congestion

⊙ **reduce congestion**

Active Traffic Management schemes are intended to reduce congestion and make journey times more reliable. In these areas the hard shoulder may be used as a running lane to ease congestion at peak times or in the event of an incident. It may appear that you could travel faster for a short distance, but keeping traffic flow at a constant speed may improve your journey time.

9.49   NI EXEMPT   *Mark **one** answer*   **R-ES 18, HC r269**

You are in an Active Traffic Management area on a motorway. When the Actively Managed mode is operating

- speed limits are only advisory
- the national speed limit will apply
- the speed limit is always 30 mph
- all speed limit signals are set

⊙ **all speed limit signals are set**

When an Active Traffic Management (ATM) scheme is operating on a motorway you MUST follow the mandatory instructions shown on the gantries above each lane. This includes the hard shoulder.

9.50   NI EXEMPT   *Mark **one** answer*   **R-ES 18, HC r258 & 269**

You are travelling on a motorway. A red cross is shown above the hard shoulder. What does this mean?

- Use this lane as a rest area
- Use this as a normal running lane
- Do not use this lane to travel in
- National speed limit applies in this lane

⊙ **Do not use this lane to travel in**

When a red cross is shown above the hard shoulder it should only be used for breakdowns or emergencies. Within Active Traffic Management (ATM) areas the hard shoulder may sometimes be used as a running lane. Speed limit signs directly above the hard shoulder will show that it's open.

Why can it be an advantage for traffic speed to stay constant over a longer distance?

- ⊙ You will do more stop-start driving
- ⊙ You will use far more fuel
- ⊙ You will be able to use more direct routes
- ⊙ Your overall journey time will normally improve

⊙ **Your overall journey time will normally improve**

When traffic travels at a constant speed over a longer distance, journey times normally improve. You may feel that you could travel faster for short periods but this won't generally improve your overall journey time. Signs will show the maximum speed at which you should travel.

You should not normally travel on the hard shoulder of a motorway. When can you use it?

- ⊙ When taking the next exit
- ⊙ When traffic is stopped
- ⊙ When signs direct you to
- ⊙ When traffic is slow moving

⊙ **When signs direct you to**

Normally you should only use the hard shoulder for emergencies and breakdowns, and at roadworks when signs direct you to do so. Active Traffic Management (ATM) areas are being introduced to ease traffic congestion. In these areas the hard shoulder may be used as a running lane when speed limit signs are shown directly above.

For what reason may you use the right-hand lane of a motorway?

- ⊙ For keeping out of the way of lorries
- ⊙ For travelling at more than 70 mph
- ⊙ For turning right
- ⊙ For overtaking other vehicles

⊙ **For overtaking other vehicles**

The right-hand lane of the motorway is for overtaking.

Sometimes you may be directed into a right-hand lane as a result of roadworks or a traffic incident. This will be indicated by signs or officers directing the traffic.

9.54

*Mark **one** answer*

R-ES 18, HC r269

On a motorway what is used to reduce traffic bunching?

- Variable speed limits
- Contraflow systems
- National speed limits
- Lane closures

⊙ **Variable speed limits**

Congestion can be reduced by keeping traffic at a constant speed. At busy times maximum speed limits are displayed on overhead gantries. These can be varied quickly depending on the amount of traffic. By keeping to a constant speed on busy sections of motorway overall journey times are normally improved.

9.55

*Mark **three** answers*

R-ES 18, HC r258 & 269-270

When should you stop on a motorway?

- If you have to read a map
- When you are tired and need a rest
- If red lights show above every lane
- When told to by the police
- If your mobile phone rings
- When signalled by a Highways Agency Traffic Officer

⊙ **If red lights show above every lane**

⊙ **When told to by the police**

⊙ **When signalled by a Highways Agency Traffic Officer**

There are some occasions when you may have to stop on the carriageway of a motorway. These include when being signalled by the police or a Highways Agency Traffic Officer, when flashing red lights show above every lane and in traffic jams.

9.56

*Mark **one** answer*

R-ES 18, HC r258 & 270

When may you stop on a motorway?

- If you have to read a map
- When you are tired and need a rest
- If your mobile phone rings
- In an emergency or breakdown

⊙ **In an emergency or breakdown**

You should not normally stop on a motorway but there may be occasions when you need to do so. If you are unfortunate enough to break down make every effort to pull up on the hard shoulder.

You are travelling on a motorway. Unless signs show a lower speed limit you must NOT exceed

- ⊙ 50 mph
- ⊙ 60 mph
- ⊙ 70 mph
- ⊙ 80 mph

⊙ **70 mph**

The national speed limit for a car or motorcycle on the motorway is 70 mph. Lower speed limits may be in force, for example at roadworks, so look out for the signs. Variable speed limits operate in some areas to control very busy stretches of motorway. The speed limit may change depending on the volume of traffic.

Motorway emergency telephones are usually linked to the police. In some areas they are now linked to

- ⊙ the local ambulance service
- ⊙ an Highways Agency control centre
- ⊙ the local fire brigade
- ⊙ a breakdown service control centre

⊙ **an Highways Agency control centre**

The controller will ask you

- the make and colour of your vehicle
- whether you are a member of an emergency breakdown service
- the number shown on the emergency telephone casing
- whether you are travelling alone.

You are on a motorway. There are red flashing lights above every lane. You must

- ⊙ pull onto the hard shoulder
- ⊙ slow down and watch for further signals
- ⊙ leave at the next exit
- ⊙ stop and wait

⊙ **stop and wait**

Red flashing lights above every lane mean you must not go on any further. You'll also see a red cross illuminated. Stop and wait. Don't

- change lanes
- continue
- pull onto the hard shoulder (unless in an emergency).

9.60   NI EXEMPT   *Mark **one** answer*   R-ES 18, HC r269

You are on a three-lane motorway. A red cross is shown above the hard shoulder and mandatory speed limits above all other lanes. This means

- ⊙ the hard shoulder can be used as a rest area if you feel tired
- ⊙ the hard shoulder is for emergency or breakdown use only
- ⊙ the hard shoulder can be used as a normal running lane
- ⊙ the hard shoulder has a speed limit of 50 mph

⊙ **the hard shoulder is for emergency or breakdown use only**

A red cross above the hard shoulder shows it is closed as a running lane and should only be used for emergencies or breakdowns. At busy times within an Active Traffic Management (ATM) area the hard shoulder may be used as a running lane. This will be shown by a mandatory speed limit on the gantry above.

9.61   NI EXEMPT   *Mark **one** answer*   R-ES 18, HC r269

You are on a three-lane motorway and see this sign. It means you can use

- ⊙ any lane except the hard shoulder
- ⊙ the hard shoulder only
- ⊙ the three right hand lanes only
- ⊙ all the lanes including the hard shoulder

⊙ **all the lanes including the hard shoulder**

Mandatory speed limit signs above all lanes including the hard shoulder, show that you are in an Active Traffic Management (ATM) area. In this case you can use the hard shoulder as a running lane. You must stay within the speed limit shown. Look out for any vehicles that may have broken down and be blocking the hard shoulder.

Case study practice 9 – Motorway rules

Max is riding his motorcycle and newly fitted sidecar. On the motorway, Max rides in the left-hand lane. He then sees flashing amber lights on the central reservation, with a sign showing '50'. Later, Max needs to exit at the next junction, so he watches for countdown markers. He then reaches the marker showing three bars.

9.1 What could be affected by the presence of the sidecar?

*Mark **one** answer*

- ⊙ Steering and braking.
- ⊙ Indicators and fairings.
- ⊙ Road tax and speed limits.
- ⊙ Fuel type and exhaust.

> **R-ES 14**

9.2 Why would Max take this position on the motorway?

*Mark **one** answer*

- ⊙ That is the only lane which is completely empty of other traffic.
- ⊙ He is travelling more slowly and doesn't want to obstruct others.
- ⊙ All traffic should do so unless they are overtaking other vehicles.
- ⊙ He's unsure when he will reach the slip road for the next junction.

> **R-ES 11, HC r264**

9.3 How should Max initially ride?

*Mark **one** answer*

- ⊙ The same as normal.
- ⊙ Slower than normal.
- ⊙ Faster than normal.
- ⊙ Only with a passenger.

R-ES 11

9.4 What is meant by the sign and lights?

*Mark **one** answer*

- ⊙ Temporary minimum speed advised.
- ⊙ Temporary maximum distance advised.
- ⊙ Temporary maximum speed advised.
- ⊙ Temporary minimum distance advised.

R-ES 11

9.5 At this marker, how far is Max from the exit he needs?

*Mark **one** answer*

- ⊙ Four hundred yards.
- ⊙ Three hundred yards.
- ⊙ Two hundred yards.
- ⊙ One hundred yards.

R-ES 11, HC p112

section **ten**
RULES OF
THE ROAD

This section covers
- Speed limits
- Lane discipline
- Parking
- Lighting

Rules of the road

It's important that everyone knows and follows the rules of the road. Some are legal requirements and some are just recommended best practice, but all help towards safer roads.

Speed limits

You must not exceed the speed limit for the road you're on or your vehicle type. Where there isn't any other limit shown, the national speed limit for cars and motorcycles is

- 60 mph (96 km/h) on a single carriageway
- 70 mph (112 km/h) on a dual carriageway or motorway.

Lower speed limits of

- 50 mph (80 km/h) on a single carriageway
- 60 mph (96 km/h) on a dual carriageway or motorway

apply for vehicles towing a trailer or caravan.

Street lights normally mean that there's a 30 mph (48 km/h) speed limit for all vehicles unless signs show otherwise. On some roads you may also find a minimum speed limit where you should travel above the limit shown on the sign unless it's unsafe to do so.

HC r124, p40 & p107

Always drive with care and according to the conditions. If you're going along a street where cars are parked, keep your speed down and beware of

- pedestrians (especially children) emerging from behind parked vehicles

- vehicles pulling out
- drivers' doors opening.

At roadworks there may be temporary speed limits to slow traffic down. Obey these signs.

R-ES 10, HC r152 & r288, KYTS p89

Lanes and junctions

Some roads have lanes reserved for specific vehicles such as cycles, buses or trams. These are marked by signs and road markings, and must only be used by those vehicles during their hours of operation.

Never drive or park in a cycle lane marked by a solid white line during its period of operation. Don't drive or park in one marked by a broken line unless it's unavoidable.

Only drive over a footpath to gain access to a property.

HC r140-141 & r145

On a dual carriageway, the right-hand lane is only for turning right or overtaking. The same rule applies to three-lane dual carriageways.

Treat all junctions with extra care. On approach, move into the appropriate position in good time. If you're going to turn left, keep well to the left as you approach the junction. Remember to check for cyclists to your left before you turn.

R-ES 9, HC r181-183

If you're turning right at a crossroads when an oncoming road user is also turning right, it's normally safer to keep the other vehicle to your right and turn behind it. If you have to pass in front of the other vehicle, take extra care as your view may be obscured.

A box junction – indicated by yellow hatched lines – should be kept clear. Only enter it if your exit road is clear. You may wait in the box if you want to turn right and are only prevented from doing so by oncoming traffic.

R-ES 7 & 9, HC r174 & r181

At crossroads where there aren't any signs or markings, no one has priority. Check very carefully in all directions before you proceed.

R-ES 9, HC r146

Roundabouts are designed to aid the flow of traffic. Follow signs and road markings as you approach and negotiate these. Normally, if you're going straight ahead

- don't signal as you approach
- signal left before you leave the roundabout, just after you pass the exit before the one you want.

Some vehicles may not follow the normal rules:

- cyclists and horse riders may stay in the left-hand lane even if they're turning right
- long vehicles may take up a different position to stop the rear of the vehicle hitting the kerb.

R-ES 9, HC r186-187

Overtaking and turning

Overtaking is a dangerous manoeuvre. Ask yourself if you really need to overtake and never do so if you're in any doubt as to whether it's safe.

You should normally overtake on the right, but in a one-way street you can overtake on either side. Take extra care if you're overtaking on a dual carriageway, as the right-hand lane can also be used by traffic turning right.

R-ES 8, HC r137-138, r163

If you're on a busy road and find that you're

- travelling in the wrong direction
- in the wrong lane at a busy junction

keep going until you can find somewhere safe, such as a quiet side road, in which to turn round.

R-ES 6 & 9, HC r200

Crossings

If someone is standing on the pavement, waiting to cross at a zebra crossing, stop, as long as it's safe to do so, and let them cross.

Pelican crossings are light-controlled. When the red light changes to flashing amber, wait for any pedestrians to get clear of the crossing before moving off. On toucan crossings, cyclists are allowed to cycle across at the same time as pedestrians walk.

R-ES 8, HC r195-199, KYTS p122

Level crossings

A level crossing, where a railway line crosses the road, may have countdown markers to warn you if the crossing is hidden, such as round a bend. Controlled crossings have traffic light signals, plus twin flashing red lights and a warning alarm for pedestrians. They may or may not have barriers.

- If the warning lights come on as you're approaching the crossing – stop
- If you're already on the crossing when the warning lights come on or a bell rings – keep going and clear the crossing
- If you're waiting at a level crossing and a train has passed but the red lights keep flashing – wait. There may be another train coming.

R-ES 7, HC r293, p109, KYTS p26-29

There are other types of level crossing without lights, such as those with user-operated gates or barriers and open crossings. Treat all types of level crossing with caution. Also take care when crossing rails – they may be slippery, particularly in wet weather.

R-ES 8, HC r295-299

Stopping and parking

At night, the safest place to park your motorcycle is in your garage, if you have one. If you're away from home, try to find secure car or motorcycle parking, or park in a well-lit area.

R-ES 9 & 10, HC r239 & p131

If you have to park on a road, you must leave your sidelights on if the speed limit on that road is over 30 mph (48 km/h). You should normally park on the left-hand side of the road so other road users can see your reflectors, but in a one-way street you can park on either side.

R-ES 13, HC r248-250

Never stop on a clearway. On an urban clearway or a road marked with double white lines (even where one of the lines is broken), you may stop only to set down and pick up passengers or to load/unload goods.

R-ES 7, HC r240

Do not park where you would cause a danger or obstruction to others, such as

- on or near the brow of a hill
- at a bus stop
- opposite a traffic island or dropped kerb
- in front of someone else's drive
- near a school entrance
- within 10 metres (32 feet) of a junction (in Northern Ireland, within 15 metres or 48 feet of a junction).

HC r242-243

Don't cause an obstruction by stopping or parking where there are restrictions such as yellow lines and associated signs or in spaces reserved for disabled drivers. In a controlled parking zone you'll have to pay to park. Park within marked bays on the days and times shown on the zone entry signs.

R-ES 7, HC r238 & r245, KYTS p45

FAQs

What do I do if there's an obstruction on my side of the road?

Give way to oncoming traffic if there isn't room for traffic on both sides to continue safely.

R-ES 8

On a dual carriageway, if a sign warns that my lane will close 800 yards ahead, when should I move over?

Move to another lane in good time – don't leave it until the last minute. When changing lanes on any dual carriageway, be aware of other traffic and don't forget to make mirror and over-the-shoulder checks.

R-ES 11, HC r288-289

At night, if a car overtakes me, when should I dip my headlights?

Dip your lights as soon as the car passes you or your lights could dazzle the other driver. If travelling abroad, remember that you'll need to fit headlight deflectors for riding on the right-hand side of the road.

HC r115

I'm on a road that's only wide enough for one vehicle and there's a car coming towards me. What do I do?

Pull into a passing place on your left, or if the nearest passing place is on your right, wait opposite it.

R-ES 10, HC r155

How can brake lights give signals to other drivers?

Brake lights show traffic behind you that you're slowing down.

R-ES 6

What do I do if I want to turn right onto a dual carriageway that has a narrow central reservation?

Wait until the road is clear in both directions or you'll obstruct traffic coming from your right.

R-ES 9, HC r173

Are there times when I have to stop by law?

Yes. You must stop

- *when involved in a road traffic incident*
- *at a red traffic light*
- *at a stop sign*
- *when signalled to do so by a police officer, traffic officer, or school crossing patrol.*

HC r195-109 & r286

In a well-lit built-up area, can I ride using sidelights only?

It's recommended that you use dipped headlights so that you can be seen easily by others. If you use reflective or hi-vis clothing as well, this will improve your visibility even more.

HC r115

10.1 *Mark one answer* R-ES 8 & 9

You are riding slowly in a town centre. Before turning left you should glance over your left shoulder to

⊙ check for cyclists

⊙ help keep your balance

⊙ look for traffic signs

⊙ check for potholes

⊙ **check for cyclists**

When riding slowly you must remember cyclists. They can travel quickly and fit through surprisingly narrow spaces. Before you turn left in slow-moving traffic it's important to check that a cyclist isn't trying to overtake on your left.

10.2 *Mark two answers* R-ES 8, HC r140 & r300

As a motorcycle rider which TWO lanes must you NOT use?

⊙ Crawler lane

⊙ Overtaking lane

⊙ Acceleration lane

⊙ Cycle lane

⊙ Tram lane

⊙ **Cycle lane**

⊙ **Tram lane**

In some towns motorcycles are permitted to use bus lanes. Check the signs carefully.

10.3 *Mark one answer* R-ES 8 & 9

You are riding on a busy dual carriageway. When changing lanes you should

⊙ rely totally on mirrors

⊙ always increase your speed

⊙ signal so others will give way

⊙ use mirrors and shoulder checks

⊙ **use mirrors and shoulder checks**

Before changing direction, as well as using your mirrors, you need to take a quick sideways glance to check for vehicles in any of your blind spots. These are areas behind and to the side of you which are not covered by the mirrors.

10.4 *Mark two answers* HC r242-243

In which TWO places should you NOT park?

⊙ Near a school entrance

⊙ Near a police station

⊙ In a side road

⊙ At a bus stop

⊙ In a one-way street

⊙ **Near a school entrance**

⊙ **At a bus stop**

It may be tempting to park where you shouldn't while you run a quick errand. Careless parking is a selfish act and could endanger other road users.

What does this sign mean?

- ⊙ No parking for solo motorcycles
- ⊙ Parking for solo motorcycles
- ⊙ Passing place for motorcycles
- ⊙ Police motorcycles only

⊙ **Parking for solo motorcycles**

In some towns and cities there are special areas reserved for parking motorcycles. Look out for these signs.

You are looking for somewhere to park your motorcycle. The area is full EXCEPT for spaces marked 'disabled use'. You can

- ⊙ use these spaces when elsewhere is full
- ⊙ park if you stay with your motorcycle
- ⊙ use these spaces, disabled or not
- ⊙ not park there unless permitted

⊙ **not park there unless permitted**

Don't be selfish. These spaces are intended for people with limited mobility. Find somewhere else to park, even if it means that you have to walk further.

You are on a road with passing places. It is only wide enough for one vehicle. There is a car coming towards you. What should you do?

- ⊙ Pull into a passing place on your right
- ⊙ Force the other driver to reverse
- ⊙ Turn round and ride back to the main road
- ⊙ Pull into a passing place on your left

⊙ **Pull into a passing place on your left**

If you meet another vehicle in a narrow road and the passing place is on your left, pull into it. If the passing place is on the right, wait opposite it.

10.8
*Mark **one** answer*

R-ES 9, HC r181

You are both turning right at this crossroads. It is safer to keep the car to your right so you can

- see approaching traffic
- keep close to the kerb
- keep clear of following traffic
- make oncoming vehicles stop

⊙ **see approaching traffic**

When turning right at this crossroads you should keep the oncoming car on your right. This will give you a clear view of the road ahead and any oncoming traffic.

10.9
*Mark **three** answers*

HC r88

When filtering through slow-moving or stationary traffic you should

- watch for hidden vehicles emerging from side roads
- continually use your horn as a warning
- look for vehicles changing course suddenly
- always ride with your hazard lights on
- stand up on the footrests for a good view ahead
- look for pedestrians walking between vehicles

⊙ **watch for hidden vehicles emerging from side roads**

⊙ **look for vehicles changing course suddenly**

⊙ **look for pedestrians walking between vehicles**

Other road users may not expect or look for motorcycles filtering through slow-moving or stationary traffic. Your view will be reduced by the vehicles around you. Watch out for, pedestrians walking between the vehicles, vehicles suddenly changing direction and vehicles pulling out of side roads.

10.10

*Mark **one** answer*

R-ES 8 & 10, HC r109

You are riding towards roadworks. The temporary traffic lights are at red. The road ahead is clear. What should you do?

- ⊙ Ride on with extreme caution
- ⊙ Ride on at normal speed
- ⊙ Carry on if approaching cars have stopped
- ⊙ Wait for the green light

⊙ **Wait for the green light**

You must obey all traffic signs and signals. Just because the lights are temporary it does not mean that you can disregard them.

10.11

*Mark **one** answer*

R-ES 19

You intend to go abroad and will be riding on the right-hand side of the road. What should you fit to your motorcycle?

- ⊙ Twin headlights
- ⊙ Headlight deflectors
- ⊙ Tinted yellow brake lights
- ⊙ Tinted red indicator lenses

⊙ **Headlight deflectors**

When abroad and riding on the right, deflectors are usually required to prevent your headlight dazzling approaching drivers.

10.12

*Mark **one** answer*

R-ES 14, HC r89 & r98

You want to tow a trailer with your motorcycle. Your engine must be more than

- ⊙ 50 cc
- ⊙ 125 cc
- ⊙ 525 cc
- ⊙ 1000 cc

⊙ **125 cc**

You must remember that towing a trailer requires special care. You must obey the restrictions which apply to all vehicles towing trailers. Do not forget it is there, especially when negotiating bends and junctions.

10.13   *Mark **one** answer*   **HC r124 & p40**

What is the national speed limit on a single carriageway?

- ⊙ 40 mph
- ⊙ 50 mph
- ⊙ 60 mph
- ⊙ 70 mph

⊙ **60 mph**

You don't have to ride at the speed limit. Use your own judgement and ride at a speed that suits the prevailing road, weather and traffic conditions.

10.14   *Mark **three** answers*   **HC r105, r109, r286-287**

On which THREE occasions MUST you stop your motorcycle?

- ⊙ When involved in a collision
- ⊙ At a red traffic light
- ⊙ When signalled to do so by a police officer
- ⊙ At a junction with double broken white lines
- ⊙ At a clear pelican crossing when the amber light is flashing

⊙ **When involved in a collision**

⊙ **At a red traffic light**

⊙ **When signalled to do so by a police officer**

Don't stop or hold up traffic unnecessarily. However there are occasions when you MUST stop by law. These include, when signalled to do so by a police officer, at a red traffic light and if you have a collision. There are many other instances where you may have to stop.

10.15   *Mark **one** answer*   **KYTS p20**

What is the meaning of this sign?

- ⊙ Local speed limit applies
- ⊙ No waiting on the carriageway
- ⊙ National speed limit applies
- ⊙ No entry to vehicular traffic

⊙ **National speed limit applies**

This sign doesn't tell you the speed limit in figures. You should know the speed limit for the type of road that you're on. Study your copy of The Highway Code.

What is the national speed limit for cars and motorcycles on a dual carriageway?

- ⊙ 30 mph
- ⊙ 50 mph
- ⊙ 60 mph
- ⊙ 70 mph

⊙ **70 mph**

Ensure that you know the speed limit for the road that you're on. The speed limit on a dual carriageway or motorway is 70 mph for cars and motorcycles, unless there are signs to indicate otherwise. The speed limits for different types of vehicles are listed in The Highway Code.

There are no speed limit signs on the road. How is a 30 mph limit indicated?

- ⊙ By hazard warning lines
- ⊙ By street lighting
- ⊙ By pedestrian islands
- ⊙ By double or single yellow lines

⊙ **By street lighting**

There is usually a 30 mph speed limit where there are street lights unless there are signs showing another limit.

There is a tractor ahead of you. You wish to overtake but you are NOT sure if it is safe to do so. You should

- ⊙ follow another overtaking vehicle through
- ⊙ sound your horn to the slow vehicle to pull over
- ⊙ speed through but flash your lights to oncoming traffic
- ⊙ not overtake if you are in doubt

⊙ **not overtake if you are in doubt**

Never overtake if you're not sure whether it's safe. Can you see far enough down the road to ensure that you can complete the manoeuvre safely? If the answer is no, DON'T GO.

10.19   *Mark **one** answer*   KYTS p21

What does this sign mean?

- ⊙ Minimum speed 30 mph
- ⊙ End of maximum speed
- ⊙ End of minimum speed
- ⊙ Maximum speed 30 mph

⊙ **End of minimum speed**

A red slash through this sign indicates that the restriction has ended. In this case the restriction was a minimum speed limit of 30 mph.

10.20   *Mark **one** answer*   HC r124 & p40

Where you see street lights but no speed limit signs the limit is usually

- ⊙ 30 mph
- ⊙ 40 mph
- ⊙ 50 mph
- ⊙ 60 mph

⊙ **30 mph**

The presence of street lights generally shows that there is a 30 mph speed limit, unless signs tell you otherwise.

10.21   *Mark **three** answers*   HC r187

Which three of the following are most likely to take an unusual course at roundabouts?

- ⊙ Horse riders
- ⊙ Milk floats
- ⊙ Delivery vans
- ⊙ Long vehicles
- ⊙ Estate cars
- ⊙ Cyclists

⊙ **Horse riders**

⊙ **Long vehicles**

⊙ **Cyclists**

Long vehicles might have to take a slightly different position when approaching the roundabout or going around it. This is to stop the rear of the vehicle cutting in and mounting the kerb.

Horse riders and cyclists might stay in the left-hand lane although they are turning right. Be aware of this and allow them room.

On a clearway you must not stop

- ⊙ at any time
- ⊙ when it is busy
- ⊙ in the rush hour
- ⊙ during daylight hours

⊙ **at any time**

Clearways are in place so that traffic can flow without the obstruction of parked vehicles. Just one parked vehicle will cause an obstruction for all other traffic. You MUST NOT stop where a clearway is in force, not even to pick up or set down passengers.

What is the meaning of this sign?

- ⊙ No entry
- ⊙ Waiting restrictions
- ⊙ National speed limit
- ⊙ School crossing patrol

⊙ **Waiting restrictions**

This sign indicates that there are waiting restrictions. It is normally accompanied by details of when restrictions are in force.

Details of most signs which are in common use are shown in The Highway Code and a more comprehensive selection is available in Know Your Traffic Signs.

You can park on the right-hand side of a road at night

- ⊙ in a one-way street
- ⊙ with your sidelights on
- ⊙ more than 10 metres (32 feet) from a junction
- ⊙ under a lamp-post

⊙ **in a one-way street**

Red rear reflectors show up when headlights shine on them. These are useful when you are parked at night but will only reflect if you park in the same direction as the traffic flow. Normally you should park on the left, but if you're in a one-way street you may also park on the right-hand side.

10.25   *Mark **one** answer*   **R-ES 8, HC r137-138**

On a three-lane dual carriageway the right-hand lane can be used for

⊙ overtaking only, never turning right

⊙ overtaking or turning right

⊙ fast-moving traffic only

⊙ turning right only, never overtaking

⊙ **overtaking or turning right**

You should normally use the left-hand lane on any dual carriageway unless you are overtaking or turning right.

When overtaking on a dual carriageway, look for vehicles ahead that are turning right. They're likely to be slowing or stopped. You need to see them in good time so that you can take appropriate action.

10.26   *Mark **one** answer*   **R-ES 6 & 9, HC r133-134**

You are approaching a busy junction. There are several lanes with road markings. At the last moment you realise that you are in the wrong lane. You should

⊙ continue in that lane

⊙ force your way across

⊙ stop until the area has cleared

⊙ use clear arm signals to cut across

⊙ **continue in that lane**

There are times where road markings can be obscured by queuing traffic, or you might be unsure which lane you need to be in.

If you realise that you're in the wrong lane, don't cut across lanes or bully other drivers to let you in. Follow the lane you're in and find somewhere safe to turn around if you need to.

10.27   *Mark **one** answer*   **R-ES 8, HC r137-138**

Where may you overtake on a one-way street?

⊙ Only on the left-hand side

⊙ Overtaking is not allowed

⊙ Only on the right-hand side

⊙ Either on the right or the left

⊙ **Either on the right or the left**

You can overtake other traffic on either side when travelling in a one-way street. Make full use of your mirrors and ensure that it's clear all around before you attempt to overtake. Look for signs and road markings and use the most suitable lane for your destination.

*Mark **one** answer*

When going straight ahead at a roundabout you should

- ⊙ indicate left before leaving the roundabout
- ⊙ not indicate at any time
- ⊙ indicate right when approaching the roundabout
- ⊙ indicate left when approaching the roundabout

⊙ **indicate left before leaving the roundabout**

When you want to go straight on at a roundabout, don't signal as you approach it, but indicate left just after you pass the exit before the one you wish to take.

---

*Mark **one** answer*

Which vehicle might have to use a different course to normal at roundabouts?

- ⊙ Sports car
- ⊙ Van
- ⊙ Estate car
- ⊙ Long vehicle

⊙ **Long vehicle**

A long vehicle may have to straddle lanes either on or approaching a roundabout so that the rear wheels don't cut in over the kerb.

If you're following a long vehicle, stay well back and give it plenty of room.

---

*Mark **one** answer*

You may only enter a box junction when

- ⊙ there are less than two vehicles in front of you
- ⊙ the traffic lights show green
- ⊙ your exit road is clear
- ⊙ you need to turn left

⊙ **your exit road is clear**

Yellow box junctions are marked on the road to prevent the road becoming blocked. Don't enter one unless your exit road is clear. You may only wait in the yellow box if your exit road is clear but oncoming traffic is preventing you from completing the turn.

10.31   *Mark* **one** *answer*   **R-ES 7, HC r174**

You may wait in a yellow box junction when

- ⊙ oncoming traffic is preventing you from turning right
- ⊙ you are in a queue of traffic turning left
- ⊙ you are in a queue of traffic to go ahead
- ⊙ you are on a roundabout

⊙ **oncoming traffic is preventing you from turning right**

The purpose of this road marking is to keep the junction clear of queuing traffic. You may only wait in the marked area when you're turning right and your exit lane is clear but you can't complete the turn because of oncoming traffic.

10.32   *Mark* **three** *answers*   **HC r105-109 & 286**

You MUST stop when signalled to do so by which THREE of these?

- ⊙ A police officer
- ⊙ A pedestrian
- ⊙ A school crossing patrol
- ⊙ A bus driver
- ⊙ A red traffic light

⊙ **A police officer**

⊙ **A school crossing patrol**

⊙ **A red traffic light**

Looking well ahead and 'reading' the road will help you to anticipate hazards. This will enable you to stop safely at traffic lights or if ordered to do so by an authorised person.

10.33   *Mark* **one** *answer*   **R-ES 8, HC r195-199, KYTS p122**

Someone is waiting to cross at a zebra crossing. They are standing on the pavement. You should normally

- ⊙ go on quickly before they step onto the crossing
- ⊙ stop before you reach the zigzag lines and let them cross
- ⊙ stop, let them cross, wait patiently
- ⊙ ignore them as they are still on the pavement

⊙ **stop, let them cross, wait patiently**

By standing on the pavement, the pedestrian is showing an intention to cross. If you are looking well down the road you will give yourself enough time to slow down and stop safely. Don't forget to check your mirrors before slowing down.

*Mark **one** answer* **R-ES 8, HC r195-199, KYTS p122**

At toucan crossings, apart from pedestrians you should be aware of

⊙ emergency vehicles emerging

⊙ buses pulling out

⊙ trams crossing in front

⊙ cyclists riding across

⊙ **cyclists riding across**

The use of cycles is being encouraged and more toucan crossings are being installed. These crossings enable pedestrians and cyclists to cross the path of other traffic. Watch out as cyclists will approach the crossing faster than pedestrians.

10.35 *Mark **one** answer* **HC r181**

You are intending to turn right at a crossroads. An oncoming driver is also turning right. It will normally be safer to

⊙ keep the other vehicle to your RIGHT and turn behind it (offside to offside)

⊙ keep the other vehicle to your LEFT and turn in front of it (nearside to nearside)

⊙ carry on and turn at the next junction instead

⊙ hold back and wait for the other driver to turn first

⊙ **keep the other vehicle to your RIGHT and turn behind it (offside to offside)**

At some junctions the layout may make it difficult to turn offside to offside. If this is the case, be prepared to pass nearside to nearside, but take extra care as your view ahead will be obscured by the vehicle turning in front of you.

10.36 *Mark **one** answer* **R-ES 8, HC r195-199, KYTS p122**

At a pelican crossing, what does a flashing amber light mean?

⊙ You must not move off until the lights stop flashing

⊙ You must give way to pedestrians still on the crossing

⊙ You can move off, even if pedestrians are still on the crossing

⊙ You must stop because the lights are about to change to red

⊙ **You must give way to pedestrians still on the crossing**

If there is no-one on the crossing when the amber light is flashing, you may proceed over the crossing. You don't need to wait for the green light to show.

10.37   *Mark one answer*   R-ES 8, HC r195-199, KYTS p122

You are waiting at a pelican crossing. The red light changes to flashing amber. This means you must

⊙ wait for pedestrians on the crossing to clear

⊙ move off immediately without any hesitation

⊙ wait for the green light before moving off

⊙ get ready and go when the continuous amber light shows

⊙ **wait for pedestrians on the crossing to clear**

This light allows time for the pedestrians already on the crossing to get to the other side in their own time, without being rushed. Don't rev your engine or start to move off while they are still crossing.

10.38   *Mark one answer*   R-ES 7, HC r240

When can you park on the left opposite these road markings?

⊙ If the line nearest to you is broken

⊙ When there are no yellow lines

⊙ To pick up or set down passengers

⊙ During daylight hours only

⊙ **To pick up or set down passengers**

You MUST NOT park or stop on a road marked with double white lines (even where one of the lines is broken) except to pick up or set down passengers.

10.39   *Mark two answers*   R-ES 8, HC r195-199, KYTS p122

Who can use a toucan crossing?

⊙ Trains

⊙ Cyclists

⊙ Buses

⊙ Pedestrians

⊙ Trams

⊙ **Cyclists**

⊙ **Pedestrians**

Toucan crossings are similar to pelican crossings but there is no flashing amber phase. Cyclists share the crossing with pedestrians and are allowed to cycle across when the green cycle symbol is shown.

You are on a road that has no traffic signs. There are street lights. What is the speed limit?

- ⊙ 20 mph
- ⊙ 30 mph
- ⊙ 40 mph
- ⊙ 60 mph

⊙ **30 mph**

If you aren't sure of the speed limit a good indication is the presence of street lights. If there is street lighting the speed limit will be 30 mph unless otherwise indicated.

You are going along a street with parked vehicles on the left-hand side. For which THREE reasons should you keep your speed down?

- ⊙ So that oncoming traffic can see you more clearly
- ⊙ You may set off car alarms
- ⊙ Vehicles may be pulling out
- ⊙ Drivers' doors may open
- ⊙ Children may run out from between the vehicles

⊙ **Vehicles may be pulling out**

⊙ **Drivers' doors may open**

⊙ **Children may run out from between the vehicles**

Travel slowly and carefully where there are parked vehicles in a built-up area.

Beware of

- vehicles pulling out, especially bicycles and other motorcycles
- pedestrians, especially children, who may run out from between cars
- drivers opening their doors.

You are on a two-lane dual carriageway. For which TWO of the following would you use the right-hand lane?

- ⊙ Turning right
- ⊙ Normal progress
- ⊙ Staying at the minimum allowed speed
- ⊙ Constant high speed
- ⊙ Overtaking slower traffic
- ⊙ Mending punctures

⊙ **Turning right**

⊙ **Overtaking slower traffic**

Normally you should travel in the left-hand lane and only use the right-hand lane for overtaking or turning right. Move back into the left lane as soon as it's safe but don't cut in across the path of the vehicle you've just passed.

10.43 — Mark **one** answer — HC r146 & 176

At a busy unmarked crossroads, which of the following has priority?

- ⊙ Vehicles going straight ahead
- ⊙ Vehicles turning right
- ⊙ None of the vehicles
- ⊙ The vehicles that arrived first

⊙ **None of the vehicles**

If there are no road signs or markings do not assume that you have priority. Remember that other drivers may assume they have the right to go. No type of vehicle has priority but it's courteous to give way to large vehicles. Also look out in particular for cyclists and motorcyclists.

10.44 — Mark **one** answer — HC r146 & 176

Who has priority at an unmarked crossroads?

- ⊙ The larger vehicle
- ⊙ No one has priority
- ⊙ The faster vehicle
- ⊙ The smaller vehicle

⊙ **No one has priority**

Practise good observation in all directions before you emerge or make a turn. Proceed only when you're sure it's safe to do so.

10.45 — NI EXEMPT — Mark **one** answer — HC r242-243

What is the nearest you may park to a junction?

- ⊙ 10 metres (32 feet)
- ⊙ 12 metres (39 feet)
- ⊙ 15 metres (49 feet)
- ⊙ 20 metres (66 feet)

⊙ **10 metres (32 feet)**

Don't park within 10 metres (32 feet) of a junction (unless in an authorised parking place). This is to allow drivers emerging from, or turning into, the junction a clear view of the road they are joining. It also allows them to see hazards such as pedestrians or cyclists at the junction.

10.46 — Mark **one** answer — R-ES 8

You meet an obstruction on your side of the road. You should

- ⊙ carry on, you have priority
- ⊙ give way to oncoming traffic
- ⊙ wave oncoming vehicles through
- ⊙ accelerate to get past first

⊙ **give way to oncoming traffic**

Take care if you have to pass a parked vehicle on your side of the road. Give way to oncoming traffic if there isn't enough room for you both to continue safely.

In which THREE places must you NOT park?

- ⊙ Near the brow of a hill
- ⊙ At or near a bus stop
- ⊙ Where there is no pavement
- ⊙ Within 10 metres (32 feet) of a junction
- ⊙ On a 40 mph road

⊙ **Near the brow of a hill**

⊙ **At or near a bus stop**

⊙ **Within 10 metres (32 feet) of a junction**

Other traffic will have to pull out to pass you. They may have to use the other side of the road, and if you park near the brow of a hill, they may not be able to see oncoming traffic. It's important not to park at or near a bus stop as this could inconvenience passengers, and may put them at risk as they get on or off the bus. Parking near a junction could restrict the view for emerging vehicles.

You are waiting at a level crossing. A train has passed but the lights keep flashing. You must

- ⊙ carry on waiting
- ⊙ phone the signal operator
- ⊙ edge over the stop line and look for trains
- ⊙ park and investigate

⊙ **carry on waiting**

If the lights at a level crossing continue to flash after a train has passed, you should still wait as there might be another train coming. Time seems to pass slowly when you're held up in a queue. Be patient and wait until the lights stop flashing.

At a crossroads there are no signs or road markings. Two vehicles approach. Which has priority?

- ⊙ Neither of the vehicles
- ⊙ The vehicle travelling the fastest
- ⊙ Oncoming vehicles turning right
- ⊙ Vehicles approaching from the right

⊙ **Neither of the vehicles**

At a crossroads where there are no 'give way' signs or road markings be very careful. No vehicle has priority, even if the sizes of the roads are different.

10.50 Mark *one* answer KYTS p38-44

What does this sign tell you?

- That it is a no-through road
- End of traffic calming zone
- Free parking zone ends
- No waiting zone ends

⊙ **No waiting zone ends**

The blue and red circular sign on its own means that waiting restrictions are in force. This sign shows that you are leaving the controlled zone and waiting restrictions no longer apply.

10.51 Mark *one* answer HC r288, KYTS p89

You are entering an area of roadworks. There is a temporary speed limit displayed. You should

- not exceed the speed limit
- obey the limit only during rush hour
- ignore the displayed limit
- obey the limit except at night

⊙ **not exceed the speed limit**

Where there are extra hazards such as roadworks, it's often necessary to slow traffic down by imposing a temporary speed limit. These speed limits aren't advisory, they must be obeyed.

10.52 Mark *one* answer R-ES 9, HC r186-187

You are going straight ahead at a roundabout. How should you signal?

- Signal right on the approach and then left to leave the roundabout
- Signal left after you leave the roundabout and enter the new road
- Signal right on the approach to the roundabout and keep the signal on
- Signal left just after you pass the exit before the one you will take

⊙ **Signal left just after you pass the exit before the one you will take**

To go straight ahead at a roundabout you should normally approach in the left-hand lane. You will not normally need to signal, but look out for the road markings. At some roundabouts the left lane on approach is marked as 'left turn only', so make sure you use the correct lane to go ahead. Signal before you leave as other road users need to know your intentions.

10.53

*Mark **one** answer*

HC r115

You are travelling on a well-lit road at night in a built-up area. By using dipped headlights you will be able to

- ⊙ see further along the road
- ⊙ go at a much faster speed
- ⊙ switch to main beam quickly
- ⊙ be easily seen by others

⊙ **be easily seen by others**

You may be difficult to see when you're travelling at night, even on a well lit road. If you use dipped headlights rather than sidelights other road users will see you more easily.

10.54

*Mark **one** answer*

R-ES 9, HC r173

The dual carriageway you are turning right onto has a very narrow central reservation. What should you do?

- ⊙ Proceed to the central reservation and wait
- ⊙ Wait until the road is clear in both directions
- ⊙ Stop in the first lane so that other vehicles give way
- ⊙ Emerge slightly to show your intentions

⊙ **Wait until the road is clear in both directions**

When the central reservation is narrow you should treat a dual carriageway as one road. Wait until the road is clear in both directions before emerging to turn right. If you try to treat it as two separate roads and wait in the middle, you are likely to cause an obstruction and possibly a collision.

10.55

*Mark **one** answer*

HC p40

What is the national speed limit on a single carriageway road for cars and motorcycles?

- ⊙ 30 mph
- ⊙ 50 mph
- ⊙ 60 mph
- ⊙ 70 mph

⊙ **60 mph**

Exceeding the speed limit is dangerous and can result in you receiving penalty points on your licence. It isn't worth it. You should know the speed limit for the road that you're on by observing the road signs. Different speed limits apply if you are towing a trailer.

10.56   Mark *one* answer   R-ES 13, HC r248-250

You park at night on a road with a 40 mph speed limit. You should park

◉ facing the traffic

◉ with parking lights on

◉ with dipped headlights on

◉ near a street light

◉ **with parking lights on**

You MUST use parking lights when parking at night on a road or lay-by with a speed limit greater than 30 mph. You MUST also park in the direction of the traffic flow and not close to a junction.

10.57   Mark *one* answer   KYTS p26-29

You will see these red and white markers when approaching

◉ the end of a motorway

◉ a concealed level crossing

◉ a concealed speed limit sign

◉ the end of a dual carriageway

◉ **a concealed level crossing**

If there is a bend just before the level crossing you may not be able to see the level crossing barriers or waiting traffic. These signs give you an early warning that you may find these hazards just around the bend.

10.58   NI EXEMPT   Mark *one* answer   R-ES 18, HC r108

You are travelling on a motorway. You MUST stop when signalled to do so by which of these?

◉ Flashing amber lights above your lane

◉ A Highways Agency Traffic Officer

◉ Pedestrians on the hard shoulder

◉ A driver who has broken down

◉ **A Highways Agency Traffic Officer**

You will find Highways Agency Traffic Officers on many of Britain's motorways. They work in partnership with the police, helping to keep traffic moving and to make your journey as safe as possible. It is an offence not to comply with the directions given by a Traffic Officer.

Case study practice 10 – Rules of the road

Ray is riding his motorcycle in the local area. At a signed mini-roundabout, Ray turns right. Later he comes to road works. There are temporary traffic lights showing red but no oncoming traffic. Once past, Ray turns right into a road containing road humps and narrowed areas. He sees a sign showing red and black arrows, asking road users to give way to oncoming traffic.

10.1 What colour would this roundabout sign be?

*Mark **one** answer*

- ⊙ Blue and white.
- ⊙ Red and white.
- ⊙ Green and white.
- ⊙ Black and white.

HC p107, KYTS p19 & p69

10.2 How should Ray act at these traffic lights?

*Mark **one** answer*

- ⊙ Go quickly as there's no oncoming traffic.
- ⊙ Stop and wait until the light turns green.
- ⊙ Get off and wheel the motorcycle through.
- ⊙ Ride slowly through while indicating.

HC p109

10.3 What should Ray do before making the turn?

*Mark **one** answer*

- ⊙ Check that his hazard lights are working.
- ⊙ Turn and look back over his left shoulder.
- ⊙ Remove his helmet so he can see clearly.
- ⊙ Take a final look over his right shoulder.

R-ES 8 & 9

10.4 What are these humps for?

*Mark **one** answer*

- ⊙ To increase reaction time.
- ⊙ To monitor tyre pressure.
- ⊙ To help slow traffic down.
- ⊙ To test the suspension.

R-ES 7

10.5 What shape would the arrowed sign be?

*Mark **one** answer*

- ⊙ Circular.
- ⊙ Triangular.
- ⊙ Rectangular.
- ⊙ Square.

KYTS p18

section **eleven**

ROAD AND TRAFFIC SIGNS

This section covers
- Road signs
- Speed limits
- Road markings
- Regulations

Road and traffic signs

Signs

You **MUST** comply with all traffic signs and road markings. Road signs can be divided into groups depending on their shape and colour. Each group means something different:

- circular signs give orders
  - blue circles give an instruction
  - red rings or circles tell you what you must not do
- triangular signs give warnings
- rectangular signs give information.

The exception to the shape rule is the 'stop' sign – this is octagonal to give it greater prominence and ensure that its meaning is understood even if partly obscured.

R-ES 7, HC r109, KYTS p9

Maximum speed limit signs are shown by red circles – you **MUST NOT** exceed the speed shown. Speed limit signs may be incorporated in other signs, such as those indicating a traffic-calmed area.

HC p106, KYTS p20

It's impossible to mention all the signs here. *Know Your Traffic Signs* shows all the signs that you're likely to come across and *The Highway Code* contains important advice and instructions surrounding current GB legislation and best practice in road safety.

HC p106-116, KYTS p9-61 & p77-89

It's important that you know these so that you don't break the law.

Road markings

Markings on the road give information, orders or warnings. As a rough guide the more paint, the more important the message.

R-ES 7, HC p127-131, KYTS p62-64

Lines along the road can be divided into

- those along the middle of the road
  - short broken white lines divide lanes
  - longer broken white lines indicate a hazard ahead: only overtake if the road ahead is clear
  - double white lines with a solid white line on your side of the road: you must not cross or straddle the line
  - white diagonal stripes or chevrons: these separate lanes of traffic or protect traffic turning right.

HC p115-116, R-ES 7

- those along the side of the road
  - a white line shows the edge of the road
  - yellow lines show waiting and stopping restrictions
  - zigzag lines (white at pedestrian crossings, yellow outside schools) mean no stopping or parking at any time.

HC p114 & p116, KYTS p62, 65 &122

Lines on or across the road can be divided into

- broken lines across the road: these mean 'give way' (at a roundabout, give way to traffic from the right)
- a solid line: this means 'stop'
- various markings on the road (give way triangles, road hump markings, arrows): these warn of a hazard.

R-ES 7, HC p114-116, KYTS p60-73

You may see areas where red tarmac has been used within a block of white lines or diagonals. This is to further highlight the area which separates traffic flowing in opposite directions.

As with signs, you should refer to *Know Your Traffic Signs* and *The Official Highway Code* to get the full picture on road markings. Reflective studs may be found on motorways and other roads. These are especially useful at night and when visibility is poor.

HC r132

Traffic lights and warning lights

At traffic lights, the sequence of lights and their meaning is

- red – stop and wait behind the stop line
- red and amber – stop and wait
- green – go, if the way is clear
- amber – stop unless you've already crossed the stop line or you're so close to it that pulling up might cause an accident

- red (as above).

R-ES 7, HC p102, KYTS p119-120

There may be a green filter arrow. This means that you can go in the direction of the arrow, even if the main light isn't showing green.

If the traffic lights are out of order, proceed with great care, as nobody has priority. This problem may be brought to your attention by a sign.

R-ES 7

You will find red flashing lights at level crossings, lifting bridges or outside fire stations. Stop when these show.

HC p102, KYTS p13, 26-29, 120

On motorways, signals on the overhead gantries or roadside may be accompanied by flashing lights:

- amber – warns you of a hazard (eg lane closures, to leave at the next exit, fog) or a temporary maximum speed limit
- red (above your lane) – tells you that the lane is closed beyond this point, so move into another lane
- red (above all the lanes, on the central reservation or roadside) – tells you to stop. You **MUST NOT** go beyond that point in any lane.

HC r255-258, p102, KYTS p89-91

Signals given by drivers and police or traffic officers

Drivers normally signal their intention to turn by using their indicators. Ensure that your indicators are cancelled after turning to avoid misleading other road users. Be aware that another driver may have left their indicator on by mistake. For example, if you're emerging from a junction and a driver coming along the main road from the right is indicating left, wait until the vehicle starts to turn before you emerge.

R-ES 6, HC r103-104

An arm signal may be used to strengthen or clarify the message, such as when

• signalling to turn right in busy traffic
• slowing down to give way at a zebra crossing.

However, don't continue with the arm signal while you are turning left or right, because you will have less control over the steering.

If you're slowing down and stopping just after a junction, wait to signal until you're passing the junction, or just after it.

Police or traffic officers may signal to you if they're directing traffic. Ensure you know all arm signals and police or traffic officer signals in case you need to use or react to them.

HC r105-109 & p104-105

The horn may be used to warn others of your presence. It must not be used between 11.30 pm and 7.00 am. Only use your horn when stationary if another vehicle is likely to cause a danger.

R-ES 6, HC r110-112

The only reason that you should flash your headlights is to warn other road users that you're there.

A police or Highways Agency traffic officer following you in a patrol vehicle may flash their headlights, indicate left and point to the left to get you to stop. Pull up on the left as soon as it's safe to do so.

Remember, you **MUST** obey any signals given by police or traffic officers, traffic wardens and signs used by school crossing patrols.

HC r105-108 & p104-105

Use of road lanes

Contraflow lanes are lanes that flow in the opposite direction to most of the traffic. Bus and cycle contraflow lanes may be found in one-way streets. They will be signed and marked on the road. Don't enter these lanes.

R-ES 7, HC r140-141, r143

You may also see contraflow lanes at roadworks. When you see the signs, reduce your speed in good time, choose an appropriate lane early and keep the correct separation distance from the vehicle in front.

R-ES 11, KYTS p128-133

The centre and right-hand lanes of a three-lane motorway are overtaking lanes. Always move back to a lane on your left after overtaking to allow other vehicles to overtake. You may not overtake on your left on a free-flowing motorway or dual carriageway.

R-ES 11, HC r264 & r268

FAQs

I've seen some signs with a brown background – does this mean anything in particular?

Signs with a brown background give tourist information.

KYTS p34, p84, p100-102

Sometimes you see lorries with large arrows on the back. What do they mean?

These are placed on slow-moving or stationary maintenance vehicles which are blocking traffic lanes. They show you which side of the vehicle you should pass.

HC r289 & p113

Can I ever cross double white lines where there's a solid white line on my side of the road?

You can cross a solid white line if you're passing a stationary vehicle or overtaking a pedal cycle, horse or road maintenance vehicle, if they're travelling at 10 mph or less.

HC r129

Can I use my hazard warning lights when I'm moving?

If you're riding on a motorway or dual carriageway, you can use your hazard warning lights to warn drivers behind you that there's an obstruction ahead.

R-ES 5 & 11, HC r116

How can traffic be controlled at roadworks?

Traffic can be controlled by

- *a police or traffic officer*
- *traffic lights*
- *a stop-go board.*

HC r288, KYTS p136

11.1 — Mark **one** answer — R-ES 7, HC r103-104 & p103

How should you give an arm signal to turn left?

Arm signals can be effective during daylight, especially when you're wearing bright clothing. Practise giving arm signals when you're learning. You need to be able to keep full control of your motorcycle with one hand off the handlebars.

11.2 — Mark **one** answer — R-ES 7, HC r103-104 & p103

You are giving an arm signal ready to turn left. Why should you NOT continue with the arm signal while you turn?

- Because you might hit a pedestrian on the corner
- Because you will have less steering control
- Because you will need to keep the clutch applied
- Because other motorists will think that you are stopping on the corner

- **Because you will have less steering control**

Consider giving an arm signal if it will help other road users. Situations where you might do this include, approaching a pedestrian crossing, in bright sunshine when your indicators may be difficult to see, when your indicators may be obscured in a traffic queue and where your indicators could cause confusion, such as when pulling up close to a side road. Don't maintain an arm signal when turning. Maintain full control by keeping both hands on the handlebars when you turn.

This sign is of particular importance to motorcyclists. It means

⊙ side winds

⊙ airport

⊙ slippery road

⊙ service area

⊙ **side winds**

Strong crosswinds can suddenly blow you off course. Keep your speed down when it's very windy, especially on exposed roads.

Which one of these signs are you allowed to ride past on a solo motorcycle?

Most regulatory signs are circular, a red circle tells you what you must NOT do.

Your indicators are difficult to see due to bright sunshine. When using them you should

⊙ also give an arm signal

⊙ sound your horn

⊙ flash your headlight

⊙ keep both hands on the handlebars

⊙ **also give an arm signal**

Arm signals should be used to confirm your intentions when you aren't sure that your indicators can be seen by other road users. Use the signals shown in The Highway Code and return your hand to the handlebars before you turn.

11.6   *Mark **one** answer*   **R-ES 7, HC r110**

When drivers flash their headlights at you it means

- ⊙ that there is a radar speed trap ahead
- ⊙ that they are giving way to you
- ⊙ that they are warning you of their presence
- ⊙ that there is something wrong with your motorcycle

⊙ **that they are warning you of their presence**

A driver flashing their headlights has the same meaning as sounding the horn, it's a warning of their presence.

11.7   *Mark **one** answer*   **R-ES 7, HC r103-104**

Why should you make sure that you cancel your indicators after turning?

- ⊙ To avoid flattening the battery
- ⊙ To avoid misleading other road users
- ⊙ To avoid dazzling other road users
- ⊙ To avoid damage to the indicator relay

⊙ **To avoid misleading other road users**

Always check that you have cancelled your indicators after turning. Failing to cancel your indicators could lead to a serious or even fatal collision. Other road users may pull out in front of you if they think you are going to turn off before you reach them.

11.8   *Mark **one** answer*   **R-ES 7, HC r103-104 & p103**

Which of these signals should you give when slowing or stopping your motorcycle?

⊙

⊙

Arm signals can be given to reinforce your flashing indicators, especially if the indicator signal could cause confusion, for example if you intend to pull up close to a side road.

287

*Mark **one** answer* **R-ES 7, HC r225**

You are riding on a motorway. There is a slow-moving vehicle ahead. On the back you see this sign. What should you do?

- ⊙ Pass on the right
- ⊙ Pass on the left
- ⊙ Leave at the next exit
- ⊙ Drive no further

⊙ **Pass on the left**

If this vehicle is in your lane you will have to move to the left. Use your mirrors and signal if necessary. When it's safe move into the lane on your left. You should always look well ahead so that you can spot such hazards early, giving yourself time to react safely.

*Mark **one** answer* **R-ES 7, HC p102-117, KYTS**

You MUST obey signs giving orders. These signs are mostly in

- ⊙ green rectangles
- ⊙ red triangles
- ⊙ blue rectangles
- ⊙ red circles

⊙ **red circles**

There are three basic types of traffic sign, those that warn, inform or give orders. Generally, triangular signs warn, rectangular ones give information or directions, and circular signs usually give orders. An exception is the eight-sided 'STOP' sign.

*Mark **one** answer* **R-ES 7, HC p102-117, KYTS**

Traffic signs giving orders are generally which shape?

⊙   ⊙

⊙   ⊙

⊙

Road signs in the shape of a circle give orders. Those with a red circle are mostly prohibitive. The 'stop' sign is octagonal to give it greater prominence. Signs giving orders MUST always be obeyed.

11.12 *Mark **one** answer* **R-ES 7, HC p102-117, KYTS**

Which type of sign tells you NOT to do something?

Signs in the shape of a circle give orders. A sign with a red circle means that you aren't allowed to do something. Study Know Your Traffic Signs to ensure that you understand what the different traffic signs mean.

11.13 *Mark **one** answer* **R-ES 7, HC p102-117, KYTS**

What does this sign mean?

- Maximum speed limit with traffic calming
- Minimum speed limit with traffic calming
- '20 cars only' parking zone
- Only 20 cars allowed at any one time

⊙ **Maximum speed limit with traffic calming**

If you're in places where there are likely to be pedestrians such as outside schools, near parks, residential areas and shopping areas, you should be extra-cautious and keep your speed down.

Many local authorities have taken measures to slow traffic down by creating traffic calming measures such as speed humps. They are there for a reason; slow down.

Which sign means no motor vehicles are allowed?

You would generally see this sign at the approach to a pedestrian-only zone.

Which of these signs means no motor vehicles?

If you are driving a motor vehicle or riding a motorcycle you MUST NOT travel past this sign. This area has been designated for use by pedestrians.

What does this sign mean?

- ⊙ Low bridge ahead
- ⊙ Tunnel ahead
- ⊙ Ancient monument ahead
- ⊙ Traffic danger spot ahead

⊙ **Tunnel ahead**

When approaching a tunnel switch on your dipped headlights. Be aware that your eyes might need to adjust to the sudden darkness. You may need to reduce your speed.

11.17

*Mark **one** answer*

R-ES 7, HC p102-117, KYTS

What does this sign mean?

- New speed limit 20 mph
- No vehicles over 30 tonnes
- Minimum speed limit 30 mph
- End of 20 mph zone

⊙ **End of 20 mph zone**

Where you see this sign the 20 mph restriction ends. Check all around for possible hazards and only increase your speed if it's safe to do so.

11.18

*Mark **one** answer*

R-ES 7, HC p102-117, KYTS

What does this sign mean?

- No overtaking
- No motor vehicles
- Clearway (no stopping)
- Cars and motorcycles only

⊙ **No motor vehicles**

A sign will indicate which types of vehicles are prohibited from certain roads. Make sure that you know which signs apply to the vehicle you're using.

*Mark **one** answer*

What does this sign mean?

- ⊙ No parking
- ⊙ No road markings
- ⊙ No through road
- ⊙ No entry

⊙ **No entry**

'No entry' signs are used in places such as one-way streets to prevent vehicles driving against the traffic. To ignore one would be dangerous, both for yourself and other road users, as well as being against the law.

---

*Mark **one** answer*

What does this sign mean?

- ⊙ Bend to the right
- ⊙ Road on the right closed
- ⊙ No traffic from the right
- ⊙ No right turn

⊙ **No right turn**

The 'no right turn' sign may be used to warn road users that there is a 'no entry' prohibition on a road to the right ahead.

---

*Mark **one** answer*

Which sign means 'no entry'?

⊙

Look out for traffic signs. Disobeying or not seeing a sign could be dangerous. It may also be an offence for which you could be prosecuted.

11.22   *Mark **one** answer*   **R-ES 7, HC p102-117, KYTS**

What does this sign mean?

- ⊙ Route for trams only
- ⊙ Route for buses only
- ⊙ Parking for buses only
- ⊙ Parking for trams only

⊙ **Route for trams only**

Avoid blocking tram routes. Trams are fixed on their route and can't manoeuvre around other vehicles and pedestrians. Modern trams travel quickly and are quiet so you might not hear them approaching.

11.23   *Mark **one** answer*   **R-ES 7, HC p102-117, KYTS**

Which type of vehicle does this sign apply to?

4.4 m
14'6"

- ⊙ Wide vehicles
- ⊙ Long vehicles
- ⊙ High vehicles
- ⊙ Heavy vehicles

⊙ **High vehicles**

The triangular shapes above and below the dimensions indicate a height restriction that applies to the road ahead.

*Mark **one** answer* **R-ES 7, HC p102-117, KYTS**

Which sign means NO motor vehicles allowed?

This sign is used to enable pedestrians to walk free from traffic. It's often found in shopping areas.

---

*Mark **one** answer* **R-ES 7, HC p102-117, KYTS**

What does this sign mean?

- ⊙ You have priority
- ⊙ No motor vehicles
- ⊙ Two-way traffic
- ⊙ No overtaking

⊙ **No overtaking**

Road signs that prohibit overtaking are placed in locations where passing the vehicle in front is dangerous. If you see this sign don't attempt to overtake. The sign is there for a reason and you must obey it.

---

*Mark **one** answer* **R-ES 7, HC p102-117, KYTS**

You are approaching a red traffic light. What will the signal show next?

- ⊙ Red and amber
- ⊙ Green alone
- ⊙ Amber alone
- ⊙ Green and amber

⊙ **Red and amber**

If you know which light is going to show next you can plan your approach accordingly. This can help prevent excessive braking or hesitation at the junction.

11.27   *Mark **one** answer*   **R-ES 7, HC p102-117, KYTS**

Which sign means no overtaking?

⊙   ⊙

⊙   ⊙

⊙

This sign indicates that overtaking here is not allowed and you could face prosecution if you ignore this prohibition.

11.28   *Mark **one** answer*   **R-ES 7, HC p102-117, KYTS**

What does this sign mean?

⊙ Waiting restrictions apply
⊙ Waiting permitted
⊙ National speed limit applies
⊙ Clearway (no stopping)

⊙ **Waiting restrictions apply**

There will be a plate or additional sign to tell you when the restrictions apply.

11.29   *Mark **one** answer*   **R-ES 7, HC p102-117, KYTS**

What does this sign mean?

⊙ Keep in one lane
⊙ Give way to oncoming traffic
⊙ Do not overtake
⊙ Form two lanes

⊙ **Do not overtake**

If you're behind a slow-moving vehicle be patient. Wait until the restriction no longer applies and you can overtake safely.

What does this sign mean?

- ⊙ Roundabout
- ⊙ Crossroads
- ⊙ No stopping
- ⊙ No entry

⊙ **No stopping**

This sign is in place to ensure a clear route for traffic. Don't stop except in an emergency.

Which sign means 'no stopping'?

⊙

Stopping where this clearway restriction applies is likely to cause congestion. Allow the traffic to flow by obeying the signs.

You have just driven past this sign. You should be aware that

- ⊙ it is a single track road
- ⊙ you cannot stop on this road
- ⊙ there is only one lane in use
- ⊙ all traffic is going one way

⊙ **all traffic is going one way**

In a one-way system traffic may be passing you on either side. Always be aware of all traffic signs and understand their meaning. Look well ahead and react to them in good time.

11.33   *Mark one answer*   R-ES 7, HC p102-117, KYTS

What does this sign mean?

- ⊙ End of restricted speed area
- ⊙ End of restricted parking area
- ⊙ End of clearway
- ⊙ End of cycle route

⊙ **End of restricted parking area**

Even though you have left the restricted area, make sure that you park where you won't endanger other road users or cause an obstruction.

11.34   *Mark one answer*   R-ES 7, HC p102-117, KYTS

You see this sign ahead. It means

- ⊙ national speed limit applies
- ⊙ waiting restrictions apply
- ⊙ no stopping
- ⊙ no entry

⊙ **no stopping**

Clearways are stretches of road where you aren't allowed to stop unless in an emergency. You'll see this sign. Stopping where these restrictions apply may be dangerous and likely to cause an obstruction. Restrictions might apply for several miles and this may be indicated on the sign.

*Mark **one** answer*

What does this sign mean?

- Distance to parking place ahead
- Distance to public telephone ahead
- Distance to public house ahead
- Distance to passing place ahead

⊙ **Distance to parking place ahead**

If you intend to stop and rest, this sign allows you time to reduce speed and pull over safely.

*Mark **one** answer*

What does this sign mean?

- Vehicles may not park on the verge or footway
- Vehicles may park on the left-hand side of the road only
- Vehicles may park fully on the verge or footway
- Vehicles may park on the right-hand side of the road only

⊙ **Vehicles may park fully on the verge or footway**

In order to keep roads free from parked cars, there are some areas where you're allowed to park on the verge. Only do this where you see the sign. Parking on verges or footways anywhere else could lead to a fine.

11.37 *Mark **one** answer* **R-ES 7, HC p102-117, KYTS**

What does this traffic sign mean?

⊙ No overtaking allowed

⊙ Give priority to oncoming traffic

⊙ Two way traffic

⊙ One-way traffic only

⊙ **Give priority to oncoming traffic**

Priority signs are normally shown where the road is narrow and there isn't enough room for two vehicles to pass. These can be at narrow bridges, road works and where there's a width restriction.

Make sure that you know who has priority, don't force your way through. Show courtesy and consideration to other road users.

11.38 *Mark **one** answer* **R-ES 7, HC p102-117, KYTS**

What is the meaning of this traffic sign?

⊙ End of two-way road

⊙ Give priority to vehicles coming towards you

⊙ You have priority over vehicles coming towards you

⊙ Bus lane ahead

⊙ **You have priority over vehicles coming towards you**

Don't force your way through. Show courtesy and consideration to other road users. Although you have priority, make sure oncoming traffic is going to give way before you continue.

What does this sign mean?

⊙ No overtaking

⊙ You are entering a one-way street

⊙ Two-way traffic ahead

⊙ You have priority over vehicles from the opposite direction

⊙ **You have priority over vehicles from the opposite direction**

Don't force your way through if oncoming vehicles fail to give way. If necessary, slow down and give way to avoid confrontation or a collision.

What shape is a STOP sign at a junction?

⊙

To make it easy to recognise, the 'stop' sign is the only sign of this shape. You must stop and take effective observation before proceeding.

What does this sign mean?

⊙ Service area 30 miles ahead

⊙ Maximum speed 30 mph

⊙ Minimum speed 30 mph

⊙ Lay-by 30 miles ahead

⊙ **Minimum speed 30 mph**

This sign is shown where slow-moving vehicles would impede the flow of traffic, for example in tunnels. However, if you need to slow down or even stop to avoid an incident or potential collision, you should do so.

11.42   *Mark **one** answer*   **R-ES 7, HC p102-117, KYTS**

At a junction you see this sign partly covered by snow. What does it mean?

⊙ Cross roads

⊙ Give way

⊙ Stop

⊙ Turn right

⊙ **Stop**

The STOP sign is the only road sign that is octagonal. This is so that it can be recognised and obeyed even if it is obscured, for example by snow.

11.43   *Mark **one** answer*   **R-ES 7, HC p102-117, KYTS**

What does this sign mean?

⊙ Give way to oncoming vehicles

⊙ Approaching traffic passes you on both sides

⊙ Turn off at the next available junction

⊙ Pass either side to get to the same destination

⊙ **Pass either side to get to the same destination**

These signs are often seen in one-way streets that have more than one lane. When you see this sign, use the route that's the most convenient and doesn't require a late change of direction.

11.44   Mark *one* answer   R-ES 7, HC p102-117, KYTS

What does this sign mean?

⊙ **Route for trams**

Take extra care when you encounter trams. Look out for road markings and signs that alert you to them. Modern trams are very quiet and you may not hear them approaching.

⊙ Route for trams
⊙ Give way to trams
⊙ Route for buses
⊙ Give way to buses

11.45   Mark *one* answer   R-ES 7, HC p102-117, KYTS

What does a circular traffic sign with a blue background do?

⊙ **Give an instruction**

Signs with blue circles give a positive instruction. These are often found in urban areas and include signs for mini-roundabouts and directional arrows.

⊙ Give warning of a motorway ahead
⊙ Give directions to a car park
⊙ Give motorway information
⊙ Give an instruction

11.46   Mark *one* answer   R-ES 7, HC p102-117, KYTS

Where would you see a contraflow bus and cycle lane?

⊙ On a dual carriageway
⊙ On a roundabout
⊙ On an urban motorway
⊙ On a one-way street

⊙ **On a one-way street**

In a contraflow lane the traffic permitted to use it travels in the opposite direction to traffic in the other lanes on the road.

11.47   *Mark **one** answer*   **R-ES 7, HC p102-117, KYTS**

What does this sign mean?

- ⊙ Bus station on the right
- ⊙ Contraflow bus lane
- ⊙ With-flow bus lane
- ⊙ Give way to buses

⊙ **Contraflow bus lane**

There will also be markings on the road surface to indicate the bus lane. You must not use this lane for parking or overtaking.

11.48   *Mark **one** answer*   **R-ES 7, HC p102-117, KYTS**

What does a sign with a brown background show?

- ⊙ Tourist directions
- ⊙ Primary roads
- ⊙ Motorway routes
- ⊙ Minor routes

⊙ **Tourist directions**

Signs with a brown background give directions to places of interest. They will often be seen on a motorway directing you along the easiest route to the attraction.

11.49   *Mark **one** answer*   **R-ES 7, HC p102-117, KYTS**

This sign means

- ⊙ tourist attraction
- ⊙ beware of trains
- ⊙ level crossing
- ⊙ beware of trams

⊙ **tourist attraction**

These signs indicate places of interest and are designed to guide you by the easiest route. They are particularly useful if you are unfamiliar with the area.

*Mark **one** answer*

What are triangular signs for?

⊙ To give warnings

⊙ To give information

⊙ To give orders

⊙ To give directions

⊙ **To give warnings**

This type of sign will warn you of hazards ahead.

Make sure you look at each sign that you pass on the road, so that you do not miss any vital instructions or information.

---

*Mark **one** answer*

What does this sign mean?

⊙ Turn left ahead

⊙ T-junction

⊙ No through road

⊙ Give way

⊙ **T-junction**

This type of sign will warn you of hazards ahead. Make sure you look at each sign and road markings that you pass, so that you do not miss any vital instructions or information. This particular sign shows there is a T-junction with priority over vehicles from the right.

---

*Mark **one** answer*

What does this sign mean?

⊙ Multi-exit roundabout

⊙ Risk of ice

⊙ Six roads converge

⊙ Place of historical interest

⊙ **Risk of ice**

It will take up to ten times longer to stop when it's icy. Where there is a risk of icy conditions you need to be aware of this and take extra care. If you think the road may be icy, don't brake or steer harshly as your tyres could lose their grip on the road.

11.53   *Mark **one** answer*   **R-ES 7, HC p102-117, KYTS**

What does this sign mean?

⊙ Crossroads

⊙ Level crossing with gate

⊙ Level crossing without gate

⊙ Ahead only

⊙ **Crossroads**

The priority through the junction is shown by the broader line. You need to be aware of the hazard posed by traffic crossing or pulling out onto a major road.

11.54   *Mark **one** answer*   **R-ES 7, HC p102-117, KYTS**

What does this sign mean?

⊙ Ring road

⊙ Mini-roundabout

⊙ No vehicles

⊙ Roundabout

⊙ **Roundabout**

As you approach a roundabout look well ahead and check all signs. Decide which exit you wish to take and move into the correct position as you approach the roundabout, signalling as required.

11.55   *Mark **one** answer*   **R-ES 7, HC p102-117, KYTS**

What does this sign mean?

⊙ Cyclists must dismount

⊙ Cycles are not allowed

⊙ Cycle route ahead

⊙ Cycle in single file

⊙ **Cycle route ahead**

Where there's a cycle route ahead, a sign will show a bicycle in a red warning triangle. Watch out for children on bicycles and cyclists rejoining the main road.

11.56

*Mark **four** answers*

Which FOUR of these would be indicated by a triangular road sign?

- ⊙ Road narrows
- ⊙ Ahead only
- ⊙ Low bridge
- ⊙ Minimum speed
- ⊙ Children crossing
- ⊙ T-junction

⊙ **Road narrows**

⊙ **Low bridge**

⊙ **Children crossing**

⊙ **T-junction**

Warning signs are there to make you aware of potential hazards on the road ahead. Act on the signs so you are prepared and can take whatever action is necessary.

11.57

*Mark **one** answer*

Which sign means that pedestrians may be walking along the road?

⊙   ⊙

⊙   ⊙

⊙

When you pass pedestrians in the road, leave plenty of room. You might have to use the right-hand side of the road, so look well ahead, as well as in your mirrors, before pulling out. Take great care if there is a bend in the road obscuring your view ahead.

11.58 · *Mark **one** answer* · R-ES 7, HC p102-117, KYTS

Which of these signs means there is a double bend ahead?

Triangular signs give you a warning of hazards ahead. They are there to give you time to prepare for the hazard, for example by adjusting your speed.

11.59 · *Mark **one** answer* · R-ES 7, HC p102-117, KYTS

What does this sign mean?

- Wait at the barriers
- Wait at the crossroads
- Give way to trams
- Give way to farm vehicles

⊙ **Give way to trams**

Obey the 'give way' signs. Trams are unable to steer around you if you misjudge when it is safe to enter the junction.

*Mark **one** answer* **R-ES 7, HC p102-117, KYTS**

What does this sign mean?

⊙ Humpback bridge

⊙ Humps in the road

⊙ Entrance to tunnel

⊙ Soft verges

⊙ **Humps in the road**

These have been put in place to slow the traffic down. They're usually found in residential areas. Slow down to an appropriate speed.

---

*Mark **one** answer* **R-ES 7, HC p102-117, KYTS**

Which of these signs means the end of a dual carriageway?

If you're overtaking make sure you move back safely into the left-hand lane before you reach the end of the dual carriageway.

---

*Mark **one** answer* **R-ES 7, HC p102-117, KYTS**

What does this sign mean?

⊙ End of dual carriageway

⊙ Tall bridge

⊙ Road narrows

⊙ End of narrow bridge

⊙ **End of dual carriageway**

Don't leave moving into the left-hand lane until the last moment. Plan ahead and don't rely on other traffic letting you in.

11.63   *Mark **one** answer*   R-ES 7, HC p102-117, KYTS

What does this sign mean?

⊙ Crosswinds

⊙ Road noise

⊙ Airport

⊙ Adverse camber

⊙ **Crosswinds**

A warning sign with a picture of a windsock will indicate there may be strong crosswinds. This sign is often found on exposed roads.

11.64   *Mark **one** answer*   R-ES 7, HC p102-117, KYTS

What does this traffic sign mean?

⊙ Slippery road ahead

⊙ Tyres liable to punctures ahead

⊙ Danger ahead

⊙ Service area ahead

⊙ **Danger ahead**

This sign is there to alert you to the likelihood of danger ahead. It may be accompanied by a plate indicating the type of hazard. Be ready to reduce your speed and take avoiding action.

You are about to overtake when you see this sign. You should

⊙ overtake the other driver as quickly as possible

⊙ move to the right to get a better view

⊙ switch your headlights on before overtaking

⊙ hold back until you can see clearly ahead

⊙ **hold back until you can see clearly ahead**

You won't be able to see any hazards that might be hidden in the dip. As well as oncoming traffic the dip may conceal

- cyclists
- horse riders
- parked vehicles
- pedestrians

in the road.

What does this sign mean?

⊙ Level crossing with gate or barrier

⊙ Gated road ahead

⊙ Level crossing without gate or barrier

⊙ Cattle grid ahead

⊙ **Level crossing with gate or barrier**

Some crossings have gates but no attendant or signals. You should stop, look both ways, listen and make sure that there is no train approaching. If there is a telephone, contact the signal operator to make sure that it's safe to cross.

11.67 Mark **one** answer R-ES 7, HC p102-117, KYTS

What does this sign mean?

⊙ No trams ahead

⊙ Oncoming trams

⊙ Trams crossing ahead

⊙ Trams only

⊙ **Trams crossing ahead**

This sign warns you to beware of trams. If you don't usually drive in a town where there are trams, remember to look out for them at junctions and look for tram rails, signs and signals.

11.68 Mark **one** answer R-ES 7, HC p102-117, KYTS

What does this sign mean?

⊙ Adverse camber

⊙ Steep hill downwards

⊙ Uneven road

⊙ Steep hill upwards

⊙ **Steep hill downwards**

This sign will give you an early warning that the road ahead will slope downhill. Prepare to alter your speed and gear. Looking at the sign from left to right will show you whether the road slopes uphill or downhill.

11.69 Mark **one** answer R-ES 7, HC p102-117, KYTS

What does this sign mean?

⊙ Uneven road surface

⊙ Bridge over the road

⊙ Road ahead ends

⊙ Water across the road

⊙ **Water across the road**

This sign is found where a shallow stream crosses the road. Heavy rainfall could increase the flow of water. If the water looks too deep or the stream has spread over a large distance, stop and find another route.

What does this sign mean?

⊙   **No through road on the left**

If you intend to take a left turn, this sign shows you that you can't get through to another route using the left-turn junction ahead.

⊙   Turn left for parking area
⊙   No through road on the left
⊙   No entry for traffic turning left
⊙   Turn left for ferry terminal

What does this sign mean?

⊙   **No through road**

You will not be able to find a through route to another road. Use this road only for access.

⊙   T-junction
⊙   No through road
⊙   Telephone box ahead
⊙   Toilet ahead

Which sign means 'no through road'?

⊙   ⊙

⊙   ⊙

⊙

This sign is found at the entrance to a road that can only be used for access.

11.73   *Mark **one** answer*   **R-ES 7, HC p102-117, KYTS**

Which is the sign for a ring road?

Ring roads are designed to relieve congestion in towns and city centres.

11.74   *Mark **one** answer*   **R-ES 7, HC p102-117, KYTS**

What does this sign mean?

- The right-hand lane ahead is narrow
- Right-hand lane for buses only
- Right-hand lane for turning right
- The right-hand lane is closed

⊙ **The right-hand lane is closed**

Yellow and black temporary signs may be used to inform you of roadworks or lane restrictions. Look well ahead. If you have to change lanes, do so in good time.

11.75   *Mark **one** answer*   **R-ES 7, HC p102-117, KYTS**

What does this sign mean?

STAY IN LANE
Max speed **30**

- Change to the left lane
- Leave at the next exit
- Contraflow system
- One-way street

⊙ **Contraflow system**

If you use the right-hand lane in a contraflow system, you'll be travelling with no permanent barrier between you and the oncoming traffic. Observe speed limits and keep a good distance from the vehicle ahead.

*Mark **one** answer*

What does this sign mean?

⊙ Leave motorway at next exit

⊙ Lane for heavy and slow vehicles

⊙ All lorries use the hard shoulder

⊙ Rest area for lorries

⊙ **Lane for heavy and slow vehicles**

Where there's a long, steep, uphill gradient on a motorway, a crawler lane may be provided. This helps the traffic to flow by diverting the slower heavy vehicles into a dedicated lane on the left.

*Mark **one** answer*

A red traffic light means

⊙ you should stop unless turning left

⊙ stop, if you are able to brake safely

⊙ you must stop and wait behind the stop line

⊙ proceed with caution

⊙ **you must stop and wait behind the stop line**

Make sure you learn and understand the sequence of traffic lights. Whatever light appears you will then know what light is going to appear next and be able to take the appropriate action. For example if amber is showing on its own you'll know that red will appear next, giving you ample time to slow and stop safely.

11.78 *Mark **one** answer* **R-ES 7, HC p102-117, KYTS**

At traffic lights, amber on its own means

⊙ prepare to go

⊙ go if the way is clear

⊙ go if no pedestrians are crossing

⊙ stop at the stop line

⊙ **stop at the stop line**

When amber is showing on its own red will appear next. The amber light means STOP, unless you have already crossed the stop line or you are so close to it that pulling up might cause a collision.

11.79 *Mark **one** answer* **R-ES 7, HC p102-117, KYTS**

You are at a junction controlled by traffic lights. When should you NOT proceed at green?

⊙ When pedestrians are waiting to cross

⊙ When your exit from the junction is blocked

⊙ When you think the lights may be about to change

⊙ When you intend to turn right

⊙ **When your exit from the junction is blocked**

As you approach the lights look into the road you wish to take. Only proceed if your exit road is clear. If the road is blocked hold back, even if you have to wait for the next green signal.

You are in the left-hand lane at traffic lights. You are waiting to turn left. At which of these traffic lights must you NOT move on?

At some junctions there may be a separate signal for different lanes. These are called 'filter' lights. They're designed to help traffic flow at major junctions. Make sure that you're in the correct lane and proceed if the way is clear and the green light shows for your lane.

What does this sign mean?

- ⊙ Traffic lights out of order
- ⊙ Amber signal out of order
- ⊙ Temporary traffic lights ahead
- ⊙ New traffic lights ahead

⊙ **Traffic lights out of order**

Where traffic lights are out of order you might see this sign. Proceed with caution as nobody has priority at the junction.

When traffic lights are out of order, who has priority?

- ⊙ Traffic going straight on
- ⊙ Traffic turning right
- ⊙ Nobody
- ⊙ Traffic turning left

⊙ **Nobody**

When traffic lights are out of order you should treat the junction as an unmarked crossroads. Be cautious as you may need to give way or stop. Keep a look out for traffic attempting to cross the junction at speed.

11.83

*Mark **three** answers*

R-ES 7, HC p102-117, KYTS

These flashing red lights mean STOP. In which THREE of the following places could you find them?

⊙ Pelican crossings

⊙ Lifting bridges

⊙ Zebra crossings

⊙ Level crossings

⊙ Motorway exits

⊙ Fire stations

⊙ **Lifting bridges**

⊙ **Level crossings**

⊙ **Fire stations**

You must always stop when the red lights are flashing, whether or not the way seems to be clear.

11.84

*Mark **one** answer*

R-ES 7, HC p102-117, KYTS

What do these zigzag lines at pedestrian crossings mean?

⊙ No parking at any time

⊙ Parking allowed only for a short time

⊙ Slow down to 20 mph

⊙ Sounding horns is not allowed

⊙ **No parking at any time**

The approach to, and exit from, a pedestrian crossing is marked with zigzag lines. You must not park on them or overtake the leading vehicle when approaching the crossing. Parking here would block the view for pedestrians and the approaching traffic.

*Mark **one** answer*

When may you cross a double solid white line in the middle of the road?

- ⊙ To pass traffic that is queuing back at a junction
- ⊙ To pass a car signalling to turn left ahead
- ⊙ To pass a road maintenance vehicle travelling at 10 mph or less
- ⊙ To pass a vehicle that is towing a trailer

- ⊙ **To pass a road maintenance vehicle travelling at 10 mph or less**

You may cross the solid white line to pass a stationary vehicle, pedal cycle, horse or road maintenance vehicle if they are travelling at 10 mph or less. You may also cross the solid line to enter into a side road or access a property.

*Mark **one** answer*

At this junction there is a stop sign with a solid white line on the road surface. Why is there a stop sign here?

- ⊙ Speed on the major road is de-restricted
- ⊙ It is a busy junction
- ⊙ Visibility along the major road is restricted
- ⊙ There are hazard warning lines in the centre of the road

- ⊙ **Visibility along the major road is restricted**

If your view is restricted at a road junction you must stop. There may also be a 'stop' sign. Don't emerge until you're sure there's no traffic approaching.

IF YOU DON'T KNOW, DON'T GO.

11.87   *Mark **one** answer*   R-ES 7, HC p102-117, KYTS

Where would you see this road marking?

- ⊙ At traffic lights
- ⊙ On road humps
- ⊙ Near a level crossing
- ⊙ At a box junction

⊙ **On road humps**

Due to the dark colour of the road, changes in level aren't easily seen. White triangles painted on the road surface give you an indication of where there are road humps.

11.88   *Mark **one** answer*   R-ES 7, HC p102-117, KYTS

Which is a hazard warning line?

⊙

You need to know the difference between the normal centre line and a hazard warning line. If there is a hazard ahead, the markings are longer and the gaps shorter. This gives you advanced warning of an unspecified hazard ahead.

11.89   *Mark **one** answer*   R-ES 7, HC p102-117, KYTS

What does this road marking mean?

- ⊙ Do not cross the line
- ⊙ No stopping allowed
- ⊙ You are approaching a hazard
- ⊙ No overtaking allowed

⊙ **You are approaching a hazard**

Road markings will warn you of a hazard ahead. A single, broken line along the centre of the road, with long markings and short gaps, is a hazard warning line. Don't cross it unless you can see that the road is clear well ahead.

You see this line across the road at the entrance to a roundabout. What does it mean?

⊙ Give way to traffic from the right

⊙ Traffic from the left has right of way

⊙ You have right of way

⊙ Stop at the line

⊙ **Give way to traffic from the right**

Slow down as you approach the roundabout and check for traffic from the right. If you need to stop and give way, stay behind the broken line until it is safe to emerge onto the roundabout.

How will a police officer in a patrol vehicle normally get you to stop?

⊙ Flash the headlights, indicate left and point to the left

⊙ Wait until you stop, then approach you

⊙ Use the siren, overtake, cut in front and stop

⊙ Pull alongside you, use the siren and wave you to stop

⊙ **Flash the headlights, indicate left and point to the left**

You must obey signals given by the police. If a police officer in a patrol vehicle wants you to pull over they will indicate this without causing danger to you or other traffic.

You approach a junction. The traffic lights are not working. A police officer gives this signal. You should

⊙ turn left only

⊙ turn right only

⊙ stop level with the officer's arm

⊙ stop at the stop line

⊙ **stop at the stop line**

If a police officer or traffic warden is directing traffic you must obey them. They will use the arm signals shown in The Highway Code. Learn what these mean and act accordingly.

11.93 *Mark **one** answer* **R-ES 7, HC p102-117, KYTS**

The driver of the car in front is giving this arm signal. What does it mean?

- ⊙ The driver is slowing down
- ⊙ The driver intends to turn right
- ⊙ The driver wishes to overtake
- ⊙ The driver intends to turn left

⊙ **The driver intends to turn left**

There might be an occasion where another driver uses an arm signal. This may be because the vehicle's indicators are obscured by other traffic. In order for such signals to be effective all drivers should know the meaning of them. Be aware that the 'left turn' signal might look similar to the 'slowing down' signal.

11.94 *Mark **one** answer* **R-ES 7, HC p102-117, KYTS**

Where would you see these road markings?

- ⊙ At a level crossing
- ⊙ On a motorway slip road
- ⊙ At a pedestrian crossing
- ⊙ On a single-track road

⊙ **On a motorway slip road**

When driving on a motorway or slip road, you must not enter into an area marked with chevrons and bordered by a solid white line for any reason, except in an emergency.

11.95 *Mark **one** answer* **R-ES 7, HC p102-117, KYTS**

What does this motorway sign mean?

- ⊙ Change to the lane on your left
- ⊙ Leave the motorway at the next exit
- ⊙ Change to the opposite carriageway
- ⊙ Pull up on the hard shoulder

⊙ **Change to the lane on your left**

On the motorway, signs sometimes show temporary warnings due to traffic or weather conditions. They may be used to indicate

- lane closures
- temporary speed limits
- weather warnings.

*Mark **one** answer*

What does this motorway sign mean?

⊙ Temporary minimum speed 50 mph

⊙ No services for 50 miles

⊙ Obstruction 50 metres (164 feet) ahead

⊙ Temporary maximum speed 50 mph

⊙ **Temporary maximum speed 50 mph**

Look out for signs above your lane or on the central reservation. These will give you important information or warnings about the road ahead. Due to the high speed of motorway traffic these signs may light up some distance from any hazard. Don't ignore the signs just because the road looks clear to you.

*Mark **one** answer*

What does this sign mean?

⊙ Through traffic to use left lane

⊙ Right-hand lane T-junction only

⊙ Right-hand lane closed ahead

⊙ 11 tonne weight limit

⊙ **Right-hand lane closed ahead**

You should move into the lanes as directed by the sign. Here the right-hand lane is closed and the left-hand and centre lanes are available. Merging in turn is recommended when it's safe and traffic is going slowly, for example at road works or a road traffic incident. When vehicles are travelling at speed this is not advisable and you should move into the appropriate lane in good time.

*Mark **one** answer*

On a motorway this sign means

⊙ move over onto the hard shoulder

⊙ overtaking on the left only

⊙ leave the motorway at the next exit

⊙ move to the lane on your left

⊙ **move to the lane on your left**

It is important to know and obey temporary signs on the motorway: they are there for a reason. You may not be able to see the hazard straight away, as the signs give warnings well in advance, due to the speed of traffic on the motorway.

11.99   *Mark **one** answer*   **R-ES 7, HC p102-117, KYTS**

What does '25' mean on this motorway sign?

- ⊙ The distance to the nearest town
- ⊙ The route number of the road
- ⊙ The number of the next junction
- ⊙ The speed limit on the slip road

⊙ **The number of the next junction**

Before you set out on your journey use a road map to plan your route. When you see advance warning of your junction, make sure you get into the correct lane in plenty of time. Last-minute harsh braking and cutting across lanes at speed is extremely hazardous.

11.100   *Mark **one** answer*   **R-ES 7, HC p102-117, r265, KYTS**

The right-hand lane of a three-lane motorway is

- ⊙ for lorries only
- ⊙ an overtaking lane
- ⊙ the right-turn lane
- ⊙ an acceleration lane

⊙ **an overtaking lane**

You should stay in the left-hand lane of a motorway unless overtaking. The right-hand lane of a motorway is an overtaking lane and not a 'fast lane'.

After overtaking, move back to the left when it is safe to do so.

11.101   *Mark **one** answer*   **R-ES 7, HC r132, KYTS**

Where can you find reflective amber studs on a motorway?

- ⊙ Separating the slip road from the motorway
- ⊙ On the left-hand edge of the road
- ⊙ On the right-hand edge of the road
- ⊙ Separating the lanes

⊙ **On the right-hand edge of the road**

At night or in poor visibility reflective studs on the road help you to judge your position on the carriageway.

323

Where on a motorway would you find green reflective studs?

⊙ Separating driving lanes

⊙ Between the hard shoulder and the carriageway

⊙ At slip road entrances and exits

⊙ Between the carriageway and the central reservation

⊙ **At slip road entrances and exits**

Knowing the colours of the reflective studs on the road will help you judge your position, especially at night, in foggy conditions or when visibility is poor.

You are travelling along a motorway. You see this sign. You should

⊙ leave the motorway at the next exit

⊙ turn left immediately

⊙ change lane

⊙ move onto the hard shoulder

⊙ **leave the motorway at the next exit**

You'll see this sign if the motorway is closed ahead. Pull into the nearside lane as soon as it is safe to do so. Don't leave it to the last moment.

What does this sign mean?

⊙ No motor vehicles

⊙ End of motorway

⊙ No through road

⊙ End of bus lane

⊙ **End of motorway**

When you leave the motorway make sure that you check your speedometer. You may be going faster than you realise. Slow down and look out for speed limit signs.

11.105   *Mark **one** answer*   R-ES 7, HC p102-117, KYTS

Which of these signs means that the national speed limit applies?

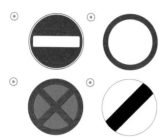

You should know the speed limit for the road on which you are travelling, and the vehicle that you are driving. The different speed limits are shown in The Highway Code.

11.106   *Mark **one** answer*   R-ES 7, HC p40, 102-117, KYTS

What is the maximum speed on a single carriageway road?

- 50 mph
- 60 mph
- 40 mph
- 70 mph

◉ **60 mph**

If you're travelling on a dual carriageway that becomes a single carriageway road, reduce your speed gradually so that you aren't exceeding the limit as you enter. There might not be a sign to remind you of the limit, so make sure you know what the speed limits are for different types of roads and vehicles.

11.107   *Mark **one** answer*   R-ES 7, HC p102, KYTS

What does this sign mean?

- End of motorway
- End of restriction
- Lane ends ahead
- Free recovery ends

◉ **End of restriction**

Temporary restrictions on motorways are shown on signs which have flashing amber lights. At the end of the restriction you will see this sign without any flashing lights.

This sign is advising you to

- follow the route diversion
- follow the signs to the picnic area
- give way to pedestrians
- give way to cyclists

⊙ **follow the route diversion**

When a diversion route has been put in place, drivers are advised to follow a symbol which may be a triangle, square, circle or diamond shape on a yellow background.

Why would this temporary speed limit sign be shown?

- To warn of the end of the motorway
- To warn you of a low bridge
- To warn you of a junction ahead
- To warn of road works ahead

⊙ **To warn of road works ahead**

In the interests of road safety, temporary speed limits are imposed at all major road works. Signs like this, giving advanced warning of the speed limit, are normally placed about three quarters of a mile ahead of where the speed limit comes into force.

11.110 *Mark **one** answer* **R-ES 7, HC p102-117, KYTS**

This traffic sign means there is

- ⊙ a compulsory maximum speed limit
- ⊙ an advisory maximum speed limit
- ⊙ a compulsory minimum speed limit
- ⊙ an advised separation distance

⊙ **a compulsory maximum speed limit**

The sign gives you an early warning of a speed restriction. If you are travelling at a higher speed, slow down in good time. You could come across queuing traffic due to roadworks or a temporary obstruction.

11.111 *Mark **one** answer* **R-ES 7, HC p102-117, KYTS**

You see this sign at a crossroads. You should

- ⊙ maintain the same speed
- ⊙ carry on with great care
- ⊙ find another route
- ⊙ telephone the police

⊙ **carry on with great care**

When traffic lights are out of order treat the junction as an unmarked crossroad. Be very careful as no one has priority and be prepared to stop.

11.112 *Mark **one** answer* **R-ES 7, HC p102-117, r176, KYTS**

You are signalling to turn right in busy traffic. How would you confirm your intention safely?

- ⊙ Sound the horn
- ⊙ Give an arm signal
- ⊙ Flash your headlights
- ⊙ Position over the centre line

⊙ **Give an arm signal**

In some situations you may feel your indicators cannot be seen by other road users. If you think you need to make your intention more clearly seen, give the arm signal shown in The Highway Code.

What does this sign mean?

⊙ Motorcycles only

⊙ No cars

⊙ Cars only

⊙ No motorcycles

⊙ **No motorcycles**

You must comply with all traffic signs and be especially aware of those signs which apply specifically to the type of vehicle you are using.

You are on a motorway. You see this sign on a lorry that has stopped in the right-hand lane. You should

⊙ move into the right-hand lane

⊙ stop behind the flashing lights

⊙ pass the lorry on the left

⊙ leave the motorway at the next exit

⊙ **pass the lorry on the left**

Sometimes work is carried out on the motorway without closing the lanes. When this happens, signs are mounted on the back of lorries to warn other road users of roadworks ahead.

11.115 *Mark one answer*   **R-ES 7, HC p102-117, r269, KYTS**

You are on a motorway. Red flashing lights appear above your lane only. What should you do?

- ⊙ Continue in that lane and look for further information
- ⊙ Move into another lane in good time
- ⊙ Pull onto the hard shoulder
- ⊙ Stop and wait for an instruction to proceed

⊙ **Move into another lane in good time**

Flashing red lights above your lane show that your lane is closed. You should move into another lane as soon as you can do so safely.

11.116 *Mark one answer*   **R-ES 7, HC p102-117, KYTS**

A red traffic light means

- ⊙ you must stop behind the white stop line
- ⊙ you may go straight on if there is no other traffic
- ⊙ you may turn left if it is safe to do so
- ⊙ you must slow down and prepare to stop if traffic has started to cross

⊙ **you must stop behind the white stop line**

The white line is generally positioned so that pedestrians have room to cross in front of waiting traffic. Don't move off while pedestrians are crossing, even if the lights change to green.

The driver of this car is giving an arm signal. What are they about to do?

- ⊙ Turn to the right
- ⊙ Turn to the left
- ⊙ Go straight ahead
- ⊙ Let pedestrians cross

⊙ **Turn to the left**

In some situations drivers may need to give arm signals, in addition to indicators, to make their intentions clear. For arm signals to be effective, all road users should know their meaning.

When may you sound the horn?

- ⊙ To give you right of way
- ⊙ To attract a friend's attention
- ⊙ To warn others of your presence
- ⊙ To make slower drivers move over

⊙ **To warn others of your presence**

Never sound the horn aggressively. You MUST NOT sound it when driving in a built-up area between 11.30 pm and 7.00 am or when you are stationary, an exception to this is when another road user poses a danger. Do not scare animals by sounding your horn.

Which sign means you have priority over oncoming vehicles?

⊙

Even though you have priority, be prepared to give way if other drivers don't. This will help to avoid congestion, confrontation or even a collision.

11.120 *Mark **one** answer* R-ES 7, HC p102-117, KYTS

What does this sign mean?

⊙ You can park on the days and times shown

⊙ No parking on the days and times shown

⊙ No parking at all from Monday to Friday

⊙ End of the urban clearway restrictions

⊙ **No parking on the days and times shown**

Urban clearways are provided to keep traffic flowing at busy times. You may stop only briefly to set down or pick up passengers. Times of operation will vary from place to place so always check the signs.

11.121 *Mark **one** answer* R-ES 7, HC p102-117, KYTS

What does this sign mean?

⊙ Quayside or river bank

⊙ Steep hill downwards

⊙ Uneven road surface

⊙ Road liable to flooding

⊙ **Quayside or river bank**

You should be careful in these locations as the road surface is likely to be wet and slippery. There may be a steep drop to the water, and there may not be a barrier along the edge of the road.

11.122 *Mark **one** answer* R-ES 7, HC p102-117, r112, KYTS

You must not use your horn when you are stationary

⊙ unless a moving vehicle may cause you danger

⊙ at any time whatsoever

⊙ unless it is used only briefly

⊙ except for signalling that you have just arrived

⊙ **unless a moving vehicle may cause you danger**

When stationary only sound your horn if you think there is a risk of danger from another road user. Don't use it just to attract someone's attention. This causes unnecessary noise and could be misleading.

A white line like this along the centre of the road is a

- ⊙ bus lane marking
- ⊙ hazard warning
- ⊙ give way marking
- ⊙ lane marking

⊙ **hazard warning**

The centre of the road is usually marked by a broken white line, with lines that are shorter than the gaps. When the lines become longer than the gaps this is a hazard warning line. Look well ahead for these, especially when you are planning to overtake or turn off.

What is the reason for the yellow criss-cross lines painted on the road here?

- ⊙ To mark out an area for trams only
- ⊙ To prevent queuing traffic from blocking the junction on the left
- ⊙ To mark the entrance lane to a car park
- ⊙ To warn you of the tram lines crossing the road

⊙ **To prevent queuing traffic from blocking the junction on the left**

Yellow 'box junctions' like this are often used where it's busy. Their purpose is to keep the junction clear for crossing traffic. Don't enter the painted area unless your exit is clear. The exception to this is when you are turning right and are only prevented from doing so by oncoming traffic or by other vehicles waiting to turn right.

11.125   *Mark **one** answer*   R-ES 7, HC p102-117, KYTS

What is the reason for the area marked in red and white along the centre of this road?

- ⊙ It is to separate traffic flowing in opposite directions
- ⊙ It marks an area to be used by overtaking motorcyclists
- ⊙ It is a temporary marking to warn of the roadworks
- ⊙ It is separating the two sides of the dual carriageway

⊙ **It is to separate traffic flowing in opposite directions**

Areas of 'hatched markings' such as these are to separate traffic streams which could be a danger to each other. They are often seen on bends or where the road becomes narrow. If the area is bordered by a solid white line, you must not enter it except in an emergency.

11.126   *Mark **one** answer*   R-ES 7, HC p102-117, r110, KYTS

Other drivers may sometimes flash their headlights at you. In which situation are they allowed to do this?

- ⊙ To warn of a radar speed trap ahead
- ⊙ To show that they are giving way to you
- ⊙ To warn you of their presence
- ⊙ To let you know there is a fault with your vehicle

⊙ **To warn you of their presence**

If other drivers flash their headlights this isn't a signal to show priority. The flashing of headlights has the same meaning as sounding the horn, it's a warning of their presence.

11.127   *Mark **one** answer*   R-ES 7, HC p102-117, r152, KYTS

In some narrow residential streets you may find a speed limit of

- ⊙ 20 mph
- ⊙ 25 mph
- ⊙ 35 mph
- ⊙ 40 mph

⊙ **20 mph**

In some built-up areas, you may find the speed limit reduced to 20 mph. Driving at a slower speed will help give you the time and space to see and deal safely with hazards such as pedestrians and parked cars.

Mark one answer

At a junction you see this signal. It means

- ⊙ cars must stop
- ⊙ trams must stop
- ⊙ both trams and cars must stop
- ⊙ both trams and cars can continue

⊙ **trams must stop**

The white light shows that trams must stop, but the green light shows that other vehicles may go if the way is clear. You may not live in an area where there are trams but you should still learn the signs. You never know when you may go to a town with trams.

Mark one answer

There is a police car following you. The police officer flashes the headlights and points to the left. What should you do?

- ⊙ Turn left at the next junction
- ⊙ Pull up on the left
- ⊙ Stop immediately
- ⊙ Move over to the left

⊙ **Pull up on the left**

You must pull up on the left as soon as it's safe to do so and switch off your engine.

Mark one answer

This broken white line painted in the centre of the road means

- ⊙ oncoming vehicles have priority over you
- ⊙ you should give priority to oncoming vehicles
- ⊙ there is a hazard ahead of you
- ⊙ the area is a national speed limit zone

⊙ **there is a hazard ahead of you**

A long white line with short gaps means that you are approaching a hazard. If you do need to cross it, make sure that the road is clear well ahead.

11.131   *Mark **one** answer*   **R-ES 7, HC p102-117, KYTS**

You see this amber traffic light ahead. Which light or lights, will come on next?

- ⊙ Red alone
- ⊙ Red and amber together
- ⊙ Green and amber together
- ⊙ Green alone

⊙ **Red alone**

At junctions controlled by traffic lights you must stop behind the white line until the lights change to green. Red and amber lights showing together also mean stop.

You may proceed when the light is green unless your exit road is blocked or pedestrians are crossing in front of you.

If you're approaching traffic lights that are visible from a distance and the light has been green for some time they are likely to change. Be ready to slow down and stop.

11.132   *Mark **one** answer*   **R-ES 7, HC p102-117, KYTS**

Where would you find these road markings?

- ⊙ At a railway crossing
- ⊙ At a junction
- ⊙ On a motorway
- ⊙ On a pedestrian crossing

⊙ **At a junction**

These markings show the direction in which the traffic should go at a mini-roundabout.

11.133   *Mark **one** answer*   **R-ES 7, HC p102-117, KYTS**

You see this signal overhead on the motorway. What does it mean?

- ⊙ Leave the motorway at the next exit
- ⊙ All vehicles use the hard shoulder
- ⊙ Sharp bend to the left ahead
- ⊙ Stop, all lanes ahead closed

⊙ **Leave the motorway at the next exit**

You will see this sign if there has been an incident ahead and the motorway is closed. You MUST obey the sign. Make sure that you prepare to leave as soon as you see the warning sign.

Don't pull over at the last moment or cut across other traffic.

What is the purpose of these yellow criss-cross lines on the road?

⊙ To make you more aware of the traffic lights

⊙ To guide you into position as you turn

⊙ To prevent the junction becoming blocked

⊙ To show you where to stop when the lights change

⊙ **To prevent the junction becoming blocked**

You MUST NOT enter a box junction until your exit road or lane is clear. The exception to this is if you want to turn right and are only prevented from doing so by oncoming traffic or by other vehicles waiting to turn right.

What MUST you do when you see this sign?

⊙ Stop, only if traffic is approaching

⊙ Stop, even if the road is clear

⊙ Stop, only if children are waiting to cross

⊙ Stop, only if a red light is showing

⊙ **Stop, even if the road is clear**

STOP signs are situated at junctions where visibility is restricted or there is heavy traffic. They MUST be obeyed. You MUST stop.

Take good all-round observation before moving off.

11.136 *Mark **one** answer* **R-ES 7, HC p102-117, KYTS**

Which shape is used for a 'give way' sign?

Other warning signs are the same shape and colour, but the 'give way' sign triangle points downwards. When you see this sign you MUST give way to traffic on the road which you are about to enter.

11.137 *Mark **one** answer* **R-ES 7, HC p102-117, KYTS**

What does this sign mean?

⊙ Buses turning
⊙ Ring road
⊙ Mini-roundabout
⊙ Keep right

⊙ **Mini-roundabout**

When you see this sign, look out for any direction signs and judge whether you need to signal your intentions. Do this in good time so that other road users approaching the roundabout know what you're planning to do.

11.138 *Mark **one** answer* **R-ES 7, HC p102-117, KYTS**

What does this sign mean?

⊙ Two-way traffic straight ahead
⊙ Two-way traffic crosses a one-way road
⊙ Two-way traffic over a bridge
⊙ Two-way traffic crosses a two-way road

⊙ **Two-way traffic crosses a one-way road**

Be prepared for traffic approaching from junctions on either side of you. Try to avoid unnecessary changing of lanes just before the junction.

What does this sign mean?

- ⊙ Two-way traffic ahead across a one-way road
- ⊙ Traffic approaching you has priority
- ⊙ Two-way traffic straight ahead
- ⊙ Motorway contraflow system ahead

⊙ **Two-way traffic straight ahead**

This sign may be at the end of a dual carriageway or a one-way street. It is there to warn you of oncoming traffic.

What does this sign mean?

- ⊙ Hump-back bridge
- ⊙ Traffic calming hump
- ⊙ Low bridge
- ⊙ Uneven road

⊙ **Hump-back bridge**

You will need to slow down. At humpback bridges your view ahead will be restricted and the road will often be narrow on the bridge. If the bridge is very steep or your view is restricted sound your horn to warn others of your approach. Going too fast over the bridge is highly dangerous to other road users and could even cause your wheels to leave the road, with a resulting loss of control.

Which of the following signs informs you that you are coming to a 'no through road'?

This sign is found at the entrance to a road that can only be used for access.

11.142   *Mark **one** answer*   **R-ES 7, KYTS**

What does this sign mean?

⊙ Direction to park-and-ride car park

⊙ No parking for buses or coaches

⊙ Directions to bus and coach park

⊙ Parking area for cars and coaches

⊙ **Direction to park-and-ride car park**

To ease the congestion in town centres, some cities and towns provide park-and-ride schemes. These allow you to park in a designated area and ride by bus into the centre.

Park-and-ride schemes are usually cheaper and easier than car parking in the town centre.

11.143   *Mark **one** answer*   **R-ES 7, HC p102-117, KYTS**

You are approaching traffic lights. Red and amber are showing. This means

⊙ pass the lights if the road is clear

⊙ there is a fault with the lights – take care

⊙ wait for the green light before you cross the stop line

⊙ the lights are about to change to red

⊙ **wait for the green light before you cross the stop line**

Be aware that other traffic might still be clearing the junction. Make sure the way is clear before continuing.

This marking appears on the road just before a

⊙ 'no entry' sign

⊙ 'give way' sign

⊙ 'stop' sign

⊙ 'no through road' sign

⊙ **'give way' sign**

Where you see this road marking you should give way to traffic on the main road. It might not be used at junctions where there is relatively little traffic. However, if there is a double broken line across the junction the 'give way' rules still apply.

At a railway level crossing the red light signal continues to flash after a train has gone by. What should you do?

⊙ Phone the signal operator

⊙ Alert drivers behind you

⊙ Wait

⊙ Proceed with caution

⊙ **Wait**

You MUST always obey red flashing stop lights. If a train passes but the lights continue to flash, another train will be passing soon. Cross only when the lights go off and the barriers open.

You are in a tunnel and you see this sign. What does it mean?

⊙ Direction to emergency pedestrian exit

⊙ Beware of pedestrians, no footpath ahead

⊙ No access for pedestrians

⊙ Beware of pedestrians crossing ahead

⊙ **Direction to emergency pedestrian exit**

If you have to leave your vehicle in a tunnel and leave by an emergency exit, do so as quickly as you can. Follow the signs directing you to the nearest exit point. If there are several people using the exit, don't panic but try to leave in a calm and orderly manner.

11.147 *Mark **one** answer* **R-ES 7, HC p102-117, KYTS**

Which of these signs shows that you are entering a one-way system?

⊙

If the road has two lanes you can use either lane and overtake on either side. Use the lane that's more convenient for your destination unless signs or road markings indicate otherwise.

11.148 *Mark **one** answer* **R-ES 7, HC p102-117, KYTS**

What does this sign mean?

⊙ With-flow bus and cycle lane
⊙ Contraflow bus and cycle lane
⊙ No buses and cycles allowed
⊙ No waiting for buses and cycles

⊙ **With-flow bus and cycle lane**

Buses and cycles can travel in this lane. In this case they will flow in the same direction as other traffic. If it's busy they may be passing you on the left, so watch out for them. Times on the sign will show its hours of operation. No times shown, or no sign at all, means it's 24 hours. In some areas other vehicles, such as taxis and motorcycles, are allowed to use bus lanes. The sign will show these.

11.149 *Mark **one** answer* **R-ES 7, HC p102-117, KYTS**

Which of these signs warns you of a zebra crossing?

⊙

Look well ahead and check the pavements and surrounding areas for pedestrians. Look for anyone walking towards the crossing. Check your mirrors for traffic behind, in case you have to slow down or stop.

*Mark **one** answer* **R-ES 7, HC p102-117, KYTS**

What does this sign mean?

- ⊙ No footpath
- ⊙ No pedestrians
- ⊙ Zebra crossing
- ⊙ School crossing

⊙ **Zebra crossing**

You need to be aware of the various signs that relate to pedestrians. Some of the signs look similar but have very different meanings. Make sure you know what they all mean and be ready for any potential hazard.

---

*Mark **one** answer* **R-ES 7, HC p102-117, KYTS**

What does this sign mean?

- ⊙ School crossing patrol
- ⊙ No pedestrians allowed
- ⊙ Pedestrian zone – no vehicles
- ⊙ Zebra crossing ahead

⊙ **Zebra crossing ahead**

Look well ahead and be ready to stop for any pedestrians crossing, or about to cross, the road. Also check the pavements for anyone who looks like they might step or run into the road.

---

*Mark **one** answer* **R-ES 7, HC p102-117, KYTS**

Which sign means there will be two-way traffic crossing your route ahead?

⊙   ⊙

⊙   ⊙

⊙

This sign is found in or at the end of a one-way system. It warns you that traffic will be crossing your path from both directions.

11.153 *Mark **one** answer* R-ES 7, HC p102-117, KYTS

Which arm signal tells you that the car you are following is going to pull up?

There may be occasions when drivers need to give an arm signal to confirm an indicator. This could include in bright sunshine, at a complex road layout, when stopping at a pedestrian crossing or when turning right just after passing a parked vehicle. You should understand what each arm signal means. If you give arm signals, make them clear, correct and decisive.

11.154 *Mark **one** answer* R-ES 7, HC p102-117, KYTS

Which of these signs means turn left ahead?

Blue circles tell you what you must do and this sign gives a clear instruction to turn left ahead. You should be looking out for signs at all times and know what they mean.

11.155 *Mark **one** answer* R-ES 7, HC p102-117, KYTS

Which sign shows that traffic can only travel in one direction on the road you're on?

This sign means that traffic can only travel in one direction. The others show different priorities on a two-way road.

Case study practice 11 – Road and traffic signs

You are riding in the town centre. There are different types of road layouts and staggered junctions with various types of sign. Some roads have 'no entry' signs, others are one-way only. At a large junction with traffic lights, there are filter arrows for traffic going left. Beyond the junction there are bus lanes on either side of the road. There are no signs showing times of operation.

11.1 What type of sign is the one for 'no entry'?

*Mark **one** answer*

- ⊙ Advisory.
- ⊙ Warning.
- ⊙ Regulatory.
- ⊙ Information.

HC p106, KYTS p16

11.2 What is meant by 'staggered'?

*Mark **one** answer*

- ⊙ The joining side roads are both narrow one-way streets.
- ⊙ The joining side roads are exactly opposite each other.
- ⊙ The joining side roads are reserved for pedestrians only.
- ⊙ The joining side roads are slightly offset from each other.

R-ES 9

11.3 What colours are used on the 'one way only' sign?

*Mark **one** answer*

⊙ White with red arrow.

⊙ Blue with white arrow.

⊙ Red with green arrow.

⊙ White with black arrow.

HC p107, KYTS p19

11.4 What colour is the filter arrow?

*Mark **one** answer*

⊙ White.

⊙ Amber.

⊙ Green.

⊙ Blue.

R-ES 7, HC p102

11.5 What is meant by the lack of bus lane signs?

*Mark **one** answer*

⊙ The lane is in operation at all times for buses.

⊙ The lane is not yet finished and still needs signs.

⊙ The lane is available for use by any vehicle.

⊙ The lane is being discontinued or removed.

HC r141

section **twelve**
DOCUMENTS

This section covers
- Licences
- Insurance
- MOT certificate

Documents

Before you can ride as a learner on a public road, you must have

- passed a Compulsory Basic Training (CBT) course, given by a Driving Standards Agency (DSA) approved training body
- a valid tax disc displayed on your vehicle. The vehicle registration documents must be correct and up to date
- a valid provisional driving licence, which must be signed
- proper insurance cover
- visible L plates (D plates in Wales)
- a valid MOT certificate, if required.

You will not be able to tax your motorcycle unless you have a valid MOT certificate and appropriate, current insurance documentation.

As a learner, you **MUST NOT** carry a pillion passenger, pull a trailer or ride your motorcycle on a motorway. You can do all three once you have passed your practical test and gained a full licence.

R-ES 2, HC r85 & p122

Licences

The Vehicle Registration Certificate (V5C) contains details of

- the vehicle (including make, model and engine size) and year of registration
- the registered keeper.

You, the registered keeper, must notify the licensing authority when you change your vehicle, your name or your permanent address. If you buy a second-hand vehicle, notify them immediately of the change of ownership.

A vehicle kept on the public road must have a valid tax disc clearly displayed. This confirms that vehicle excise duty has been paid. If you do not intend to use your vehicle on the public road, you will not have to pay road tax as long as you advise DVLA in advance. This is called a SORN declaration (Statutory Off Road Notification) and lasts for 12 months.

Before riding on a public road, a learner must have a valid provisional driving licence and CBT pass certificate. The CBT certificate is valid for two years. If you do not pass a practical test within that time, you will have to retake the CBT training.

R-ES 2, HC p122

You **MUST** notify the licensing authority if

- your health is likely to affect your riding
- your eyesight does not meet the required standard.

R-ES 1, HC r90

Insurance

You must have at least third party insurance cover before riding on public roads.
This covers

- injury to another person
- damage to someone else's property
- damage to other vehicles.

Riding without insurance is a criminal offence. It can lead to a maximum fine of £5,000, and possibly also disqualification.

R-ES 2, HC p121-122

You'll need to show your insurance certificate when you're taxing your vehicle or if a police officer asks you for it. You may be issued with a temporary cover note until you receive your insurance certificate.

The cost of your insurance is generally less if you are over 25 years old. Your insurance policy may have an excess of a certain amount, say £100. This means that you'll have to pay the first £100 of any claim.

Remember, before you ride anyone else's motorcycle, make sure that the vehicle is insured for your use.

R-ES 2, HC p121-122

MOT

Motorcycles must first have an MOT test when they're three years old (four in Northern Ireland). If your motorcycle has a sidecar, the MOT costs slightly more. Trailers don't need an MOT, but they do need to be kept in good order. MOT certificates are valid for one year.

You can ride your motorcycle without an MOT certificate when driving to an appointment at an MOT centre.

If your vehicle needs an MOT certificate and you don't have one

- you won't be able to renew your road tax
- you could be prosecuted
- it could invalidate your insurance.

R-ES 2, HC p121

FAQs

What happens if the police ask to see my documents and I don't have them with me?

You can produce them at a police station within seven days.

R-ES 16, HC p122

I've heard that I'm on probation for two years after I've passed my test. What does this mean?

If you get six or more penalty points within two years of passing your practical test, you'll lose your licence. You'll then have to

- *reapply for a provisional licence*
- *retake your theory and practical tests (and your CBT) again.*

Any points on your provisional licence will be transferred onto your new licence when you pass your test.

HC p127

12.1   Mark *three* answers   R-ES 2, HC p122

Which of the following information is found on your motorcycle registration document?

⊙ Make and model
⊙ Service history record
⊙ Ignition key security number
⊙ Engine size and number
⊙ Purchase price
⊙ Year of first registration

⊙ **Make and model**

⊙ **Engine size and number**

⊙ **Year of first registration**

Each motorcycle has a registration document which describes the vehicle's make, model and other details; it also gives details of the registered keeper. If you buy a new motorcycle the dealer will register your motorcycle with the licensing authority, who will send the registration document to you.

12.2   Mark *three* answers   R-ES 2, HC p120

You have a duty to contact the licensing authority when

⊙ you go abroad on holiday
⊙ you change your motorcycle
⊙ you change your name
⊙ your job status is changed
⊙ your permanent address changes
⊙ your job involves travelling abroad

⊙ **you change your motorcycle**

⊙ **you change your name**

⊙ **your permanent address changes**

The licensing authority will need to keep their records up to date. They send out a reminder when your road tax is due and need your current address for this purpose. Every motorcycle in the country is registered, so it is possible to trace its history.

12.3   Mark *one* answer   R-ES 2

Before riding anyone else's motorcycle you should make sure that

⊙ the owner has third party insurance cover
⊙ your own motorcycle has insurance cover
⊙ the motorcycle is insured for your use
⊙ the owner has the insurance documents with them

⊙ **the motorcycle is insured for your use**

If you borrow a motorcycle you must make sure that you are insured. Find out yourself. Don't take anyone else's word for it.

Vehicle excise duty is often called 'Road Tax' or 'The Tax Disc'. You must

- ⊙ keep it with your registration document
- ⊙ display it clearly on your motorcycle
- ⊙ keep it concealed safely in your motorcycle
- ⊙ carry it on you at all times

⊙ **display it clearly on your motorcycle**

You must display a current, valid tax disc on your vehicle. It can't be transferred from one vehicle to another. A vehicle that is exempt from duty must display a valid nil licence instead.

Your motorcycle is insured third party only. This covers

- ⊙ damage to your motorcycle
- ⊙ damage to other vehicles
- ⊙ injury to yourself
- ⊙ injury to others
- ⊙ all damage and injury

⊙ **damage to other vehicles**

⊙ **injury to others**

Third party insurance cover is usually cheaper than fully comprehensive. However, it does not cover any damage to your own motorcycle or property and it does not provide cover if your motorcycle is stolen.

Which THREE pieces of information are found on a registration document?

- ⊙ Registered keeper
- ⊙ Make of the motorcycle
- ⊙ Service history details
- ⊙ Date of the MOT
- ⊙ Type of insurance cover
- ⊙ Engine size

⊙ **Registered keeper**

⊙ **Make of the motorcycle**

⊙ **Engine size**

Every motorcycle used on the road has a registration document issued by the Driver and Vehicle Licensing Agency (DVLA) or Driver and Vehicle Agency (DVA) in Northern Ireland. It is used to record any change of ownership and gives, date of first registration, registration number, previous keeper, registered keeper, make of motorcycle, engine size and frame number, year of manufacture and colour.

12.7   NI EXEMPT   *Mark one answer*   R-ES 2, HC p118-119

Compulsory Basic Training (CBT) can only be carried out by

⊙ any ADI (Approved Driving Instructor)
⊙ any road safety officer
⊙ any DSA (Driving Standards Agency) approved training body
⊙ any motorcycle main dealer

⊙ **any DSA (Driving Standards Agency) approved training body**

CBT courses can only be given by training bodies that are approved by DSA. The standard of training is monitored by DSA examiners. The course is designed to give you basic skills before going on the road.

12.8   NI EXEMPT   *Mark one answer*   R-ES 2, HC p121

Motorcycles must FIRST have an MOT test certificate when they are

⊙ one year old
⊙ three years old
⊙ five years old
⊙ seven years old

⊙ **three years old**

Any motorcycle you ride must be in good condition and roadworthy. If it's over three years old it must have a valid MOT test certificate.

12.9   *Mark one answer*   R-ES 2, HC p121

What is the legal minimum insurance cover you must have to ride on public roads?

⊙ Third party, fire and theft
⊙ Fully comprehensive
⊙ Third party only
⊙ Personal injury cover

⊙ **Third party only**

The minimum insurance cover required by law is third party only. This covers other people and vehicles involved in a collision, but not you or your vehicle. Also basic third party insurance won't cover you for theft or fire damage. Make sure you carefully read and understand your policy.

12.10   *Mark one answer*   R-ES 2, HC p121-122

When you apply to renew your vehicle excise licence (tax disc) what must you have?

⊙ Valid insurance
⊙ The old tax disc
⊙ The vehicle handbook
⊙ A valid driving licence

⊙ **Valid insurance**

Tax discs can be renewed online, at most post offices, your nearest vehicle registration office or by post to the licensing authority. Make sure you have or take all the relevant documents with your application.

12.11
*Mark **one** answer*

R-ES 2, HC p122

A Vehicle Registration Document will show

- the service history
- the year of first registration
- the purchase price
- the tyre sizes

⊙ **the year of first registration**

A Vehicle Registration Document contains a number of details that are unique to a particular vehicle. You must notify DVLA (or DVA in Northern Ireland) of any changes to, for example, the registered keeper, registration number or any modifications to the vehicle.

12.12
*Mark **one** answer*

R-ES 2, HC p121

What is the purpose of having a vehicle test certificate (MOT)?

- To make sure your motorcycle is roadworthy
- To certify how many miles per gallon it does
- To prove you own the motorcycle
- To allow you to park in restricted areas

⊙ **To make sure your motorcycle is roadworthy**

It is your responsibility to make sure that any motorcycle you ride is in a roadworthy condition. Any faults that develop should be promptly corrected. If your motorcycle fails an MOT test, it should not be used on the road unless you're taking it to have the faults repaired or for a previously arranged retest.

12.13   NI EXEMPT   *Mark **one** answer*

R-ES 2, HC p118

Before taking a practical motorcycle test you need

- a full moped licence
- a full car licence
- a CBT (Compulsory Basic Training) certificate
- 12 months riding experience

⊙ **a CBT (Compulsory Basic Training) certificate**

The purpose of a CBT (Compulsory Basic Training) course is to teach you basic theory and practical skills before riding on the road, on your own, for the first time. They can only be given by Approved Training Bodies (ATBs).

12.14

*Mark **three** answers*

R-ES 2, HC r90

You must notify the licensing authority when

⊙ your health affects your riding
⊙ your eyesight does not meet a set standard
⊙ you intend lending your motorcycle
⊙ your motorcycle requires an MOT certificate
⊙ you change your motorcycle

⊙ **your health affects your riding**

⊙ **your eyesight does not meet a set standard**

⊙ **you change your motorcycle**

The Driver and Vehicle Licensing Agency (DVLA) hold the records of all vehicles, drivers and riders in Great Britain (DVA in Northern Ireland). They need to know of any change in circumstances so they can keep their records up to date. Your health might affect your ability to ride safely. Don't put yourself or other road users at risk.

12.15

*Mark **two** answers*

R-ES 2, HC p127 & p133-4

You have just passed your practical motorcycle test. This is your first full licence. Within two years you get six penalty points. You will have to

⊙ retake only your theory test
⊙ retake your theory and practical tests
⊙ retake only your practical test
⊙ reapply for your full licence immediately
⊙ reapply for your provisional licence

⊙ **retake your theory and practical tests**

⊙ **reapply for your provisional licence**

If, during your first two years of holding a full licence, the number of points on your licence reaches six or more, your licence will be revoked. This includes offences you committed before you passed your test. You may ride only as a learner until you pass both the theory and practical tests again.

12.16

*Mark **three** answers*

R-ES 2, HC r85, r253 & p123

You hold a provisional motorcycle licence. This means you must NOT

⊙ exceed 30 mph
⊙ ride on a motorway
⊙ ride after dark
⊙ carry a pillion passenger
⊙ ride without 'L' plates displayed

⊙ **ride on a motorway**

⊙ **carry a pillion passenger**

⊙ **ride without 'L' plates displayed**

Provisional entitlement means that restrictions apply to your use of motorcycles. The requirements are there to protect you and other road users. Make sure you are aware of all the restrictions that apply before you ride your motorcycle on the road.

12.17

*Mark **one** answer*

R-ES 2, HC p118-120

A full category A1 licence will allow you to ride a motorcycle up to

- ⊙ 125 cc
- ⊙ 250 cc
- ⊙ 350 cc
- ⊙ 425 cc

⊙ **125 cc**

When you pass your test on a motorcycle between 75 cc and 125 cc you will be issued with a full light motorcycle licence of category A1. You will then be allowed to ride any motorcycle up to 125 cc and with a power output of 11 Kw (14.6 bhp).

12.18   NI EXEMPT   *Mark **one** answer*

R-ES 2, HC p118-120

You want a licence to ride a large motorcycle via Direct Access. You will

- ⊙ not require L-plates if you have passed a car test
- ⊙ require L-plates only when learning on your own machine
- ⊙ require L-plates while learning with a qualified instructor
- ⊙ not require L-plates if you have passed a moped test

⊙ **require L-plates while learning with a qualified instructor**

While training through the Direct Access scheme you must be accompanied by an instructor on another motorcycle and be in radio contact. You must display L-plates on your motorcycle and follow all normal learner restrictions.

12.19   NI EXEMPT   *Mark **three** answers*

R-ES 2, HC r85

A motorcyclist may only carry a pillion passenger when

- ⊙ the rider has successfully completed CBT (Compulsory Basic Training)
- ⊙ the rider holds a full licence for the category of motorcycle
- ⊙ the motorcycle is fitted with rear footrests
- ⊙ the rider has a full car licence and is over 21
- ⊙ there is a proper passenger seat fitted
- ⊙ there is no sidecar fitted to the machine

⊙ **the rider holds a full licence for the category of motorcycle**

⊙ **the motorcycle is fitted with rear footrests**

⊙ **there is a proper passenger seat fitted**

Before carrying a passenger on a motorcycle the rider must hold a full licence for the category being ridden. They must also ensure that a proper passenger seat and footrests are fitted.

12.20 NI EXEMPT *Mark **one** answer* **R-ES 2, HC p118**

You have a CBT (Compulsory Basic Training) certificate. How long is it valid?

⊙ one year
⊙ two years
⊙ three years
⊙ four years

⊙ **two years**

All new learner motorcycle and moped riders must complete a Compulsory Basic Training (CBT) course before riding on the road. This can only be given by an Approved Training Body (ATB). If you don't pass your practical test within two years you will need to retake and pass CBT to continue riding.

12.21 *Mark **one** answer* **R-ES 2**

Your road tax disc is due to expire. To renew it you may need a renewal form, the fee, and valid MOT (if required). What else will you need?

⊙ Proof of purchase receipt
⊙ Compulsory Basic Training certificate
⊙ A valid certificate of insurance
⊙ A complete service record

⊙ **A valid certificate of insurance**

You will normally be sent a reminder automatically by the DVLA (DVA in Northern Ireland) close to the time of renewal. Make sure that all your documentation is correct, up to date and valid. You can renew, by post, in person, by phone or online.

12.22 *Mark **one** answer* **R-ES 2, HC r85**

You want to carry a pillion passenger on your motorcycle. To do this

⊙ your motorcycle must be larger than 125 cc
⊙ they must be a full motorcycle licence-holder
⊙ you must have passed your test for a full motorcycle licence
⊙ you must have three years motorcycle riding experience

⊙ **you must have passed your test for a full motorcycle licence**

As a learner motorcyclist you are not allowed to carry a pillion passenger, even if they hold a full motorcycle licence. You MUST NOT carry a pillion, or tow a trailer, until you have passed your test.

*Mark **one** answer*

A friend asks you to give them a lift on your motorcycle. What conditions apply?

⊙ Your motorcycle must be larger than 125 cc

⊙ You must have three years motorcycle riding experience

⊙ The pillion must be a full motorcycle licence-holder

⊙ You must have passed your test for a full motorcycle licence

⊙ **You must have passed your test for a full motorcycle licence**

By law, you can only carry a pillion passenger after you have gained a full motorcycle licence. Even if they hold a full licence it makes no difference. As a learner you are also restricted from towing a trailer.

---

*Mark **one** answer*

Your motorcycle insurance policy has an excess of £100. What does this mean?

⊙ The insurance company will pay the first £100 of any claim

⊙ You will be paid £100 if you do not have a crash

⊙ Your motorcycle is insured for a value of £100 if it is stolen

⊙ You will have to pay the first £100 of any claim

⊙ **You will have to pay the first £100 of any claim**

This is a method used by insurance companies to keep annual premiums down. Generally, the higher the excess you choose to pay, the lower the annual premium you will be charged.

---

*Mark **one** answer*

An MOT certificate is normally valid for

⊙ three years after the date it was issued

⊙ 10,000 miles

⊙ one year after the date it was issued

⊙ 30,000 miles

⊙ **one year after the date it was issued**

Make a note of the date that your MOT certificate expires. Some garages remind you that your vehicle is due an MOT but not all do. You may take your vehicle for MOT up to one month in advance and have the certificate post dated.

12.26 *Mark **one** answer*   R-ES 2, HC p121-122

A cover note is a document issued before you receive your

- ⊙ driving licence
- ⊙ insurance certificate
- ⊙ registration document
- ⊙ MOT certificate

⊙ **insurance certificate**

Sometimes an insurance company will issue a temporary insurance certificate called a cover note. It gives you the same insurance cover as your certificate, but lasts for a limited period, usually one month.

12.27 *Mark **two** answers*   R-ES 1 & 2, HC p127 & p134

You have just passed your practical test. You do not hold a full licence in another category. Within two years you get six penalty points on your licence. What will you have to do?

- ⊙ Retake only your theory test
- ⊙ Retake your theory and practical tests
- ⊙ Retake only your practical test
- ⊙ Reapply for your full licence immediately
- ⊙ Reapply for your provisional licence

⊙ **Retake your theory and practical tests**

⊙ **Reapply for your provisional licence**

If you accumulate six or more penalty points within two years of gaining your first full licence it will be revoked. The six or more points include any gained due to offences you committed before passing your test. If this happens you may only drive as a learner until you pass both the theory and practical tests again.

12.28 *Mark **one** answer*   R-ES 2, HC p122

How long will a Statutory Off Road Notification (SORN) last for?

- ⊙ 12 months
- ⊙ 24 months
- ⊙ 3 years
- ⊙ 10 years

⊙ **12 months**

A SORN declaration allows you to keep a vehicle off road and untaxed for 12 months. If you want to keep your vehicle off road beyond that you must send a further SORN form to DVLA, or DVA in Northern Ireland. If the vehicle is sold SORN will end and the new owner becomes responsible immediately.

What is a Statutory Off Road Notification (SORN) declaration?

⊙ A notification to tell VOSA that a vehicle does not have a current MOT

⊙ Information kept by the police about the owner of the vehicle

⊙ A notification to tell DVLA that a vehicle is not being used on the road

⊙ Information held by insurance companies to check the vehicle is insured

⊙ **A notification to tell DVLA that a vehicle is not being used on the road**

If you want to keep a vehicle off the public road you must declare SORN. It is an offence not to do so. You then won't have to pay road tax. If you don't renew the SORN declaration or re-license the vehicle, you will incur a penalty.

A Statutory Off Road Notification (SORN) declaration is

⊙ to tell DVLA that your vehicle is being used on the road but the MOT has expired

⊙ to tell DVLA that you no longer own the vehicle

⊙ to tell DVLA that your vehicle is not being used on the road

⊙ to tell DVLA that you are buying a personal number plate

⊙ **to tell DVLA that your vehicle is not being used on the road**

This will enable you to keep a vehicle off the public road for 12 months without having to pay road tax. You must send a further SORN declaration after 12 months.

A Statutory Off Road Notification (SORN) is valid

⊙ for as long as the vehicle has an MOT

⊙ for 12 months only

⊙ only if the vehicle is more than 3 years old

⊙ provided the vehicle is insured

⊙ **for 12 months only**

If you want to keep a vehicle off the public road you must declare SORN. It is an offence not to do so. You then won't have to pay road tax for that vehicle. You will incur a penalty after 12 months if you don't renew the SORN declaration, or re-license the vehicle. If you sell the vehicle the SORN declaration ends and the new owner should declare SORN or re-license the vehicle.

12.32 *Mark **one** answer*   R-ES 2, HC p122

A Statutory Off Road Notification (SORN) will last

⊙ for the life of the vehicle
⊙ for as long as you own the vehicle
⊙ for 12 months only
⊙ until the vehicle warranty expires

⊙ **for 12 months only**

If you are keeping a vehicle, or vehicles, off road and don't want to pay road tax you must declare SORN. You must still do this even if the vehicle is incapable of being used, for example it may be under restoration or being stored. After 12 months you must send another SORN declaration or re-license your vehicle. You will be fined if you don't do this. The SORN will end if you sell the vehicle and the new owner will be responsible immediately.

12.33 *Mark **one** answer*   R-ES 2, HC p121-122 & p126

What is the maximum specified fine for driving without insurance?

⊙ £50
⊙ £500
⊙ £1,000
⊙ £5,000

⊙ **£5,000**

It is a serious offence to drive without insurance. As well as a heavy fine you may be disqualified or incur penalty points.

12.34 *Mark **one** answer*   R-ES 2, HC p122

Who is legally responsible for ensuring that a Vehicle Registration Certificate (V5C) is updated?

⊙ The registered vehicle keeper
⊙ The vehicle manufacturer
⊙ Your insurance company
⊙ The licensing authority

⊙ **The registered vehicle keeper**

It is your legal responsibility to keep the details of your Vehicle Registration Certificate (V5C) up to date. You should tell the licensing authority of any changes. These include your name, address, or vehicle details. If you don't do this you may have problems when you sell your vehicle.

For which of these MUST you show your insurance certificate?

- When making a SORN declaration
- When buying or selling a vehicle
- When a police officer asks you for it
- When having an MOT inspection

⊙ **When a police officer asks you for it**

You MUST be able to produce your valid insurance certificate when requested by a police officer. If you can't do this immediately you may be asked to take it to a police station. Other documents you may be asked to produce are your driving licence and MOT certificate.

You must have valid insurance before you can

- make a SORN declaration
- buy or sell a vehicle
- apply for a driving licence
- obtain a tax disc

⊙ **obtain a tax disc**

You MUST have valid insurance before you can apply for a tax disc. Your vehicle will also need to have a valid MOT certificate, if applicable. You can apply on-line, at certain post offices or by post. It is illegal and can be dangerous to drive without valid insurance or an MOT.

When you apply to renew your Vehicle Excise Duty (tax disc) you must have

- valid insurance
- the old tax disc
- the handbook
- a valid driving licence

⊙ **valid insurance**

Tax discs can be renewed at post offices, vehicle registration offices, online, or by post. When applying make sure you have all the relevant valid documents, including MOT where applicable.

When should you update your Vehicle Registration Certificate?

- When you pass your driving test
- When you move house
- When your vehicle needs an MOT
- When you have a collision

⊙ **When you move house**

As the registered keeper of a vehicle it is up to you to inform DVLA (DVA in Northern Ireland) of any changes in your vehicle or personal details, for example, change of name or address. You do this by completing the relevant section of the Registration Certificate and sending it to them.

12.39   *Mark three answers*   **R-ES 2, HC p122**

Which THREE of these do you need before you can use a vehicle on the road legally?

⊙ A valid driving licence
⊙ A valid tax disc clearly displayed
⊙ Proof of your identity
⊙ Proper insurance cover
⊙ Breakdown cover
⊙ A vehicle handbook

⊙ **A valid driving licence**

⊙ **A valid tax disc clearly displayed**

⊙ **Proper insurance cover**

Using a vehicle on the road illegally carries a heavy fine and can lead to penalty points on your licence. Things you MUST have include a valid driving licence, a current valid tax disc, and proper insurance cover.

12.40   *Mark one answer*   **R-ES 2, HC p122**

Your vehicle needs a current MOT certificate. Until you have one you will NOT be able to

⊙ renew your driving licence
⊙ change your insurance company
⊙ renew your road tax disc
⊙ notify a change of address

⊙ **renew your road tax disc**

If your vehicle is required to have an MOT certificate you will need to make sure this is current before you are able to renew your tax disc (also known as vehicle excise duty). You can renew online, by phone or by post.

12.41   *Mark one answer*   **R-ES 2, HC p122**

A police officer asks to see your documents. You do not have them with you. You may be asked to take them to a police station within

⊙ 5 days
⊙ 7 days
⊙ 14 days
⊙ 21 days

⊙ **7 days**

You don't have to carry the documents for your vehicle around with you. If a police officer asks to see them and you don't have them with you, you may be asked to produce them at a police station within seven days.

Case study practice 12 – Documents

Casey's old motorcycle has just failed an MOT and needs some repair work. Casey rides the failed motorcycle to a local repairer a few miles away from the MOT centre. The parts can be ordered and the repairer can do the work. The repair takes five days. A week later, Casey has the motorcycle retested. It successfully passes the second MOT. Casey has the cheapest type of insurance cover available.

12.1 For how long does an MOT certificate last?

*Mark **one** answer*

- ⊙ Six months.
- ⊙ Twelve months.
- ⊙ Two years.
- ⊙ Three years.

R-ES 2, HC p121

12.2 Why could Casey ride to the repairer?

*Mark **one** answer*

- ⊙ It's allowed during daylight hours but not at night.
- ⊙ It's allowed but only until vehicle excise duty expires.
- ⊙ It's allowed in order to get the machine to a repairer.
- ⊙ It's allowed for a period of seven days after failure.

HC p121

12.3 Which of these **MUST** be displayed on the vehicle?

*Mark **one** answer*

- ⊙ Vehicle Excise Duty.
- ⊙ Name and address details.
- ⊙ MOT certificate.
- ⊙ Registration document.

R-ES 2, HC p120-122

12.4 What does the law say about insurance?

*Mark **one** answer*

- ⊙ It is a provisional requirement.
- ⊙ It is a security requirement.
- ⊙ It is a voluntary requirement.
- ⊙ It is a legal requirement.

R-ES 2, HC p121

12.5 What is the cheapest insurance cover called?

*Mark **one** answer*

- ⊙ Third policy.
- ⊙ Third practice.
- ⊙ Third party.
- ⊙ Third procedure.

R-ES 2, HC p121-122

section **thirteen**

INCIDENTS, ACCIDENTS AND EMERGENCIES

This section covers

- First aid
- Warning devices
- Reporting procedures
- Safety regulations

Incidents, accidents and emergencies

Breakdowns

If a warning light on the instrument panel of your vehicle comes on while you're riding, stop (as soon as you can do so safely) and check out the problem.

If a tyre bursts or you've a puncture while you're riding, hold the handlebars firmly and then gently roll to a stop at the side of the road.

R-ES 16, HC p128

If this or any other emergency occurs on a motorway, try to get onto the hard shoulder and call for help from an emergency telephone. Marker posts will point you to the nearest phone. The police or Highways Agency will answer and ask you

- the phone number
- details of yourself and your vehicle
- whether you belong to a motoring organisation.

R-ES 16, HC r270 & r275

A person who has a disability which affects their mobility may display a HELP pennant if they're unable to reach an emergency phone.

HC r278

If you break down on a level crossing, get yourself, any passenger and your motorcycle off the crossing area immediately. If you can't move your motorcycle, get yourself and any passenger clear of the crossing, then phone the signal operator and follow any instructions given to you. If you're waiting at a level crossing and the red light signal continues to flash after a train has gone by, wait, as there may be another train coming.

R-ES 7, HC r 293 & r299, KYTS p27

Safety in tunnels

Before riding through a tunnel, remove any sunglasses or sun visors and make sure your dipped headlights are on. It's particularly important to keep a safe distance from the vehicle in front when riding in a tunnel, even if it's congested. Look out for variable message signs that warn of incidents or congestion.

If your motorcycle, or the vehicle in front, is involved in an incident or breaks down in a tunnel, switch off the engine, put your hazard warning lights on, then go and call for help immediately from the nearest emergency telephone point.

R-ES 8

Warning others of a breakdown or incident

Use your hazard warning lights

- if you need to slow down or stop on a motorway or high-speed road because of a road traffic incident or hazard ahead

- when you're broken down or stopped and temporarily obstructing traffic.

If you've a warning triangle, place it at least 45 metres (147 feet) behind your motorcycle. This will warn other road users that you've broken down. However, never use a warning triangle on a motorway.

R-ES 5, 11 & 16, HC r116 & r274

Stopping at an incident

If you're the first to arrive at the scene of an incident or crash, stop and warn other traffic. Switch on your hazard warning lights. Don't put yourself at risk:

- make sure the emergency services are called as soon as possible

- ensure that the engines of any vehicles at the scene are switched off

- move uninjured people away from the accident scene.

R-ES 16, HC r283

A vehicle carrying dangerous goods will display an orange label or a hazard warning plate on the back. Report what it says when you call the emergency services. The different plates are shown in *The Highway Code.*

R-ES 16, HC p117

First aid

Even if you don't know any first aid, you can help any injured people by

- keeping them warm and comfortable

- keeping them calm by talking to them reassuringly

- making sure that they're not left alone.

R-ES 16, HC p131

Don't move them as long as the area is safe. Only move them if they're in obvious danger, and then with extreme care. If a motorcyclist is involved, never remove their helmet unless it's essential in order to keep them alive, because removal of the helmet could cause more serious injury. Always seek medical assistance and never offer a casualty any food or drink, or a cigarette to calm them down.

R-ES 16, HC p131-133

There are three vital priorities - ensure a clear airway, check for breathing, and try to stop any heavy bleeding. If someone is unconscious, follow the '**DR ABC**' code as follows

D – Danger – check for danger before you approach

R – Response – gently shake the shoulders, check for response

A – Airway – check the airway is clear

B – Breathing – check for breathing for up to 10 seconds

C – Compressions – use two hands in the centre of the chest, press down 4-5cm at a rate of 100 per minute. Use one hand, gently for a small child (two fingers for an infant).

If they're not breathing, consider giving mouth-to-mouth resuscitation:

- check and if necessary clear their mouth and airway
- gently tilt their head back as far as possible
- pinch their nostrils together.

Only stop when they can breathe without help. If the casualty is a small child, breathe very gently. Once the casualty is breathing normally, place them in the recovery position and check the airway to make sure it is clear. Keep checking, and don't leave them alone. If they're bleeding, apply firm pressure to the wound, then raise the limb as long as it isn't broken. This will help reduce the bleeding. If someone is suffering from burns, douse the burns thoroughly with cool non-toxic liquid for at least 10 minutes. Don't remove anything sticking to the burn.

People at the scene may be suffering from shock. Warning signs include a rapid pulse, sweating and pale grey skin.

- Reassure them constantly.
- Keep them warm.
- Loosen any tight clothing.
- Avoid moving them unless it's necessary
- Make sure they're not left alone.

Reporting

If you're involved in an incident, stop. It's an offence not to stop and call the police if any other person is injured or there's damage to another vehicle, property or animal. If you don't do this at the time, you **MUST** report the incident to the police within 24 hours (immediately in Northern Ireland). If another vehicle is involved, find out

- the make and registration number of the vehicle and whether the other driver owns it
- the other driver's name, address and telephone number and details of their insurance.

Following an incident (or at any other time) the police may ask you to produce your insurance certificate, the MOT certificate for the vehicle you're riding and your driving licence.

R-ES 16, HC r286

FAQs

What should I do if my engine catches fire?

Pull up as quickly and safely as possible. Get yourself and any passenger away from the motorcycle. Then call the fire brigade.

R-ES 11, HC r280

What should I do if I see something fall from a lorry on the motorway?

Stop at the next emergency telephone and report the hazard to the police or Highways Agency. Do the same if anything falls from your own motorcycle – don't try to retrieve it yourself.

R-ES 16

What would you suggest I carry for use in an emergency?

It's useful to have a first aid kit, a warning triangle and a fire extinguisher. This equipment could be invaluable and is a small price to pay if it helps to prevent or lessen an injury.

R-ES 16

What should I do if I smell petrol?

Stop and investigate as soon as you can do so safely. Don't ignore it. It can be useful to carry a fire extinguisher, which may help in tackling a small fire, but don't take any risks.

R-ES 16

13.1 Mark *one* answer — R-ES 11, HC r275

Your motorcycle has broken down on a motorway. How will you know the direction of the nearest emergency telephone?

⊙ By walking with the flow of traffic

⊙ By following an arrow on a marker post

⊙ By walking against the flow of traffic

⊙ By remembering where the last phone was

⊙ **By following an arrow on a marker post**

If you break down on a motorway pull onto the hard shoulder and stop as far over to the left as you can. Switch on hazard lights (if fitted) and go to the nearest emergency telephone. Marker posts spaced every 100 metres will show you where the nearest telephone is.

13.2 Mark *one* answer — R-ES 5

You should use the engine cut-out switch to

⊙ stop the engine in an emergency

⊙ stop the engine on short journeys

⊙ save wear on the ignition switch

⊙ start the engine if you lose the key

⊙ **stop the engine in an emergency**

Most motorcycles are fitted with an engine cut-out switch. This is designed to stop the engine in an emergency and so reduce the risk of fire.

13.3 Mark *one* answer — HC r116

You are riding on a motorway. The car in front switches on its hazard warning lights whilst moving. This means

⊙ they are going to take the next exit

⊙ there is a danger ahead

⊙ there is a police car in the left lane

⊙ they are trying to change lanes

⊙ **there is a danger ahead**

When riding on a motorway, or a dual carriageway subject to a national speed limit, vehicles may switch on their hazard warning lights to warn following traffic of an obstruction ahead.

13.4   *Mark **three** answers*   R-ES 11, HC r275

You have broken down on a motorway. When you use the emergency telephone you will be asked

- for the number on the telephone that you are using
- for your driving licence details
- for the name of your vehicle insurance company
- for details of yourself and your motorcycle
- whether you belong to a motoring organisation

- ⊙ **for the number on the telephone that you are using**

- ⊙ **for details of yourself and your motorcycle**

- ⊙ **whether you belong to a motoring organisation**

Have these details ready before you phone and be sure to give the correct information. For your own safety face the traffic when you speak on the telephone.

13.5   *Mark **one** answer*   R-ES 11, HC r116

You are on a motorway. When can you use hazard warning lights?

- When a vehicle is following too closely
- When you slow down quickly because of danger ahead
- When you are being towed by another vehicle
- When riding on the hard shoulder

- ⊙ **When you slow down quickly because of danger ahead**

Hazard lights will warn the traffic behind you that there is a potential hazard ahead. Don't forget to turn them off again when your signal has been seen.

13.6   *Mark **one** answer*   R-ES 16, HC r116 & r126

Your motorcycle breaks down in a tunnel. What should you do?

- Stay with your motorcycle and wait for the Police
- Stand in the lane behind your motorcycle to warn others
- Stand in front of your motorcycle to warn oncoming drivers
- Switch on hazard lights then go and call for help immediately

- ⊙ **Switch on hazard lights then go and call for help immediately**

Any broken down vehicle in a tunnel can cause serious congestion and danger to other traffic and drivers. If you break down you should get help without delay. Switch on your hazard warning lights and then go to an emergency telephone point to call for help.

13.7

You are riding through a tunnel. Your motorcycle breaks down. What should you do?

- ⊙ Switch on hazard warning lights
- ⊙ Remain on your motorcycle
- ⊙ Wait for the police to find you
- ⊙ Rely on CCTV cameras seeing you

⊙ **Switch on hazard warning lights**

If your motorcycle breaks down in a tunnel it could present a danger to other traffic. First switch on your hazard warning lights and then call for help from an emergency telephone point. Don't rely on being found by the police or being seen by a CCTV camera.

13.8

You are travelling on a motorway. A bag falls from your motorcycle. There are valuables in the bag. What should you do?

- ⊙ Go back carefully and collect the bag as quickly as possible
- ⊙ Stop wherever you are and pick up the bag, but only when there is a safe gap
- ⊙ Stop on the hard shoulder and use the emergency telephone to inform the authorities
- ⊙ Stop on the hard shoulder and then retrieve the bag yourself

⊙ **Stop on the hard shoulder and use the emergency telephone to inform the authorities**

You must never walk on a motorway, however important you think retrieving your property may be. Your bag might be creating a hazard but not as great a hazard as you would be.

13.9

You are on a motorway. Luggage falls from your motorcycle. What should you do?

- ⊙ Stop at the next emergency telephone and report the hazard
- ⊙ Stop on the motorway and put on hazard lights while you pick it up
- ⊙ Walk back up the motorway to pick it up
- ⊙ Pull up on the hard shoulder and wave traffic down

⊙ **Stop at the next emergency telephone and report the hazard**

If any of your luggage falls onto the road, pull onto the hard shoulder near an emergency telephone and phone for assistance. Don't stop on the carriageway or attempt to retrieve anything.

You are in collision with another vehicle. Someone is injured. Your motorcycle is damaged. Which FOUR of the following should you find out?

- ⊙ Whether the driver owns the other vehicle involved
- ⊙ The other driver's name, address and telephone number
- ⊙ The make and registration number of the other vehicle
- ⊙ The occupation of the other driver
- ⊙ The details of the other driver's vehicle insurance
- ⊙ Whether the other driver is licensed to drive

⊙ **Whether the driver owns the other vehicle involved**

⊙ **The other driver's name, address and telephone number**

⊙ **The make and registration number of the other vehicle**

⊙ **The details of the other driver's vehicle insurance**

If you are involved in a collision where someone is injured, your first priority is to warn other traffic and call the emergency services.

When exchanging details, make sure you have all the information you need before you leave the scene. Don't ride your motorcycle if it is unroadworthy.

You see a car on the hard shoulder of a motorway with a HELP pennant displayed. This means the driver is most likely to be

- ⊙ a disabled person
- ⊙ first aid trained
- ⊙ a foreign visitor
- ⊙ a rescue patrol person

⊙ **a disabled person**

If a disabled driver's vehicle breaks down and they are unable to walk to an emergency phone, they are advised to stay in their car and switch on the hazard warning lights. They may also display a 'Help' pennant in their vehicle.

On the motorway, the hard shoulder should be used

- ⊙ to answer a mobile phone
- ⊙ when an emergency arises
- ⊙ for a short rest when tired
- ⊙ to check a road atlas

⊙ **when an emergency arises**

Pull onto the hard shoulder and use the emergency telephone to report your problem. This lets the emergency services know your exact location so they can send help. Never cross the carriageway to use the telephone on the other side.

13.13   *Mark one answer*   R-ES 5, 11, 16, HC r116 & 274

When are you allowed to use hazard warning lights?

- ⊙ When stopped and temporarily obstructing traffic
- ⊙ When travelling during darkness without headlights
- ⊙ When parked for shopping on double yellow lines
- ⊙ When travelling slowly because you are lost

⊙ **When stopped and temporarily obstructing traffic**

You must not use hazard warning lights when moving, except when slowing suddenly on a motorway or unrestricted dual carriageway to warn the traffic behind.

Never use hazard warning lights to excuse dangerous or illegal parking.

13.14   *Mark one answer*   R-ES 8, HC r126

You are going through a congested tunnel and have to stop. What should you do?

- ⊙ Pull up very close to the vehicle in front to save space
- ⊙ Ignore any message signs as they are never up to date
- ⊙ Keep a safe distance from the vehicle in front
- ⊙ Make a U-turn and find another route

⊙ **Keep a safe distance from the vehicle in front**

It's important to keep a safe distance from the vehicle in front at all times. This still applies in congested tunnels even if you are moving very slowly or have stopped. If the vehicle in front breaks down you may need room to manoeuvre past it.

13.15   *Mark two answers*   R-ES 5, 11, 16, HC r116 & 274

For which TWO should you use hazard warning lights?

- ⊙ When you slow down quickly on a motorway because of a hazard ahead
- ⊙ When you have broken down
- ⊙ When you wish to stop on double yellow lines
- ⊙ When you need to park on the pavement

⊙ **When you slow down quickly on a motorway because of a hazard ahead**

⊙ **When you have broken down**

Hazard warning lights are fitted to all modern cars and some motorcycles. They should only be used to warn other road users of a hazard ahead.

*Mark **one** answer*

You arrive at the scene of a crash. Someone is bleeding badly from an arm wound. There is nothing embedded in it. What should you do?

- ⊙ Apply pressure over the wound and keep the arm down
- ⊙ Dab the wound
- ⊙ Get them a drink
- ⊙ Apply pressure over the wound and raise the arm

⊙ **Apply pressure over the wound and raise the arm**

If possible, lay the casualty down. Check for anything that may be in the wound. Apply firm pressure to the wound using clean material, without pressing on anything which might be in it. Raising the arm above the level of the heart will also help to stem the flow of blood.

*Mark **one** answer*

You are at an incident where a casualty is unconscious. Their breathing should be checked. This should be done for at least

- ⊙ 2 seconds
- ⊙ 10 seconds
- ⊙ 1 minute
- ⊙ 2 minutes

⊙ **10 seconds**

Once the airway is open, check breathing. Listen and feel for breath. Do this by placing your cheek over their mouth and nose, and look to see if the chest rises. This should be done for up to 10 seconds.

*Mark **one** answer*

Following a collision someone has suffered a burn. The burn needs to be cooled. What is the shortest time it should be cooled for?

- ⊙ 5 minutes
- ⊙ 10 minutes
- ⊙ 15 minutes
- ⊙ 20 minutes

⊙ **10 minutes**

Check the casualty for shock and if possible try to cool the burn for at least ten minutes. Use a clean, cold non-toxic liquid preferably water.

13.19   *Mark **one** answer*   R-ES 16, HC p131-133

After a collision someone has suffered a burn. The burn needs to be cooled. What is the shortest time it should be cooled for?

◉ 30 seconds
◉ 60 seconds
◉ 5 minutes
◉ 10 minutes

◉ **10 minutes**

It's important to cool a burn for at least ten minutes. Use a clean, cold non-toxic liquid preferably water. Bear in mind the person may also be in shock.

13.20   *Mark **one** answer*   R-ES 16, HC p131-133

A casualty is not breathing normally. Chest compressions should be given. At what rate?

◉ 50 per minute
◉ 100 per minute
◉ 200 per minute
◉ 250 per minute

◉ **100 per minute**

If a casualty is not breathing normally chest compressions may be needed to maintain circulation. Place two hands on the centre of the chest and press down about 4-5 centimetres, at the rate of 100 per minute.

13.21   *Mark **one** answer*   R-ES 16, HC p131-133

A person has been injured. They may be suffering from shock. What are the warning signs to look for?

◉ Flushed complexion
◉ Warm dry skin
◉ Slow pulse
◉ Pale grey skin

◉ **Pale grey skin**

The effects of shock may not be immediately obvious. Warning signs are rapid pulse, sweating, pale grey skin and rapid shallow breathing.

*Mark **one** answer*

You suspect that an injured person may be suffering from shock. What are the warning signs to look for?

⊙ Warm dry skin

⊙ Sweating

⊙ Slow pulse

⊙ Skin rash

⊙ **Sweating**

Sometimes you may not realise that someone is in shock. The signs to look for are rapid pulse, sweating, pale grey skin and rapid shallow breathing.

*Mark **one** answer*

An injured person has been placed in the recovery position. They are unconscious but breathing normally. What else should be done?

⊙ Press firmly between the shoulders

⊙ Place their arms by their side

⊙ Give them a hot sweet drink

⊙ Check the airway is clear

⊙ **Check the airway is clear**

After a casualty has been placed in the recovery position, their airway should be checked to make sure it's clear. Don't leave them alone until medical help arrives. Where possible do NOT move a casualty unless there's further danger.

*Mark **one** answer*

An injured motorcyclist is lying unconscious in the road. You should always

⊙ remove the safety helmet

⊙ seek medical assistance

⊙ move the person off the road

⊙ remove the leather jacket

⊙ **seek medical assistance**

If someone has been injured, the sooner proper medical attention is given the better. Send someone to phone for help or go yourself. An injured person should only be moved if they're in further danger. An injured motorcyclist's helmet should NOT be removed unless it is essential.

13.25 *Mark one answer* **R-ES 11, HC r279-280**

You are on a motorway. A large box falls onto the road from a lorry. The lorry does not stop. You should

⊙ go to the next emergency telephone and report the hazard

⊙ catch up with the lorry and try to get the driver's attention

⊙ stop close to the box until the police arrive

⊙ pull over to the hard shoulder, then remove the box

⊙ **go to the next emergency telephone and report the hazard**

Lorry drivers can be unaware of objects falling from their vehicles. If you see something fall onto a motorway look to see if the driver pulls over. If they don't stop, do not attempt to retrieve it yourself. Pull on to the hard shoulder near an emergency telephone and report the hazard. You will be connected to the police or a Highways Agency control centre.

13.26 *Mark one answer* **R-ES 7, HC r126**

You are going through a long tunnel. What will warn you of congestion or an incident ahead?

⊙ Hazard warning lines

⊙ Other drivers flashing their lights

⊙ Variable message signs

⊙ Areas marked with hatch markings

⊙ **Variable message signs**

Follow the instructions given by the signs or by tunnel officials.

In congested tunnels a minor incident can soon turn into a major one with serious or even fatal results.

13.27 *Mark one answer* **R-ES 16, HC p131-133**

An adult casualty is not breathing. To maintain circulation, compressions should be given. What is the correct depth to press?

⊙ 1 to 2 centimetres

⊙ 4 to 5 centimetres

⊙ 10 to 15 centimetres

⊙ 15 to 20 centimetres

⊙ **4 to 5 centimetres**

An adult casualty is not breathing normally. To maintain circulation place two hands on the centre of the chest. Then press down 4 to 5 centimetres at a rate of 100 times per minute.

*Mark **two** answers* **R-ES 16, HC p131-133**

You are the first to arrive at the scene of a crash. Which TWO of these should you do?

⊙ Leave as soon as another motorist arrives

⊙ Make sure engines are switched off

⊙ Drag all casualties away from the vehicles

⊙ Call the emergency services promptly

⊙ **Make sure engines are switched off**

⊙ **Call the emergency services promptly**

At a crash scene you can help in practical ways, even if you aren't trained in first aid. Make sure you do not put yourself or anyone else in danger. The safest way to warn other traffic is by switching on your hazard warning lights.

---

*Mark **one** answer* **R-ES 16, HC p131-133**

At the scene of a traffic incident you should

⊙ not put yourself at risk

⊙ go to those casualties who are screaming

⊙ pull everybody out of their vehicles

⊙ leave vehicle engines switched on

⊙ **not put yourself at risk**

It's important that people at the scene of a collision do not create further risk to themselves or others. If the incident is on a motorway or major road, traffic will be approaching at speed. Do not put yourself at risk when trying to help casualties or warning other road users.

---

*Mark **three** answers* **R-ES 16, HC p131-133**

You are the first person to arrive at an incident where people are badly injured. Which THREE should you do?

⊙ Switch on your own hazard warning lights

⊙ Make sure that someone telephones for an ambulance

⊙ Try and get people who are injured to drink something

⊙ Move the people who are injured clear of their vehicles

⊙ Get people who are not injured clear of the scene

⊙ **Switch on your own hazard warning lights**

⊙ **Make sure that someone telephones for an ambulance**

⊙ **Get people who are not injured clear of the scene**

If you're the first to arrive at a crash scene the first concerns are the risk of further collision and fire. Ensuring that vehicle engines are switched off will reduce the risk of fire. Use hazard warning lights so that other traffic knows there's a need for caution. Make sure the emergency services are contacted, don't assume this has already been done.

13.31   *Mark one answer*   R-ES 16, HC p131-133

You arrive at the scene of a motorcycle crash. The rider is injured. When should the helmet be removed?

⊙ Only when it is essential

⊙ Always straight away

⊙ Only when the motorcyclist asks

⊙ Always, unless they are in shock

⊙ **Only when it is essential**

DO NOT remove a motorcyclist's helmet unless it is essential. Remember they may be suffering from shock. Don't give them anything to eat or drink but do reassure them confidently.

13.32   *Mark three answers*   R-ES 16, HC p131-133

You arrive at a serious motorcycle crash. The motorcyclist is unconscious and bleeding. Your THREE main priorities should be to

⊙ try to stop the bleeding

⊙ make a list of witnesses

⊙ check their breathing

⊙ take the numbers of other vehicles

⊙ sweep up any loose debris

⊙ check their airways

⊙ **try to stop the bleeding**

⊙ **check their breathing**

⊙ **check their airways**

Further collisions and fire are the main dangers immediately after a crash. If possible get others to assist you and make the area safe. Help those involved and remember DR ABC, Danger, Response, Airway, Breathing, Compressions. This will help when dealing with any injuries.

13.33   *Mark one answer*   R-ES 16, HC p131-133

You arrive at an incident. A motorcyclist is unconscious. Your FIRST priority is the casualty's

⊙ breathing

⊙ bleeding

⊙ broken bones

⊙ bruising

⊙ **breathing**

At the scene of an incident always be aware of danger from further collisions or fire. The first priority when dealing with an unconscious person is to ensure they can breathe. This may involve clearing their airway if you can see an obstruction, or if they're having difficulty breathing.

13.34
Mark **one** answer

R-ES 16, HC p131-133

Which of the following should you NOT do at the scene of a collision?

- ⊙ Warn other traffic by switching on your hazard warning lights
- ⊙ Call the emergency services immediately
- ⊙ Offer someone a cigarette to calm them down
- ⊙ Ask drivers to switch off their engines

⊙ **Offer someone a cigarette to calm them down**

Keeping casualties or witnesses calm is important, but never offer a cigarette because of the risk of fire. Bear in mind they may be in shock. Don't offer an injured person anything to eat or drink. They may have internal injuries or need surgery.

13.35
Mark **three** answers

R-ES 16, HC p131-133

You arrive at the scene of an incident. It has just happened and someone is unconscious. Which THREE of these should be given urgent priority to help them?

- ⊙ Clear the airway and keep it open
- ⊙ Try to get them to drink water
- ⊙ Check that they are breathing
- ⊙ Look for any witnesses
- ⊙ Stop any heavy bleeding
- ⊙ Take the numbers of vehicles involved

⊙ **Clear the airway and keep it open**

⊙ **Check that they are breathing**

⊙ **Stop any heavy bleeding**

Make sure that the emergency services are called immediately. Once first aid has been given, stay with the casualty.

13.36
Mark **two** answers

R-ES 16, HC p131-133

There has been a collision. A driver is suffering from shock. What TWO of these should you do?

- ⊙ Give them a drink
- ⊙ Reassure them
- ⊙ Not leave them alone
- ⊙ Offer them a cigarette
- ⊙ Ask who caused the incident

⊙ **Reassure them**

⊙ **Not leave them alone**

Be aware they could have an injury that is not immediately obvious. Ensure the emergency services are called. Reassure and stay with them until the experts arrive.

13.37   *Mark **three** answers*   R-ES 16, HC p131-133

You have stopped at an incident to give help. Which THREE things should you do?

⊙ Keep injured people warm and comfortable

⊙ Keep injured people calm by talking to them reassuringly

⊙ Keep injured people on the move by walking them around

⊙ Give injured people a warm drink

⊙ Make sure that injured people are not left alone

⊙ **Keep injured people warm and comfortable**

⊙ **Keep injured people calm by talking to them reassuringly**

⊙ **Make sure that injured people are not left alone**

There are a number of things you can do to help, even without expert training. Be aware of further danger and fire, make sure the area is safe. People may be in shock. Don't give them anything to eat or drink. Keep them warm and comfortable and reassure them. Don't move injured people unless there is a risk of further danger.

13.38   *Mark **three** answers*   R-ES 16, HC p131-133

At an incident someone is unconscious. Your THREE main priorities should be to

⊙ sweep up the broken glass

⊙ take the names of witnesses

⊙ count the number of vehicles involved

⊙ check the airway is clear

⊙ make sure they are breathing

⊙ stop any heavy bleeding

⊙ **check the airway is clear**

⊙ **make sure they are breathing**

⊙ **stop any heavy bleeding**

Remember this procedure by saying DR ABC. This stands for Danger, Response, Airway, Breathing, Compressions.

13.39   *Mark **one** answer*   R-ES 16, HC p131-133

You have to treat someone for shock at the scene of an incident. You should

⊙ reassure them constantly

⊙ walk them around to calm them down

⊙ give them something cold to drink

⊙ cool them down as soon as possible

⊙ **reassure them constantly**

Stay with the casualty and talk to them quietly and firmly to calm and reassure them. Avoid moving them unnecessarily in case they are injured. Keep them warm, but don't give them anything to eat or drink.

*Mark **three** answers*

At an incident a casualty is unconscious. Which THREE of these should you check urgently?

⊙ Circulation
⊙ Airway
⊙ Shock
⊙ Breathing
⊙ Broken bones

⊙ **Circulation**

⊙ **Airway**

⊙ **Breathing**

Remember DR ABC. An unconscious casualty may have difficulty breathing. Check that their airway is clear by tilting the head back gently and unblock it if necessary. Then make sure they are breathing. If there is bleeding, stem the flow by placing clean material over any wounds but without pressing on any objects in the wound. Compressions may need to be given to maintain circulation.

*Mark **three** answers*

You arrive at an incident. It has just happened and someone is injured. Which THREE should be given urgent priority?

⊙ Stop any severe bleeding
⊙ Give them a warm drink
⊙ Check they are breathing
⊙ Take numbers of vehicles involved
⊙ Look for witnesses
⊙ Clear their airway and keep it open

⊙ **Stop any severe bleeding**

⊙ **Check they are breathing**

⊙ **Clear their airway and keep it open**

The first priority with a casualty is to make sure their airway is clear and they are breathing. Any wounds should be checked for objects and then bleeding stemmed using clean material. Ensure the emergency services are called, they are the experts. If you're not first aid trained consider getting training. It might save a life.

13.42 — Mark **one** answer — R-ES 16, HC p131-133

You arrive at the scene of a motorcycle crash. No other vehicle is involved. The rider is unconscious and lying in the middle of the road. The FIRST thing you should do is

⊙ move the rider out of the road
⊙ warn other traffic
⊙ clear the road of debris
⊙ give the rider reassurance

⊙ **warn other traffic**

The motorcyclist is in an extremely vulnerable position, exposed to further danger from traffic. Approaching vehicles need advance warning in order to slow down and safely take avoiding action or stop. Don't put yourself or anyone else at risk. Use the hazard warning lights on your vehicle to alert other road users to the danger.

13.43 — Mark **one** answer — R-ES 16, HC p131-133

At an incident a small child is not breathing. To restore normal breathing you should breathe into their mouth

⊙ sharply
⊙ gently
⊙ heavily
⊙ rapidly

⊙ **gently**

If a young child has stopped breathing, first check that the airway is clear. Then give compressions to the chest using one hand (two fingers for an infant) and begin mouth to mouth resuscitation. Breathe very gently and continue the procedure until they can breathe without help.

13.44 — Mark **three** answers — R-ES 16, HC p131-133

At an incident a casualty is not breathing. To start the process to restore normal breathing you should

⊙ tilt their head forward
⊙ clear the airway
⊙ turn them on their side
⊙ tilt their head back gently
⊙ pinch the nostrils together
⊙ put their arms across their chest

⊙ **clear the airway**
⊙ **tilt their head back gently**
⊙ **pinch the nostrils together**

It's important to ensure that the airways are clear before you start mouth to mouth resuscitation. Gently tilt their head back and use your finger to check for and remove any obvious obstruction in the mouth.

13.45

Mark **one** answer

You arrive at an incident. There has been an engine fire and someone's hands and arms have been burnt. You should NOT

- ⊙ douse the burn thoroughly with clean cool non-toxic liquid
- ⊙ lay the casualty down on the ground
- ⊙ remove anything sticking to the burn
- ⊙ reassure them confidently and repeatedly

⊙ **remove anything sticking to the burn**

This could cause further damage and infection to the wound. Your first priority is to cool the burn with a clean, cool, non-toxic liquid, preferably water. Don't forget the casualty may be in shock.

13.46

Mark **one** answer

You arrive at an incident where someone is suffering from severe burns. You should

- ⊙ apply lotions to the injury
- ⊙ burst any blisters
- ⊙ remove anything stuck to the burns
- ⊙ douse the burns with clean cool non-toxic liquid

⊙ **douse the burns with clean cool non-toxic liquid**

Use a liquid that is clean, cold and non-toxic, preferably water. Its coolness will help take the heat out of the burn and relieve the pain. Keep the wound doused for at least ten minutes. If blisters appear don't attempt to burst them as this could lead to infection.

13.47

Mark **two** answers

You arrive at an incident. A pedestrian has a severe bleeding leg wound. It is not broken and there is nothing in the wound. What TWO of these should you do?

- ⊙ Dab the wound to stop bleeding
- ⊙ Keep both legs flat on the ground
- ⊙ Apply firm pressure to the wound
- ⊙ Raise the leg to lessen bleeding
- ⊙ Fetch them a warm drink

⊙ **Apply firm pressure to the wound**

⊙ **Raise the leg to lessen bleeding**

First check for anything that may be in the wound such as glass. If there's nothing in it apply a pad of clean cloth or bandage. Raising the leg will lessen the flow of blood. Don't tie anything tightly round the leg. This will restrict circulation and can result in long-term injury.

13.48 — *Mark **one** answer* — R-ES 16, HC p131-133

At an incident a casualty is unconscious but still breathing. You should only move them if

- ⊙ an ambulance is on its way
- ⊙ bystanders advise you to
- ⊙ there is further danger
- ⊙ bystanders will help you to

⊙ **there is further danger**

Do not move a casualty unless there is further danger, for example, from other traffic or fire. They may have unseen or internal injuries. Moving them unnecessarily could cause further injury. Do NOT remove a motorcyclists helmet unless it's essential.

13.49 — *Mark **one** answer* — R-ES 16, HC p131-133

At a collision you suspect a casualty has back injuries. The area is safe. You should

- ⊙ offer them a drink
- ⊙ not move them
- ⊙ raise their legs
- ⊙ not call an ambulance

⊙ **not move them**

Talk to the casualty and keep them calm. Do not attempt to move them as this could cause further injury. Call an ambulance at the first opportunity.

13.50 — *Mark **one** answer* — R-ES 16, HC p131-133

At an incident it is important to look after any casualties. When the area is safe, you should

- ⊙ get them out of the vehicle
- ⊙ give them a drink
- ⊙ give them something to eat
- ⊙ keep them in the vehicle

⊙ **keep them in the vehicle**

When the area is safe and there's no danger from other traffic or fire it's better not to move casualties. Moving them may cause further injury.

13.51
Mark one answer

R-ES 16, HC p117

A tanker is involved in a collision. Which sign shows that it is carrying dangerous goods?

⊙ LONG VEHICLE

⊙

⊙

⊙

⊙

There will be an orange label on the side and rear of the tanker. Look at this carefully and report what it says when you phone the emergency services. Details of hazard warning plates are given in The Highway Code.

13.52
Mark three answers

HC r286 & p122

You are involved in a collision. Because of this which THREE of these documents may the police ask you to produce?

⊙ Vehicle registration document
⊙ Driving licence
⊙ Theory test certificate
⊙ Insurance certificate
⊙ MOT test certificate
⊙ Vehicle service record

⊙ **Driving licence**

⊙ **Insurance certificate**

⊙ **MOT test certificate**

You MUST stop if you have been involved in a collision which results in injury or damage. The police may ask to see your documents at the time or later at a police station.

13.53
Mark one answer

R-ES 16, HC p131-133

After a collision someone is unconscious in their vehicle. When should you call the emergency services?

⊙ Only as a last resort
⊙ As soon as possible
⊙ After you have woken them up
⊙ After checking for broken bones

⊙ **As soon as possible**

It is important to make sure that emergency services arrive on the scene as soon as possible. When a person is unconscious, they could have serious injuries that are not immediately obvious.

13.54

A casualty has an injured arm. They can move it freely but it is bleeding. Why should you get them to keep it in a raised position?

⊙ Because it will ease the pain

⊙ It will help them to be seen more easily

⊙ To stop them touching other people

⊙ It will help to reduce the blood flow

⊙ **It will help to reduce the blood flow**

If a casualty is bleeding heavily, raise the limb to a higher position. This will help to reduce the blood flow. Before raising the limb you should make sure that it is not broken.

13.55

You are going through a tunnel. What systems are provided to warn of any incidents, collisions or congestion?

⊙ Double white centre lines

⊙ Variable message signs

⊙ Chevron 'distance markers'

⊙ Rumble strips

⊙ **Variable message signs**

Take notice of any instructions given on variable message signs or by tunnel officials. They will warn you of any incidents or congestion ahead and advise you what to do.

13.56

A collision has just happened. An injured person is lying in a busy road. What is the FIRST thing you should do to help?

⊙ Treat the person for shock

⊙ Warn other traffic

⊙ Place them in the recovery position

⊙ Make sure the injured person is kept warm

⊙ **Warn other traffic**

The most immediate danger is further collisions and fire. You could warn other traffic by displaying an advance warning triangle or sign (but not on a motorway), switching on hazard warning lights or by any other means that does not put you or others at risk.

13.57

Mark **two** answers

R-ES 16, HC p131-133

At an incident a casualty has stopped breathing. You should

- remove anything that is blocking the mouth
- keep the head tilted forwards as far as possible
- raise the legs to help with circulation
- try to give the casualty something to drink
- tilt the head back gently to clear the airway

- **remove anything that is blocking the mouth**
- **tilt the head back gently to clear the airway**

Unblocking the airway and gently tilting the head back will help the casualty to breathe. They will then be in the correct position if mouth-to-mouth resuscitation is required. Don't move a casualty unless there's further danger.

13.58

Mark **four** answers

R-ES 16, HC p131-133

You are at the scene of an incident. Someone is suffering from shock. You should

- reassure them constantly
- offer them a cigarette
- keep them warm
- avoid moving them if possible
- avoid leaving them alone
- give them a warm drink

- **reassure them constantly**
- **keep them warm**
- **avoid moving them if possible**
- **avoid leaving them alone**

The signs of shock may not be immediately obvious. Prompt treatment can help to minimise the effects. Lay the casualty down, loosen tight clothing, call an ambulance and check their breathing and pulse.

13.59

Mark **one** answer

R-ES 16, HC p131-133

There has been a collision. A motorcyclist is lying injured and unconscious. Unless it's essential, why should you usually NOT attempt to remove their helmet?

- Because they may not want you to
- This could result in more serious injury
- They will get too cold if you do this
- Because you could scratch the helmet

- **This could result in more serious injury**

When someone is injured, any movement which is not absolutely necessary should be avoided since it could make injuries worse. Unless it is essential, it's generally safer to leave a motorcyclist's helmet in place.

Case study practice 13 – Incidents, accidents and emergencies

John witnesses an incident involving a car and a motorcycle. The car driver is unhurt. The motorcyclist is lying against the kerb with his helmet still on. He is conscious but very dazed, bruised and shocked. John leaves his own motorcycle standing on the road with the hazard warning lights on. He calls the emergency services and stays with both victims until the services arrive. He then gives his contact details to a police officer.

13.1 What condition could still affect the car driver?

*Mark **one** answer*

- ⊙ Head injury.
- ⊙ Stomach pain.
- ⊙ Broken bones.
- ⊙ Shock symptoms.

HC p131

13.2 Why should the helmet stay on for the time being?

*Mark **one** answer*

- ⊙ Someone might steal the helmet if he takes it off.
- ⊙ The helmet may get lost on the way to hospital.
- ⊙ Because removing it could cause further injuries.
- ⊙ The helmet will keep his head from getting cold.

HC p131

13.3 Why did John leave his motorcycle positioned in this way?

*Mark **one** answer*

⊙ To warn following traffic of the incident hazard.

⊙ To ensure that the battery stays fully charged.

⊙ To highlight the incident for the emergency services.

⊙ To help him locate the motorcycle again later.

R-ES 16, HC r283

13.4 How should you deal with people suffering from shock?

*Mark **one** answer*

⊙ Offer them a cigarette.

⊙ Give them a drink.

⊙ Keep them warm.

⊙ Leave them alone.

R-ES 16, HC p131

13.5 Why did John provide his details?

*Mark **one** answer*

⊙ He was in a hurry to leave.

⊙ He witnessed the incident.

⊙ He wanted to be involved.

⊙ He left his licence at home.

R-ES 16

section **fourteen**
MOTORCYCLE LOADING

This section covers

o Stability
o Towing regulations

Motorcycle loading

Stability

You, as a rider, are responsible for making sure that your motorcycle isn't overloaded. Overloading can seriously affect the handling, especially steering and braking.

> **R-ES 14, HC r98**

Securely fasten any loads carried in saddle bags, panniers, tank bags and top boxes. If you use a luggage rack, the load **MUST** be securely fastened before riding. It is an offence to travel with an insecure load.

A heavy load will reduce the stability of your motorcycle. Throwover saddle bags can make your motorcycle unstable. A tank bag can affect your ability to steer whilst a heavily loaded top box can cause low-speed wobble or high-speed weave.

When carrying a heavy load on your luggage rack, your tyre pressures, headlight and suspension may also need adjusting.

> **R-ES 14**

Sidecars

Before fitting a sidecar, you need to make sure your motorcycle is suitable. Once fitted, you must make sure the sidecar is correctly aligned before riding.

When riding for the first time with a sidecar fitted, keep your speed down and be careful when negotiating bends, corners and junctions. A motorcycle with a sidecar handles very differently to a solo motorcycle.

Remember that your stopping distance may also be increased due to the extra weight of the sidecar.

> **R-ES 14**

Pillion passengers

A pillion passenger **MUST** wear a helmet which is correctly fastened. They **MUST** sit astride the machine facing forwards, on a proper passenger seat. Rear footrests should also be fitted.

You **MUST NOT** carry a pillion passenger unless

- you have passed a practical motorcycle test
- you have a full motorcycle licence for the category of motorcycle being ridden.

> **R-ES 14, HC, r83 & r85**

Your pillion passenger needs to understand that they should lean with you when going round bends. If the passenger is riding for the first time, instruct them on what to do and how to hold onto either your waist or the passenger grab rail.

Children should only be carried as pillion passengers when they can reach the handholds and footrests. They **MUST** also wear a helmet of suitable size, securely fastened, and sit properly on the pillion seat, facing forwards.

The extra weight of a passenger may increase your stopping distance, so keep well back when following other traffic. Ride with extra care until you get used to carrying a passenger. You may also need to adjust the preload on the rear shock absorbers and check the headlight alignment.

Your passenger's clothing should be warm, waterproof and bright or reflective. Don't allow them to wear a trailing scarf or belt as this could be very dangerous.

R-ES 14

Towing a trailer

If you're planning to tow a trailer, you must have a full motorcycle licence, and your motorcycle must have an engine capacity of more than 125 cc. A motorcycle trailer must be no wider than one metre (3 ft 3 in). Remember also that your stopping distance may increase due to the extra weight of the trailer.

If the trailer starts to swerve or snake as you're riding along, ease off the throttle and reduce your speed gradually to regain control.

On a three-lane motorway, towing vehicles are restricted to

- a 60 mph (96 km/h) speed limit
- the left-hand and centre lanes only – they must not use the right-hand lane.

R-ES 14, HC r98 & p40

FAQs

Should my tyres always be inflated to the same pressure?

Inflate your tyres to a higher pressure when you're carrying a heavy load or pillion passenger or if you're driving fast for a long distance, such as on a motorway.

Your vehicle handbook should tell you the correct pressure for different circumstances.

R-ES 14 & 15

14.1
Mark **one** answer
R-ES 14, HC r98

If a trailer swerves or snakes when you are towing it you should

⊙ ease off the throttle and reduce your speed

⊙ let go of the handlebars and let it correct itself

⊙ brake hard and hold the brake on

⊙ increase your speed as quickly as possible

⊙ **ease off the throttle and reduce your speed**

Don't be tempted to use harsh braking to stop swerving or snaking as this won't help the situation. You should reduce your speed by easing off the throttle.

14.2
Mark **two** answers
R-ES 14

When riding with a sidecar attached for the first time you should

⊙ keep your speed down

⊙ be able to stop more quickly

⊙ accelerate quickly round bends

⊙ approach corners more carefully

⊙ **keep your speed down**

⊙ **approach corners more carefully**

A motorcycle with a sidecar will feel very different to ride than a solo motorcycle. Keep your speed down until you get used to the outfit, especially when negotiating bends and junctions.

14.3
Mark **three** answers
R-ES 14

When carrying extra weight on a motorcycle, you may need to make adjustments to the

⊙ headlight

⊙ gears

⊙ suspension

⊙ tyres

⊙ footrests

⊙ **headlight**

⊙ **suspension**

⊙ **tyres**

Carrying extra weight such as luggage or a pillion passenger, will probably affect the aim of the headlight. Adjust this so that it does not dazzle other road users. The feel and balance will also be affected so you may need to adjust the suspension and tyre pressures to help overcome this.

To obtain the full category 'A' licence through the accelerated or direct access scheme, your motorcycle must be

⊙ solo with maximum power 25kw (33 bhp)

⊙ solo with maximum power of 11kw (14.6 bhp)

⊙ fitted with a sidecar and have minimum power of 35kw (46.6 bhp)

⊙ solo with minimum power of 35 kw (46.6 bhp)

⊙ **solo with minimum power of 35 kw (46.6 bhp)**

From the age of 21 you may take a category A test via the Direct or Accelerated Access schemes. The motorcycle you use for your practical test under the Direct or Accelerated Access scheme is one that has an engine with a minimum power output of 35 kw (46.6 bhp).

Any load that is carried on a luggage rack MUST be

⊙ securely fastened when riding

⊙ carried only when strictly necessary

⊙ visible when you are riding

⊙ covered with plastic sheeting

⊙ **securely fastened when riding**

Don't risk losing any luggage while riding: it could fall into the path of following vehicles and cause danger. It is an offence to travel with an insecure load.

Pillion passengers should

⊙ have a provisional motorcycle licence

⊙ be lighter than the rider

⊙ always wear a helmet

⊙ signal for the rider

⊙ **always wear a helmet**

Pillion passengers must sit astride the machine on a proper passenger seat and rear footrests should be fitted. They must wear a safety helmet which is correctly fastened.

14.7 *Mark **one** answer* R-ES 14

Pillion passengers should

⊙ give the rider directions
⊙ lean with the rider when going round bends
⊙ check the road behind for the rider
⊙ give arm signals for the rider

⊙ **lean with the rider when going round bends**

When riding with a pillion passenger, your motorcycle may feel unbalanced and the acceleration and braking distance may also be affected. Make sure your passenger knows they must lean with you while cornering. If they don't, they could cause the motorcycle to become unstable and difficult to control.

14.8 *Mark **one** answer* R-ES 14

When you are going around a corner your pillion passenger should

⊙ give arm signals for you
⊙ check behind for other vehicles
⊙ lean with you on bends
⊙ lean to one side to see ahead

⊙ **lean with you on bends**

A pillion passenger should not give signals or look round for you.

If your passenger has never been on a motorcycle before, make sure they know that they need to lean with you while going around bends.

14.9 *Mark **one** answer* R-ES 14

Which of these may need to be adjusted when carrying a pillion passenger?

⊙ Indicators
⊙ Exhaust
⊙ Fairing
⊙ Headlight

⊙ **Headlight**

Your headlight must be properly adjusted to avoid dazzling other road users. You will probably need to do this when carrying a heavy load or the extra weight of a pillion passenger. You may also need to adjust suspension and tyre pressures.

You are towing a trailer with your motorcycle. You should remember that your

⊙ stopping distance may increase
⊙ fuel consumption will improve
⊙ tyre grip will increase
⊙ stability will improve

⊙ **stopping distance may increase**

When you tow a trailer remember that you must obey the relevant speed limits. Ensure that the trailer is hitched correctly and that any load in the trailer is secure. You should also bear in mind that your stopping distance may increase.

Heavy loads in a motorcycle top box may

⊙ improve stability
⊙ cause low-speed wobble
⊙ cause a puncture
⊙ improve braking

⊙ **cause low-speed wobble**

Carrying heavy loads in your top box could make your motorcycle unstable because the weight is high up and at the very back of the machine. Take extra care.

Who is responsible for making sure that a motorcycle is not overloaded?

⊙ The rider of the motorcycle
⊙ The owner of the items being carried
⊙ The licensing authority
⊙ The owner of the motorcycle

⊙ **The rider of the motorcycle**

Correct loading is the responsibility of the rider. Overloading a motorcycle can seriously affect the control and handling. It could result in a crash with serious or even fatal consequences.

14.13   *Mark **one** answer*   R-ES 14

Before fitting a sidecar to a motorcycle you should

- ⊙ have the wheels balanced
- ⊙ have the engine tuned
- ⊙ pass the extended bike test
- ⊙ check that the motorcycle is suitable

⊙ **check that the motorcycle is suitable**

Make sure that the sidecar is fixed securely and properly aligned. If your motorcycle is registered on or after 1 August 1981 the sidecar must be fitted on the left-hand side of the motorcycle.

14.14   *Mark **one** answer*   R-ES 14

You are using throwover saddlebags. Why is it important to make sure they are evenly loaded?

- ⊙ They will be uncomfortable for you to sit on
- ⊙ They will slow your motorcycle down
- ⊙ They could make your motorcycle unstable
- ⊙ They will be uncomfortable for a pillion passenger to sit on

⊙ **They could make your motorcycle unstable**

Panniers or saddlebags should be loaded so that you carry about the same weight in each bag. Uneven loading could affect your balance, especially when cornering.

14.15   *Mark **one** answer*   R-ES 14

You are carrying a bulky tank bag. What could this affect?

- ⊙ Your ability to steer
- ⊙ Your ability to accelerate
- ⊙ Your view ahead
- ⊙ Your insurance premium

⊙ **Your ability to steer**

If your tank bag is too bulky it could get in the way of your arms or restrict the movement of the handlebars.

To carry a pillion passenger you must

⊙ hold a full car licence

⊙ hold a full motorcycle licence

⊙ be over the age of 21

⊙ be over the age of 25

⊙ **hold a full motorcycle licence**

The law requires you to have a full licence for the category of motorcycle you are riding before you can carry a pillion passenger.

When carrying a heavy load on your luggage rack, you may need to adjust your

⊙ carburettor

⊙ fuel tap

⊙ seating position

⊙ tyre pressures

⊙ **tyre pressures**

The load will increase the overall weight that your motorcycle is carrying. You may need to adjust your tyre pressures according to the manufacturer's instructions to allow for this. You may also need to adjust your headlight beam alignment.

You are carrying a pillion passenger. When following other traffic, which of the following should you do?

⊙ Keep to your normal following distance

⊙ Get your passenger to keep checking behind

⊙ Keep further back than you normally would

⊙ Get your passenger to signal for you

⊙ **Keep further back than you normally would**

The extra weight of a passenger may increase your stopping distance. Allow for this when following another vehicle by increasing the separation distance.

14.19 *Mark **one** answer* R-ES 14

You should only carry a child as a pillion passenger when

- ⊙ they are over 14 years old
- ⊙ they are over 16 years old
- ⊙ they can reach the floor from the seat
- ⊙ they can reach the handholds and footrests

⊙ **they can reach the handholds and footrests**

Any passenger you carry must be able to reach footrests and handholds properly to remain safe on your machine. Ensure they are wearing protective weatherproof kit and a properly fitting helmet.

14.20 *Mark **one** answer* R-ES 14

You have fitted a sidecar to your motorcycle. You should make sure that the sidecar

- ⊙ has a registration plate
- ⊙ is correctly aligned
- ⊙ has a waterproof cover
- ⊙ has a solid cover

⊙ **is correctly aligned**

If the sidecar is not correctly aligned to the mounting points it will result in the outfit being difficult to control and even dangerous.

Riding with a sidecar attached requires a different technique to riding a solo motorcycle and you should keep your speed down while learning this skill.

14.21 *Mark **one** answer* R-ES 14

You are riding a motorcycle and sidecar. The extra weight

- ⊙ will allow you to corner more quickly
- ⊙ will allow you to brake later for hazards
- ⊙ may increase your stopping distance
- ⊙ will improve your fuel consumption

⊙ **may increase your stopping distance**

You will need to adapt your riding technique when riding a motorcycle fitted with a sidecar. The extra weight will affect the handling and may increase your overall stopping distance.

You are carrying a pillion passenger. To allow for the extra weight which of the following is most likely to need adjustment?

- ⊙ Preload on the front forks
- ⊙ Preload on the rear shock absorber(s)
- ⊙ The balance of the rear wheel
- ⊙ The front and rear wheel alignment

⊙ **Preload on the rear shock absorber(s)**

When carrying a passenger or other extra weight, you may need to make adjustments, particularly to the rear shock absorber(s), tyre pressures and headlight alignment. Check your owner's handbook for details.

A trailer on a motorcycle must be no wider than

- ⊙ 0.5 metres (1 foot 8 inches)
- ⊙ 1 metre (3 feet 3 inches)
- ⊙ 1.5 metres (4 feet 11 inches)
- ⊙ 2 metres (6 feet 6 inches)

⊙ **1 metre (3 feet 3 inches)**

When you're towing a trailer you must remember that you may not be able to filter through traffic. Don't forget that the trailer is there, especially when riding round bends and negotiating junctions.

You want to tow a trailer with your motorcycle. Which one applies?

- ⊙ The motorcycle should be attached to a sidecar
- ⊙ The trailer should weigh more than the motorcycle
- ⊙ The trailer should be fitted with brakes
- ⊙ The trailer should NOT be more than 1 metre (3 feet 3 inches) wide

⊙ **The trailer should NOT be more than 1 metre (3 feet 3 inches) wide**

To tow a trailer behind a motorcycle you must have, a full motorcycle licence and a motorcycle with an engine larger than 125 cc. Motorcycle trailers must not exceed 1 metre (3 feet 3 inches) in width.

14.25 *Mark one answer* R-ES 14

You have a sidecar fitted to your motorcycle. What effect will it have?

⊙ Reduce stability

⊙ Make steering lighter

⊙ Increase stopping distance

⊙ Increase fuel economy

⊙ **Increase stopping distance**

If you want to fit a sidecar to your motorcycle make sure that your motorcycle is suitable to cope with the extra load. Make sure that the sidecar is fixed correctly and properly aligned. A sidecar will alter the handling considerably. Give yourself time to adjust to the different characteristics.

14.26 *Mark three answers* R-ES 14

Which THREE must a learner motorcyclist under 21 NOT do?

⊙ Ride a motorcycle with an engine capacity greater than 125 cc

⊙ Pull a trailer

⊙ Carry a pillion passenger

⊙ Ride faster than 30 mph

⊙ Use the right-hand lane on dual carriageways

⊙ **Ride a motorcycle with an engine capacity greater than 125 cc**

⊙ **Pull a trailer**

⊙ **Carry a pillion passenger**

Learner motorcyclists are not allowed to pull a trailer or carry a pillion passenger. In addition, if you are a learner motorcyclist under 21, you may not ride a motorcycle on the road with an engine capacity of more than 125 cc.

14.27 *Mark one answer* R-ES 14

Carrying a heavy load in your top box may

⊙ cause high speed-weave

⊙ cause a puncture

⊙ use less fuel

⊙ improve stability

⊙ **cause high speed-weave**

Carrying a heavy weight high up and at the very back of the motorcycle can make it unstable, especially when travelling at high speeds.

You want to tow a trailer behind your motorcycle. You should

- ⊙ display a 'long vehicle' sign
- ⊙ fit a larger battery
- ⊙ have a full motorcycle licence
- ⊙ ensure that your engine is more than 125 cc
- ⊙ ensure that your motorcycle has shaft drive

- ⊙ **have a full motorcycle licence**

- ⊙ **ensure that your engine is more than 125 cc**

When you tow a trailer your stopping distance will be increased. Any load on the trailer must be secure and the trailer must be fitted to the motorcycle correctly. You must obey the lower speed limit restrictions that apply to vehicles with trailers. Any trailer towed by a motorcycle must be no wider than 1 metre. The laden weight should be no greater than 150 kg or two-thirds of the kerbside weight of the motorcycle, whichever is less.

To carry a pillion passenger your motorcycle should be fitted with

- ⊙ rear footrests
- ⊙ an engine of 250 cc or over
- ⊙ a top box
- ⊙ a grab handle
- ⊙ a proper pillion seat

- ⊙ **rear footrests**

- ⊙ **a proper pillion seat**

When carrying a pillion there are certain things they should NOT do. Before carrying a pillion tell them NOT to, give hand signals, lean away from the rider when cornering, fidget or move around, put their feet down to try and support the machine when you stop, or wear long, loose items that might get caught in the rear wheel or drive chain.

Overloading your motorcycle can seriously affect the

- ⊙ gearbox
- ⊙ weather protection
- ⊙ handling
- ⊙ battery life

- ⊙ **handling**

Any load will affect the handling of your motorcycle by changing its centre of gravity. Try to keep any load as low as possible. When using panniers spread the weight evenly. Avoid carrying heavy items in a top box, as this could make your steering dangerously light.

14.31

*Mark **one** answer*

R-ES 14, HC r85

You hold a provisional motorcycle licence. Are you allowed to carry a pillion passenger?

⊙ Only if the passenger holds a full licence

⊙ Not at any time

⊙ Not unless you are undergoing training

⊙ Only if the passenger is under 21

⊙ **Not at any time**

You are not allowed to carry a pillion passenger until you hold a full motorcycle licence. This allows you to gain riding experience. Even when you've passed, don't carry a passenger if you are not confident of being able to do so safely. You are responsible for their safety.

14.32

*Mark **three** answers*

R-ES 14

Your motorcycle is fitted with a top box. It is unwise to carry a heavy load in the top box because it may

⊙ reduce stability

⊙ improve stability

⊙ make turning easier

⊙ cause high-speed weave

⊙ cause low-speed wobble

⊙ increase fuel economy

⊙ **reduce stability**

⊙ **cause high-speed weave**

⊙ **cause low-speed wobble**

Carrying a heavy weight high up and at the very back of the motorcycle can cause problems in maintaining control.

14.33

*Mark **two** answers*

R-ES 14, HC r98 & p40

You are towing a small trailer on a busy three-lane motorway. All the lanes are open. You must

⊙ not exceed 60 mph

⊙ not overtake

⊙ have a stabiliser fitted

⊙ use only the left and centre lanes

⊙ **not exceed 60 mph**

⊙ **use only the left and centre lanes**

You should be aware of the motorway regulations for vehicles towing trailers. These state that a vehicle towing a trailer must not

- use the right-hand lane of a three-lane motorway unless directed to do so, for example, at roadworks or due to a lane closure

- exceed 60 mph.

Case study practice 14 – Vehicle loading

Sandy and Chris are taking a road trip on their motorcycle. Sandy carefully connects up and checks their loaded trailer while Chris carefully packs the rigid panniers evenly. They go to the service station to buy fuel and make final checks. Once on the motorway, they travel at the speed limit when it is safe to do so and leave a good separation distance from the vehicle in front. They do not use the right-hand lane.

14.1 Why does Sandy check the trailer?

*Mark **one** answer*

⊙ To ensure it is securely shut and locked.

⊙ To ensure the paintwork is not scratched.

⊙ To ensure it is correctly connected up.

⊙ To ensure the colour matches the motorcycle.

R-ES 14

14.2 Why would Chris pack the panniers in this manner?

*Mark **one** answer*

⊙ So that nothing rattles while they are riding.

⊙ Uneven load distribution can affect balance.

⊙ So that they have not forgotten anything.

⊙ Even loads on each side look much better.

R-ES 14, HC r98, r160 & r265

14.3 What is the speed limit for their machine?

*Mark **one** answer*

- ⊙ 40 mph.
- ⊙ 50 mph.
- ⊙ 60 mph.
- ⊙ 70 mph.

R-ES 14

14.4 Why would Sandy leave more distance?

*Mark **one** answer*

- ⊙ The trailer might become detached from the motorcycle.
- ⊙ Chris doesn't like Sandy riding too close to other vehicles.
- ⊙ The motorway is not very busy so there's plenty of room.
- ⊙ Stopping distance is increased on a fully loaded vehicle.

R-ES 14

14.5 Why would they not use this lane?

*Mark **one** answer*

- ⊙ Their trailer might cause buffeting and wind resistance.
- ⊙ That lane must not be used by vehicles with trailers.
- ⊙ Only cars towing trailers can use the right-hand lane.
- ⊙ They do not want to travel at a very high speed.

HC r265

annex one
CASE STUDY

Some of the questions within the test will be presented as a case study.

You will be presented with a set of facts – the case study – which will appear on the left-hand side of the screen. The set of facts or scenario will be presented in a text format and may be accompanied by a supporting picture or diagram.

As you move within the case study and answer each question, you can be assured that the facts and the scenario content will not change, although you do have the opportunity to re-read the scenario throughout the case study should you wish to do so. The questions will appear, one by one, on the right-hand side of the screen, and you will be asked to respond.

An example of the type of scenario and questions you will be asked is given below (answers to these questions, and those for the practice studies at the end of each question section, can be found on pages 415–416).

CASE STUDY 1

You decide to visit your friend who lives about 20 miles away.

The journey will take you on various roads including country lanes and A-roads.

You've been before so think you know the way. You also have a mobile phone with you, so will be able to ring for directions if you get lost.

During the journey you go the wrong way and need to turn round. Later on, you decide to ring your friend to make sure you are still travelling in the right direction.

1. To turn round after going the wrong way, you decide to make a U-turn in the road. Before doing this, what should you do?

Mark one answer

☐ Give an arm signal as well as using indicators

☐ Signal so that other road users can slow down for you

☐ Look over your shoulder for a final check

☐ Select a higher gear than normal

◄ **Previous**   **! Flag**   👓 **Review**   **Next** ►

CASE STUDY 1

You decide to visit your friend who lives about 20 miles away.

The journey will take you on various roads including country lanes and A-roads.

You've been before so think you know the way. You also have a mobile phone with you, so will be able to ring for directions if you get lost.

During the journey you go the wrong way and need to turn round. Later on, you decide to ring your friend to make sure you are still travelling in the right direction.

2. What should you do as you approach this bridge on your journey?

Mark three answers

☐ Move into the middle of the road to get a better view

☐ Slow down

☐ Consider using the horn

☐ Find another route

☐ Beware of pedestrians

 Previous   **Flag**   **Review**   **Next**

CASE STUDY 1

You decide to visit your friend who lives about 20 miles away.

The journey will take you on various roads including country lanes and A-roads.

You've been before so think you know the way. You also have a mobile phone with you, so will be able to ring for directions if you get lost.

During the journey you go the wrong way and need to turn round. Later on, you decide to ring your friend to make sure you are still travelling in the right direction.

3. During your journey, you ring your friend. What is the safest way for you to use your mobile phone?

Mark one answer

☐ Use hands-free equipment

☐ Find a suitable place to stop

☐ Travel slowly on a quiet road

☐ Direct your call through the operator

Previous   **Flag**   **Review**   **Next**

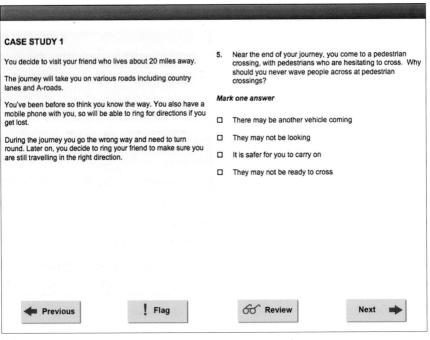

CASE STUDY 1

You decide to visit your friend who lives about 20 miles away.

The journey will take you on various roads including country lanes and A-roads.

You've been before so think you know the way. You also have a mobile phone with you, so will be able to ring for directions if you get lost.

During the journey you go the wrong way and need to turn round. Later on, you decide to ring your friend to make sure you are still travelling in the right direction.

4. You are travelling along a country road. A horse and rider are approaching. What should you do?

Mark two answers

☐ Increase your speed

☐ Sound your horn

☐ Flash your headlights

☐ Go slowly past

☐ Give plenty of room

☐ Rev your engine

Previous   ! Flag   66 Review   Next ➡

CASE STUDY 1

You decide to visit your friend who lives about 20 miles away.

The journey will take you on various roads including country lanes and A-roads.

You've been before so think you know the way. You also have a mobile phone with you, so will be able to ring for directions if you get lost.

During the journey you go the wrong way and need to turn round. Later on, you decide to ring your friend to make sure you are still travelling in the right direction.

5. Near the end of your journey, you come to a pedestrian crossing, with pedestrians who are hesitating to cross. Why should you never wave people across at pedestrian crossings?

Mark one answer

☐ There may be another vehicle coming

☐ They may not be looking

☐ It is safer for you to carry on

☐ They may not be ready to cross

Previous   ! Flag   66 Review   Next ➡

annex two
LIST OF THEORY TEST CENTRES

England
Aldershot
Barnstaple
Barrow
Basildon
Basingstoke
Bath
Berwick-upon-Tweed
Birkenhead
Birmingham
Blackpool
Bolton
Boston
Bournemouth
Bradford
Brighton
Bristol
Bury St Edmunds
Cambridge
Canterbury
Carlisle
Chatham
Chelmsford
Cheltenham
Chester
Chesterfield
Colchester
Coventry
Crawley
Derby
Doncaster
Dudley

Durham
Eastbourne
Exeter
Fareham
Gloucester
Grantham
Grimsby
Guildford
Harlow
Harrogate
Hastings
Hereford
Huddersfield
Hull
Ipswich
Isle of Wight
Isles of Scilly
King's Lynn
Leeds
Leicester
Lincoln
Liverpool
London
– Croydon
– Ilford
– Kingston
– Southgate
– Southwark
– Staines
– Uxbridge
Lowestoft
Luton

Manchester
Mansfield
Middlesbrough
Milton Keynes
Morpeth
Newcastle
Northampton
Norwich
Nottingham
Oldham
Oxford
Penzance
Peterborough
Plymouth
Portsmouth
Preston
Reading
Redditch
Runcorn
Salford
Salisbury
Scarborough
Scunthorpe
Sheffield
Shrewsbury
Sidcup
Slough
Solihull
Southampton
Southend-on-Sea
Southport
St Helens

Stevenage
Stockport
Stoke-on-Trent
Stratford-upon-Avon
Sunderland
Sutton Coldfield
Swindon
Taunton
Torquay
Truro
Watford
Weymouth
Wigan
Wolverhampton
Worcester
Workington
Worthing
Yeovil
York

Scotland
Aberdeen
Ayr
Clydebank
Dumfries
Dundee

Dunfermline
Edinburgh
Elgin
Fort William
Gairloch
Galashiels
Glasgow
Greenock
Helmsdale
Huntly
Inverness
Isle of Arran
Isle of Barra
Isle of Benbecula
Isle of Islay, Bowmore
Isle of Mull, Salen
Isle of Tiree
Kirkwall
Kyle of Lochalsh
Lerwick
Motherwell
Oban
Pitlochry
Portree
Stirling
Stornoway

Stranraer
Tarbert, Argyllshire
Tongue
Ullapool
Wick

Wales
Aberystwyth
Bangor
Builth Wells
Cardiff
Haverfordwest
Merthyr Tydfil
Newport
Rhyl
Swansea

Northern Ireland
Ballymena
Belfast
Londonderry
Newry
Omagh
Portadown

annex three
SERVICE STANDARDS

We judge our performance against the following standards (printed in our Business Plan) which we review each year

- 95% of calls to booking offices will make contact with our automated call-handling system without receiving an engaged tone
- after a call has gone through our automated call-handling system, we will answer 90% of all incoming calls to booking offices in no more than 20 seconds
- we will give 95% of candidates an appointment at their preferred centre within two weeks of their preferred date
- our online booking service will be available 99% of the time over 24 hours, 7 days a week
- we will keep 99.5% of all theory test appointments
- we will answer 90% of all letters and e-mails within 10 working days
- we will pay 95% of all refunds within 15 days of receiving a valid claim.

Complaints guide – we aim to give our customers the best possible service. Please tell us when we have done well or if you're not satisfied.

Your comments can help us to improve the service we offer.

If you have any questions about your theory test, please contact us using the numbers below.

For DSA:
Tel 0300 200 1122, fax 0300 200 1177
Minicom 0300 200 1144
Welsh speakers 0300 200 1133

For DVA (Testing) in Northern Ireland:
Tel 0845 600 6700, fax 0870 010 4372

If you have any complaints about how your theory test was carried out, or any aspect of our customer service, please call the Customer Services section on 0300 200 1188. Alternatively you can write to the Customer Services Manager at the following address:

Customer Services
Driving Theory Test
PO Box 381
Manchester M50 3UW

If you're dissatisfied with the reply you can write to the Managing Director at the same address.

If you're still not satisfied, you can take up your complaint with:

The Chief Executive
Driving Standards Agency
The Axis Building
112 Upper Parliament Street
Nottingham NG1 6LP

In Northern Ireland you should write to

The Chief Executive
Driver and Vehicle Agency (Testing)
Balmoral Road
Belfast BT12 6QL

None of this removes your right to take your complaint to your Member of Parliament, who may decide to raise your case personally with the DSA or DVA Chief Executive, the Minister or the Parliamentary Commissioner for Administration (the Ombudsman). Please refer to our leaflet *Customer Service – a Guide to our Service Standards*.

DSA is a Trading Fund and we are required to cover our costs from the driving test fee.

We don't have a quota for test passes or fails and if you demonstrate the standard required, you'll pass your test.

Refunding fees and expenses – DSA will normally refund the test fee, or rearrange another test at no further cost to you, if

• we cancel your test
• you cancel and give us at least three clear working days' notice
• you keep the test appointment but the test doesn't take place, or isn't finished, for a reason that isn't your fault.

We'll also repay you the expenses that you had to pay on the day of the test if we cancelled your test at short notice. We'll consider reasonable claims for

• the cost of travelling to and from the test centre

• any standard pay or earnings you lost through taking unpaid holiday leave (usually for half a day), after tax and national insurance contributions.

Please write to the address below and send a receipt showing travel costs and an employer's letter, which shows what earnings you lost. If you think you're entitled to fees and expenses write to:

Customer Services
Driving Theory Test
PO Box 381
Manchester M50 3UW

This reimbursement policy doesn't affect your existing legal rights.

DVA has a different reimbursement policy.

annex four
CASE STUDY PRACTICE – ANSWERS

Section 1 – Alertness

1.1 To help her be seen by others.
1.2 Check carefully and proceed with great care.
1.3 Lifesaver.
1.4 Obstruct her view of the road.
1.5 Stop her vehicle and wait patiently.

Section 2 – Attitude

2.1 60 mph.
2.2 Carefully, while increasing the distance from the vehicle in front.
2.3 Slowly, leaving plenty of room.
2.4 To allow the driver to see him in the mirrors.
2.5 Doctor attending emergency call.

Section 3 – Safety and your motorcycle

3.1 Continue using protective gear.
3.2 White with a full-face visor.
3.3 With visibility and safety.
3.4 So that her view is completely unobstructed.
3.5 At least 1mm over three-quarters of the tread breadth and all around.

Section 4 – Safety margins

4.1 Tyre pressures and headlight angle.
4.2 Blow them off-course.
4.3 Swerve to avoid cracks and holes.
4.4 With more care.
4.5 Check over his right shoulder for overtaking vehicles.

Section 5 – Hazard awareness

5.1 Convex.
5.2 Stick to soft drinks the whole time.
5.3 By making you less visible to others.
5.4 Red and yellow.
5.5 Four seconds.

Section 6 – Vulnerable road users

6.1 Turn the engine off and wait until the animals have crossed.
6.2 Stop and wait patiently until they have crossed.
6.3 Wait until the pedestrians have crossed safely.
6.4 A vehicle which is slow-moving.
6.5 By waiting until the road is clear of oncoming traffic.

Section 7 – Other types of vehicle

7.1 By using dipped headlights.
7.2 Allow it to pull out if it is safe to do so.
7.3 The lines could be very slippery in wet weather.
7.4 Diamond.
7.5 Pull a little over to the right.

Section 8 – Motorcycle handling

8.1 The extra weight can affect your balance.
8.2 Headlights.
8.3 Stop, then edge forward slowly until you can see clearly.
8.4 Lean with you when going round bends.
8.5 You might need more room in which to stop safely.

415

Section 9 – Motorway rules

9.1 Steering and braking.
9.2 All traffic should do so unless they are overtaking other vehicles.
9.3 Slower than normal.
9.4 Temporary maximum speed advised.
9.5 Three hundred yards.

Section 10 – Rules of the road

10.1 Blue and white.
10.2 Stop and wait until the light turns green.
10.3 Take a final look over his right shoulder.
10.4 To help slow traffic down.
10.5 Circular.

Section 11 – Road and traffic signs

11.1 Regulatory.
11.2 The joining side roads are slightly offset from each other.
11.3 Blue with white arrow.
11.4 Green.
11.5 The lane is in operation at all times for buses.

Section 12 – Documents

12.1 Twelve months.
12.2 It's allowed in order to get the machine to a repairer.
12.3 Vehicle Excise Duty.
12.4 It is a legal requirement.
12.5 Third party.

Section 13 – Incidents, accidents and emergencies

13.1 Shock symptoms.
13.2 Because removing it could cause further injuries.
13.3 To warn following traffic of the incident hazard.
13.4 Keep them warm.
13.5 He witnessed the incident.

Section 14 – Motorcycle loading

14.1 To ensure it is correctly connected up.
14.2 Uneven load distribution can affect balance.
14.3 60 mph.
14.4 Stopping distance is increased on a fully loaded vehicle.
14.5 That lane must not be used by vehicles with trailers.

Case study page 408 - 410

1   Look over your shoulder for a final check
2   Slow down
    Consider using the horn
    Beware of pedestrians
3   Find a suitable place to stop
4   Go past slowly
    Give plenty of room
5   There may be another vehicle coming

XTSO
information & publishing solutions

The **OFFICIAL DSA**

THEORY TEST
for Motorcyclists

2011 WIN BIKE GEAR COMPETITION*

TSO, DSA's official publishing partner, is offering you the chance to win new bike clothing or accessories.

Please send the entry form to:

2011 Win Bike Gear Competition, TSO, Freepost, ANG 4748, Norwich, NR3 1YX (No stamp required).

2011 Competition Entry Form

To enter, simply answer the questions and tell us in 25 words or less how learning to ride will make a difference to your life. The winner will be the entrant who answers the first 3 questions below correctly and writes the most apt and original 25 word essay, as decided by the judges.

1. You are following a vehicle on a wet road. You should leave a time gap of at least how many seconds?

....

2. What is the legal minimum depth of tread for motorcycle tyres in millimetres?

....

3. Why should you check over your shoulder before turning right into a side road?

....

....

Tie Breaker: Learning to ride will change my life.... (complete in 25 words or less)

....

....

....

....

When are you planning/ hoping to take your theory test?
Within a fortnight ☐ Within a month ☐ In 1-3 months ☐ In 3-6 months ☐
In 6-12 months ☐ In 12+ months ☐

When are you planning/ hoping to take your practical test?
Within a fortnight ☐ Within a month ☐ In 1-3 months ☐ In 3-6 months ☐
In 6-12 months ☐ 12+ months ☐

Do you already own a moped/ motorcycle?
Yes ☐ No ☐

If Yes, is the moped/ motorcycle...
New ☐ Second-hand ☐

What type of moped/ motorcycle is it?

....

Do you plan to buy a moped/ motorcycle when you pass?
Yes ☐ No ☐

If Yes, will the moped/ motorcycle be...
New ☐ Second-hand ☐

What type of moped/ motorcycle are you looking to own?

....

For what purposes do you propose to use your moped/ motorcycle?
Leisure ☐ Commuting ☐ For your work ☐ On-road ☐ Off-road ☐
Touring/ Holidays ☐ Sports/ Racing/ Track days ☐ Attending bike events ☐

Which publications do you read?

....

Name of shop or website that you bought this product from?

....

How would you improve this, or any other DSA product?

....

....

Name ....

Address ....

.... Date of birth ....

Daytime tel. .... Email ....

Mobile tel. ....

Signature .... Date ....

Competition Rules

The following rules apply to this competition. By entering this competition, entrants will be deemed to have accepted these rules and to agree to be bound by them.

1. Only one entry will be accepted per purchase of The Official DSA Theory Test for Motorcyclists.
2. All entries must be on original official entry forms. No photocopies will be accepted.
3. Entries must be received by the Promoter by no later than 5.00pm on Monday, 5 September 2011 (**Closing Date**). Entries must be submitted by ordinary post to the Promoter's free mailing address at: TSO, Freepost, ANG 4748, Norwich, NR3 1YX.
4. The competition will run from 2 August 2010 to 5 September 2011 and one prize shall be awarded to a winner chosen from valid entries received by the Promoter by the Closing Date. No responsibility can be taken by the Promoter for lost, late, misdirected or stolen entries.
5. The prize awarded to the winner will be a range of bike clothing to a value of approximately £1000 (at the time of these rules going to press). The Promoter may in its absolute discretion substitute this prize with a similar prize of approximate equivalent value. There will be one prize only and accordingly only one winner. Prizes cannot be transferred or exchanged and there is no cash alternative.
6. Only entrants over the age of 16 and resident in the United Kingdom are eligible to enter the competition. The Promoter reserves the right to request evidence of proof of age and residence from the winner before any prize will be awarded.
7. The winning entry will be decided by the judges in their absolute discretion from correct entries submitted by eligible entrants received by the Closing Date. A "correct" entry means a fully completed entry, with the first three questions answered correctly, the most apt and original essay and otherwise in compliance with these rules.
8. The winner will be notified by 23 September 2011. Only the winner will be contacted personally via the email address or telephone number they provide.
9. If the winner cannot be contacted by the means provided, the Promoter reserves the right to have the judges decide on an alternative winner from other correct entries received by the Closing Date, using the same criteria as for the original "winner" and subject to these rules.
10. The winner's name will be published on the Promoter's website at www.tso.co.uk on or about 23 September 2011 for a period of approximately 60 days.
11. The prize will be made available within six weeks of the Closing Date by arrangement between the Promoter and the winner, provided that the Promoter shall not be responsible for any delivery costs.
12. By entering this competition, an entrant agrees that if they accept any Prize, they will be deemed to consent to:
    (a)   the use for promotional and other purposes (without further payment and except as prohibited by law) of their name, city/town/county of residence, likeness and Prize information; and
    (b)   participate in the Promoter's reasonable marketing and promotional activities.
    The entrant agrees that all rights including copyright in all works created by the entrant as part of the competition entry shall be owned by the Promoter absolutely without the need for any payment to the entrant. They further agree to waive unconditionally and irrevocably all moral rights pursuant to the Copyright, Designs and Patents Act of 1988 and under any similar law in force from time to time anywhere in the world in respect of all such works.
13. No entries will be returned to entrants by the Promoter. Therefore, entrants may wish to retain a copy.
14. The Promoter reserves the right to cancel this competition or amend these rules at any stage without prior notice, if deemed necessary in its opinion, especially if circumstances arise outside of its control. Any such cancellation or changes to the rules will be notified on the Promoter's website.
15. This competition is not open to employees or contractors of the Promoter or the Driving Standards Agency or any person directly involved in the organisation or running of the competition, or their direct family members. Any such entries will be invalid.
16. By entering this competition, entrants warrant that all information submitted by them is true and correct and that they are eligible and have legal capacity to enter this competition. The Promoter reserves the right to disqualify any entrant if it has reasonable grounds to believe that the entrant has breached these rules.
17. Any personal data provided in any entry will be dealt with by the Promoter in accordance with the requirements of the Data Protection Act 1998, provided that the winner expressly consents to the information set out in rule 12(a) being used in the manner specified therein.
18. The judges' and the Promoter's decisions in relation to any aspect of this competition are final and no correspondence will be entered into. Neither the judges nor the Promoter will have any liability to any person in relation to their decisions or any damage, loss, injury or disappointment suffered arising from the competition (except to the extent that such liability cannot be limited or excluded by law).
19. The competition and these rules shall be governed by English law.
20. The "Promoter" means The Stationery Office Limited, St Crispins, Duke Street, Norwich, NR3 1PD (the publishers of The Official DSA Learner Range). The competition judging panel will be made up of a combination of the Promoter's employees and independent judge(s).

Other Official DSA Publications available to order

Better Biking: the Official DSA Training Aid DVD
ISBN 9780115529559   **£10.99**

This official training DVD is suitable for all motorcyclists and will help to advance your biking expertise whilst watching expert trainers deliver post-test training and the assessment for the Enhanced Rider Scheme (ERS).

The Official DSA Guide to Riding – the essential skills
Book   **ISBN 9780115526442**   **£12.99**
Downloadable PDF*   **ISBN 9780115530616**   **£12.99**

Suitable for new and experienced riders, this guide will help you acquire and maintain the skills necessary to keep you safe on the road. Includes the latest information on ecosafe riding, and avoiding and dealing with congestion.

The Official DSA Guide to Learning to Ride
Book   **ISBN 9780115530562**   **£7.99**
Downloadable PDF*   **ISBN 9780115530630**   **£7.99**

This is the only official guide which explains the standards required to complete the CBT course and pass the new modular practical motorcycle test. Being well prepared will make it more likely you will pass first time while also improving your skills for the future.

The Official Highway Code
Book   **ISBN 9780115528149**   **£2.50**
Interactive CD-ROM   **ISBN 9780115528460**   **£9.99**
British Sign Language DVD and Book Pack   **ISBN 9780115529849**   **£9.99**

Essential reading for all road users – not just for learners. This current edition contains the latest rules of the road, many of these are legal requirements and must be adhered to.

TSO (The Stationery Office) is proud to be DSA's official publishing partner.

6 Easy Ways To Order:

- Online: Visit tsoshop.co.uk/dsa
- Email: Email your order to customer.services@tso.co.uk
- Telephone: Please call 0870 243 0123. Please quote reference CQD when ordering
- Fax: Fax your order to 0870 243 0129
- Post: Marketing, TSO, Freepost, ANG 4748, Norwich NR3 1YX (No stamp required)
- Shops: Available from all good High Street book stores (including TSO shop) or online book stores.
              For interactive products please also visit selected computer software retailers.

Prices, images and publication dates are correct at time of going to press but may be subject to change without notice.
*PDF downloads provide immediate access at the press of a button. Available direct from TSO - visit tsoshop.co.uk/PDF

 Visit our Facebook page at **facebook.com/learningtodrive**

 Follow us on Twitter **twitter.com/DSA_Publishers**

TSO
information & publishing solutions